Early Modern Manchester

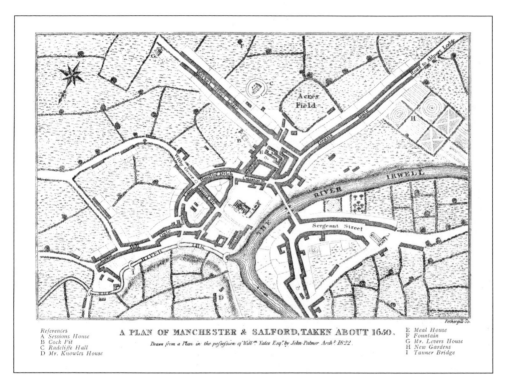

References
A Sessions House
B Cock Pit
C Radcliffe Hall
D Mr. Knowles House

A PLAN OF MANCHESTER & SALFORD, TAKEN ABOUT 1650.

Drawn from a Plan in the possession of Will.ᵐ Yates Esqʳ by John Palmer Archᵗ 1822.

E Meal House
F Fountain
G Mr. Levers House
H New Gardens
I Tanner Bridge

Manchester Region History Review

Volume 19
2008

ISSN 0952–4320

ISBN 13: 978–1–85936–184–9

Typeset by Carnegie Book Production, Lancaster.
Printed and bound by Cromwell Press, Trowbridge, Wiltshire.

Contents

The editors would like to thank the Manchester European Research Institute for its support in the preparation of this volume.

Illustrations

We are grateful to the following for their help and permission in reproducing illustrations: Manchester Archives and Local Studies centre, Manchester Reference Library; County Archivist, Lancashire Record Office; Kenneth Greene Library, Manchester Metropolitan University; Chetham's Library, Manchester; Alan G. Crosby. Every effort has been made to contact the copyright holders but if any have been inadvertently overlooked, the editors will be pleased to make the necessary arrangements at the first opportunity.

Notes for contributors

If you would like to contribute to this journal, please contact the editors before submitting copy. Authors should consult http://www.mcrh.mmu.ac.uk/pubs/guidelines.doc. Conventional articles should not exceed 8,000 words including footnotes, although they can be much shorter. We encourage a variety of contributions and are willing to discuss ideas and draft articles at an early stage. Intending contributors to the Libraries, Museums and Societies sections should consult the editors in the first instance. Book reviews should be sent to the Book Reviews editor. All submitted work should be in Word format.

Advertisements

For details of advertising rates, please contact the editors.

Indexing

Articles appearing in this journal are abstracted and indexed in HISTORICAL ABSTRACTS and AMERICA: HISTORY AND LIFE.

Contributors' Notes

Stephen Bowd lectures in European history at the University of Edinburgh. He has written widely on the history of Italian (especially Venetian) religion, politics and culture during the Renaissance and is Council member of the Society for Renaissance Studies.

Alan G. Crosby holds honorary research fellowships in the School of History, University of Liverpool; and the Centre for North-West Regional Studies, Lancaster University. He is editor of *The Local Historian* and has written numerous books and articles on the local and regional history of north-west England. His current research interests include the Lancashire landscape and the history of food and diet in Lancashire. He was the editor and co-author of *Leading the way: a history of Lancashire's roads* (1998).

Craig Horner's first research interests were in eighteenth-century Manchester. He has transcribed the diary of the Manchester wigmaker, Edmund Harrold (fl. 1712–15) to be published by Ashgate. He is co-editor of the *Manchester Region History Review* and guest co-editor of *Visual Resources* (forthcoming, 2008). He is currently researching popular motoring and society in the UK before World War I.

Kazuhiko Kondo is Professor of History at the University of Tokyo and has special interest in the social and political history of eighteenth-century Manchester. He is also chairman of the Anglo-Japanese Conference of Historians.

Bob Mather gained a BA in History at Manchester Metropolitan University and is now carrying out post-graduate research there on occupational activity in early eighteenth-century Manchester. He is also transcribing the diary of John Moss, an eighteenth-century Manchester woollen draper.

Catherine Nunn has worked for many years on the history of the parishes of east Cheshire, and particularly the impact of the civil war and interregnum on parish life. Recently she has broadened the scope of her research to include southern Lancashire and is currently working on the evidence to be found in churchwardens' accounts for parochial response to national politics. She is also a contributor to *The Oxford Dictionary of National Biography*.

Michael Powell is Librarian of Chetham's Library.

John Sculley is Museums and Heritage Services Manager at Salford Museum and Art Gallery.

Jon Stobart's research ranges across the economic, social and cultural history of England in the long eighteenth century. Key publications include: *The first industrial region* (MUP, 2004); *Towns, regions and industries*, edited with Neil Raven (MUP, 2005); and *Spaces of consumption*, with Andrew Hann and Victoria Morgan (Routledge, 2007). He is currently working on two projects: advertising and the second-hand trade; and the identity, social networks and consumption practices of the gentry in the eighteenth century.

Timothy Underhill works for the international division of Cambridge Assessment, a department of Cambridge University. He wrote his PhD dissertation on John Byrom and is preparing a new edition of Byrom's writing.

Matthew Yeo studied Modern History at St Catherine's College, Oxford and Princeton University. He is now a collaborative doctoral student at Chetham's Library, where he is undertaking a PhD on the Library's acquisitions from its foundation in 1655 until the death of the Library's first supplier, Robert Littlebury, at the end of the seventeenth century.

Introduction

The scholar and general reader is spoilt for choice when it comes to studies of the history of Manchester. Almost all of them, though, concentrate on the nineteenth century, at a time when Manchester was the 'shock city'. This is all the more surprising, since recent work has shown that understanding the development of the town, especially during the early modern period, is vital if we are understand why and how Manchester became so important and famous from the late eighteenth and nineteenth centuries.

This volume starts to address this deficit. It does so by considering a wide range of issues which are intended to show that studying a town as important as Manchester should not be confined to economic analyses or explanations for Manchester's part in the industrial revolution. Important as those are, Manchester can only be understood by reference to the totality of the experience of its inhabitants. Here, then, we provocatively publish a range of essays on subjects as diverse as John Dee, transport, John Byrom and his shorthand, the '15, non-conformism, and the networks of the Manchester region. Our other sections are themed too: a shorter 'discussion paper', introduced in this volume, is on the subject of the analysis of wills for the Manchester area. Our regular features – Museums, Libraries and Archives – consider early modern topics, as do all of the texts in our extended Long Reviews section.

The essays derive from the proceedings of a conference, 'The greatest mere village in England': networks, religion and politics in early modern Manchester, held in the greatest mere village itself in April 2005. This brought together historians of the north west for the early modern period and we are delighted to be able to publish extended versions of some of their papers here.

This is the third themed volume of the *Manchester Region History Review* and, following on from the previous two guest-edited numbers by Professors Brian Maidment and John Pickstone, has made for a hard act to follow. However, the confidence and enthusiasm expressed by the editorial board in the publication of a volume on Manchester for the early modern period demonstrate how important the area is now considered.

We are also grateful for Carnegie Publishing's continued support. This is our third collaborative effort, and the expertise and patience of everyone at Carnegie is most welcome. I have also had the benefit of my co-editor Melanie Tebbutt's wisdom, guidance and patience in putting this volume together.

Craig Horner
December 2007

OBITUARY
Neil Richardson, 1948–2006

The death of Neil Richardson on 21 August 2006 robbed the Greater Manchester area of one of its most important publishers of local history. His publications added flesh to the bare skeleton of facts, and gave the opportunity for local people to tell their story as well as enabling local historians to find a publisher for the results of their research.

Neil came into publishing through his involvement with CAMRA and the editorship of 'What's Doing', making the latter an important source of information on local pubs and breweries. When he started, his early publications concentrated on the histories of public houses in the Manchester and Salford area, but gradually other towns were added to the growing list of books in the series. Later, the histories of individual breweries were published. At the time Neil started his series of pubs, there was little information easily available except on the better known ones, and even some of this was suspect. His publications on pubs brought his name to a wider readership not only interested in their local pub, but – as pubs form part of the local history – that of their own areas generally. As a result of Neil's work, it is now possible to discover something about many pubs and breweries in the Greater Manchester area.

Another early venture was the reprinting of some long out-of-print local publications like Ogden's *A stranger's guide to Manchester*, Partington's *Tolls bars of Manchester* and several early Manchester and Salford directories. It was not only books that Neil published, for another of his projects was to reprint several early maps of Manchester and Salford, and the Greater Manchester sheets of the first 6 inches to the mile OS map, making such maps generally available for the first time so local historians could consult them in their own homes rather than in libraries. It also meant that libraries could reduce the use of their over-used originals with the new reprints.

Gradually Neil moved from publishing books on pubs, breweries and reprints into those that were the result of specific research, or were reminiscences of life in the first half of the twentieth century. These were often where the author had not been able to find a publisher but which Neil felt were worthy of a wider readership. The result has been the publication of information that would otherwise have remained in personal collections or even lost forever. For some areas it was the first time there had been material available in print and, moreover, easily available at an affordable price. Neil always had a helpful word for budding authors, and if he thought the work had potential he would take it on, illustrating it from his own large collection of illustrations and ephemera.

The death of Neil has resulted in a gap in the field of local history publishing that will take time to fill. In the meantime, his widow Sue is hoping to continue the business and everyone wishes her well in this.

Chris E. Makepeace

ARTICLES
The regional road network and the growth of Manchester in the sixteenth and seventeenth centuries

Alan G. Crosby

Introduction: urban growth in the pre-industrial period

The significance of the late sixteenth and seventeenth centuries in the history of north-west England was long overshadowed in the work of historians by the dominance of the Industrial Revolution. In the past quarter of a century, however, research on a wide range of themes, and using different areas as case-studies, has demonstrated that many of the phenomena traditionally regarded as characteristic of the second half of the eighteenth century were, in reality, apparent much earlier. From the 1750s onwards, when they expanded to become larger in scale, and with a more dramatic visible presence, processes such as urbanisation and industrialisation understandably enough attracted the attention of contemporaries. Now, however, we can appreciate more clearly that phenomena such as proto-industrialisation, nascent urban growth, demographic take-off and the improvement of infrastructure were already evident in many parts of the region by the end of the sixteenth century, and were of considerable significance half a century later. As a result of this reappraisal, the image of sudden and explosive change in the last quarter of the eighteenth century has been superseded by a picture of steadily gaining momentum over at least 150 years before the conventional start of the Industrial Revolution. It is apparent that the revolutionary image is far from reliable, perhaps implausible.[1]

Among the most important changes during the century and a half from the 1550s were the crystallisation of the hierarchy of towns and the emergence of two linked zones of vigorous urban growth, in the Manchester basin and along the lower Mersey. Chester, traditionally the largest and most important town in the north west, began to lose its pre-eminence, and although the image of stagnation and moribundity implied by some nineteenth- and early twentieth-century writers is a false one, its relative position unquestionably declined as the new commercial centres climbed the rungs of the urban ladder.[2] The substantial reshaping of the hierarchy which is often implied in the popular literature was essentially a post-1760 development and is frequently misunderstood. During the earlier stage in the urbanisation process the challengers to Chester were not upstart newcomers – mushrooming industrial communities springing up from nothing and nowhere – but were themselves ancient and well-established places, where industry, commerce, business and service activities were grafted onto the existing morphology and socio-economic structure of successful medieval market towns. This process of diversification among older urban areas was central to the process of town growth and, with the attendant demographic transformation, it produced in Manchester and Liverpool a phenomenon which by 1700 was attracting the fascinated attention of outsiders. Until the 1770s these processes did relatively little to alter the urban hierarchy within Lancashire itself. Although Liverpool's position undoubtedly showed a major improvement, the county's other leading towns in the 1750s – Manchester, Preston, Wigan, Lancaster, Bolton and Warrington – occupied the same place as they had done two centuries earlier, even though their populations had increased very considerably during that period.

Great historical significance therefore attaches to the absolute growth of the expanding towns. They became a great deal larger in a short space of time, and thus began to influence regional and sub-regional economic and social patterns in unprecedented fashion. Quantifying the scale of growth is notoriously difficult, given the absence of census data until 1801 and the unreliability of those listings and head-counts which are available. The hearth tax returns provide the most comprehensive coverage of households. In 1664 the number of households in Manchester and Salford together was at least 1,067. Applying a multiplier of 4.5 per household gives a population of approximately 4,800, while a multiplier of 5 per household gives 5,330. Neither of these figures is precisely accurate, of course, but whatever interpretation is placed upon the hearth tax returns it is reasonably certain that the combined population of the urban area was in the order of 5,000. Here, as elsewhere, much depends on the degree to which exempt households were accurately recorded: recent work on, for example, the returns for Norwich suggests that while named households are divided into taxable and exempt, there was also a large, but unquantifiable, category of households which were so poor that they were simply ignored by the assessors – they were not even worth listing.[3] If that is the case more widely, as it may well be, the population of Manchester-cum-Salford was probably significantly more than 5,300. For the sake of comparison, Table 1 gives some statistics for other towns in Lancashire and Cheshire using the same multipliers:

Table 1:
Possible
population
size of some
north-western
towns, 1664[4]

Town	Households	Population range
Chester	1686	7587 – 8430
Manchester with Salford	1067	4800 – 5335
Macclesfield	585	2632 – 2925
Wigan	458	2060 – 2290
Preston	400	1800 – 2000
Bolton	352	1584 – 1760
Stockport	308	1386 – 1540
Liverpool	284	1278 – 1420

Estimates of population size from earlier and later periods are much more tentative. It is commonly suggested that Manchester with Salford may have had about 2,000 people in the middle decades of the sixteenth century, while the usual figure proposed for the 1720s is roughly 9,500.[5] These absolute figures, and the rates of growth implied, do not seem at first glance to be notably impressive, but the probability is that the population of Manchester with Salford almost trebled in the 120 years between 1550 and 1670, and then doubled again over the following fifty years, at a time when nationally the demographic pattern was one of stagnation or decline. These were unprecedented rates of growth, and the impact of such a change (to which can be added that of smaller neighbours such as Stockport, Macclesfield and Bolton) on the local and regional economy and its supporting infrastructure deserves further consideration.

From the point of view of infrastructure, which is the main theme of this paper, the most important consequence is that at some stage in the early seventeenth century, Manchester passed the invisible and unquantifiable threshold between comparative self-sufficiency and comparative dependence, after which it started to draw ever-increasing quantities of raw materials, fuel and foodstuffs from the surrounding areas and from longer distances. Its economic impact in the wider sense – and in particular, its role in the fast-expanding textile industry and its commercial structures – is well-documented and researched, but it is also clear that by the time of the Civil War the influence of Manchester as a consumer of prosaic but essential products had begun to affect communities more widely across south-east Lancashire. This, in turn, increased local awareness of the problems associated with the infrastructure of which the town was a focus.

The road network in the early modern period

Infrastructure, in the context of the first half of the seventeenth century, means roads and bridges. Comparatively little attention has been given to the pre-turnpike road network of north-west England. Indeed, the infrastructure which supported proto-industrialisation has been largely overlooked in analyses of this complex and fundamental phase in the development of the economy of the region. That is surprising, given the depth and scale of research on the infrastructure of the Industrial Revolution period. The importance of the emergent canal system, and the parallel development of a dense and effective turnpike network, have rightly been the focus of a great deal of valuable work, but the earlier road system has been largely ignored.

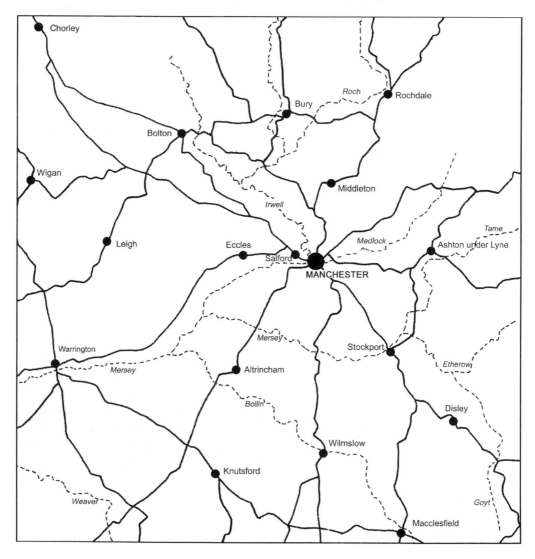

Yet during the key years from the mid sixteenth century to the early eighteenth, as towns began to grow and new industries emerged, water transport (with the exception of estuarine shipping) was almost non-existent in the region and therefore all economic change and growth was dependent upon the road network. In 1980 David Hey drew our attention to the major importance of the packhorse routes and their carriers in the Peak District, from east Cheshire to the southern West Riding.[6] In a detailed discussion of the industrial traffic which was carried by these routes he pointed to their central role in the textile trades of the sixteenth and seventeenth centuries as well as their importance to the producers of lead, coal, iron, salt and lime. There has been no comparable study for the Lancashire Pennines, but there is no reason to doubt the relevance of Hey's findings to the Manchester region.

Another merit of Hey's book is its coverage of the physical form of the roads, with explanation of features such as hollow ways, causeways and bridges, and the varied responsibility for their repair and upkeep. These have a direct bearing upon the circumstances of Manchester's development, because the early seventeenth century saw a developing conflict between, on the one hand, the pressures and demands of an expanding central place, and on the other the conservative and localist framework of the statutory measures which regulated the upkeep of highways. In this context, the exceptional significance of Manchester in terms of the regional road network is a crucial theme (see Figure 1). In the Roman period the town was the meeting place of at least seven roads and was among the most important nodal points on the national network.[7] The continued use of parts of these routes in the post-Roman and medieval periods merits further investigation. My own earlier work on the roads of Lancashire in the early modern period included some analysis of the ways in which roads were created, improved and managed in the two centuries before the advent of turnpikes (and, since the latter were slow to develop, for several decades thereafter in many cases).[8] Detailed case studies of specific roads are potentially feasible, provided that sufficient documentary evidence is available,[9] but in many instances fieldwork is impossible because later reconstruction has eliminated all physical trace of the older forms of roads. Only when earlier routes have been bypassed by later improvements, or have fallen into disuse, is some semblance of their original character still evident, and perhaps unavoidably such places tend to be in remote upland locations, rather than on or near key interurban routes. This is a considerable limitation, for while enough lengths of packhorse routes survive across moorlands and fellsides for us to be reasonably confident of their physical form, there is no reason to suppose that lowland interurban routes necessarily

Figure 1:
The main road
network of the
Manchester
area in the early
seventeenth
century

shared those characteristics – they may, for example, have been much wider, or differently surfaced, or better delineated, or with superior drainage.[10]

These issues bear upon our understanding of how the highway infrastructure in south-east Lancashire was gradually adapted as the growth of Manchester made the town the destination and origin of increasing volumes of road traffic. Under the Highways Act of 1555 all parishes (or, in northern counties, townships) had to appoint a highway surveyor and each community was given responsibility for all highways within its boundaries. The upkeep of roads was to be determined purely by local policy and local financial circumstances and the physical work was to be undertaken by statute labour or hired labour. The latter, and any materials and other costs, were to be paid for by levying highway rates. In principle, highway surveyors' accounts would provide us with invaluable information about the work being done on the roads from the reign of Mary I onwards, but in reality the survival of such sources before the late seventeenth century is very unusual anywhere, and no examples seem to exist from townships in Salford hundred before 1700. The documentary evidence for such a study is therefore found mainly among the quarter sessions records, which are held at the Lancashire Record Office and which provide continuous coverage from the mid 1620s onwards.

The role of the county magistrates in highway matters was mainly one of arbitration and adjudication rather than direct action. There

Church Brow,
Mottram in
Longdendale:
although
published
in 1818, this
engraving
powerfully
conveys the
character and
quality of the
unimproved
road network
of south-east
Lancashire
and north-east
Cheshire in the
seventeenth
and eighteenth
centuries. The
upgrading of
roads such
as these, by
incremental
local works and
eventually by
turnpiking, was
a major element
of transport
improvement
before and
during the
Industrial
Revolution
(from George
Ormerod's
*History of
Cheshire*, vi
[1818])

were some county bridges, paid for by a rate levied across Lancashire as a whole and repairable by the inhabitants at large. These bridges were on trunk roads over major rivers, as at Walton-le-Dale on the Ribble. There were also significant numbers of hundred bridges, maintainable by the inhabitants of, for example, Salford hundred and usually on main roads over smaller rivers. However, apart from these, all responsibility was borne by local communities, while the county magistrates or hundreds had no responsibility for any stretches of road except for the immediate approaches to certain bridges. This system survived until 1835, although the growth of the turnpike network from the end of the seventeenth century took substantial stretches of major roads, and some secondary ones, out of local or community control. The 1555 system was a pragmatic solution to problems of highway maintenance, but in areas where roads were heavily used, or where the terrain and topography presented challenges, it was very difficult to keep roads and bridges in good repair. It was also a very fragmented system, since individual townships only had responsibility for their own short stretches of route and no coordination over longer distances was feasible. Between Manchester and Bolton, for example, the old main road via Prestwich and Radcliffe passed through eleven townships, each of which was a separate highway jurisdiction.

There were several reasons why the justices might become involved in highway matters. Petitions could be presented by individual townships, asking for assistance from the county rate or other amelioration of financial burdens. Justices might be called upon to arbitrate in disputes between townships over liability and jurisdiction. They might also receive petitions from aggrieved parties complaining about specific problems. Finally, they might take direct action, often initiated by themselves, to address particular problems such as impassable roads or unsafe or destroyed bridges. The formal business of individual cases was dealt with at the quarterly meetings of the sessions, but there was a continuous process of administration in between these sessions. Road and bridge business formed a major component of the civil work of the justices and, in consequence, documentation is abundant.

The petitions and other documents presented to the Lancashire quarter sessions during the reign of Charles I and the Commonwealth period provide useful evidence for the impact of Manchester on the regional highway network. They use phraseology which suggests that the growth of Manchester was, even in the 1630s and 1640s, noteworthy among contemporaries. Manchester was perceived within a geographical network, a physical and tangible entity which paralleled and interacted with the networks of social, political and cultural connections into which the town was increasingly woven. By considering the words of contemporaries, albeit those expressed through the partisan perspective of a petition to the magistrates, we can begin to appreciate something of their awareness of Manchester as a phenomenon, and to understand how, 150 years before the Industrial Revolution, the country market town was changing its identity and its place in the regional and sub-regional networks.[11]

Between the summer of 1626 and the end of 1651 the county justices at their various sittings (in Lancaster, Preston, Wigan or Ormskirk, and Manchester) dealt with some 225 highway cases, an average of nine per year. The load was far from evenly spread chronologically and there was, not unexpectedly, a sharp reduction for much of the 1640s. Quite a few of these cases dealt with the same sections of road or the same bridges, with evidence of repeated cost-cutting and consequent failure to do a satisfactory job, leading to a new presentation of the same case some years later. Even allowing for this, the quantity of detailed documentary evidence is probably sufficient to allow convincing conclusions to be drawn. The geographical distribution of the cases was very uneven. Figure 2 maps them and also indicates places where road or bridge problems recurred. The pattern is clear. There were notable concentrations of activity in a few key areas of the county: the road up the Lune valley from Caton to Kirkby Lonsdale; the area between Warrington, Burtonwood and Prescot; the vicinity of Leigh; and the Irwell valley from Bolton down to Manchester and beyond. For much of the rest of the county there were only isolated examples of complaints and consequent improvements, and for substantial areas such as the south Fylde, the Ribble valley, and Rossendale, almost nothing.

Explaining this pattern is relatively straightforward. In the Lune valley, on the main highway from Lancaster to Yorkshire, frequent flood damage was a problem, while in the Sankey and Burtonwood area, drainage of mossland and the enclosure and improvement of commons had impeded and obstructed the existing highway network. In Leigh and adjacent townships, though, important new traffic flows were beginning to emerge as proto-industrialisation gathered pace. In that area mining and metal-working were assuming greater significance and it was also a crossroads, with growing longer-distance traffic flows on the main north-south and east-west axes. In the context of Manchester, special significance attaches to the Irwell valley, because the roads leading down from Bolton and beyond were not only heavily trafficked but also involved notoriously difficult river crossings. A great deal of attention was therefore given to the bridges at Ringley and Darcy Lever, over the Irwell and the Croal respectively, and to lesser bridges on other watercourses in and around Bolton. All of these experienced frequent damage from the flash floods, to which the Irwell was particularly prone because of its large upland catchment.

Manchester in 1728 (detail from the engraving by Samuel and Nathaniel Buck): the fine high-arched stone bridge over the Irwell was built in the fourteenth century and remained the only crossing of the river in the Manchester area until the early nineteenth century. Across it was channelled all the traffic reaching Manchester from the north west

At the same time, some of the roads into Manchester were beginning to suffer from growing volumes of heavy commercial traffic, especially those linking the town with other important commercial centres such as Warrington and Rochdale, or which formed part of inter-regional routes such as what is now Ashton Old Road, the first stage of the way to south Yorkshire.

The wider significance of the Irwell bridges was recognised by their being classed as repairable by the entire hundred of Salford, although such collective responsibility was very often challenged by more distant townships. In 1627, for example, the repair of Farnworth bridge was long overdue and the magistrates requested Sir Thomas Barton of Smithills and four other gentlemen to assess the costs of the work 'as they shall thinke fit for the reparinge of the same upon thinhabitantes [sic] of this hundred of Salford yf in case they shall conceave that it ought to bee repayred at the chardge of the cuntrie'.[12] The most pressing need was to rebuild wooden bridges in stone, which would not only be more durable but would bear the increasing weight of the heavy commercial traffic using these routes. The hazards of the location were well illustrated by the problems of the bridge over the river at Prestolee or Ringley, which was specifically singled out by Lord Strange in 1628 as being in urgent need of repair. In 1632 work began on a new stone structure with two arches, but in January 1633 'it pleased god Almightie the disposer and finisher of all good

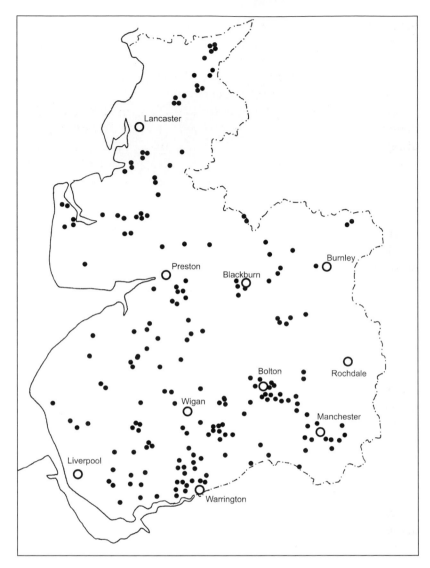

Figure 2: The geographical distribution of highway business transacted by the Lancashire quarter sessions, 1626–1652

workes to send a great raine upon the earth, which caused such an extreame high flood that the same worke ... was altogether perished, & overthrowne'. The importance of Darcy Lever bridge, which not only linked Bolton with Manchester but was also on the main road to Bury, Rochdale and Yorkshire, is reflected in frequent complaints about its condition and numerous orders made for urgent repair and strengthening.[13] The improvement of infrastructure during this period was always sporadic and to a considerable extent ineffectual. It invariably followed major problems, rather than being anticipatory, and it depended very much upon the willingness of local people to take action and to make financial contributions. That the latter were frequently avoided will occasion no surprise. Nevertheless, even townships close to destroyed bridges were conspicuously reluctant to contribute to reconstruction. In 1628 the constable of Pilkington refused to hand over the money collected in that township, which was less than a mile from the bridge, as did the inhabitants of Chadderton and Rivington among other places.[14]

For a place such as Manchester, which was increasingly reliant upon the accessibility afforded by the regional road network, highway disrepair and bridge failure were a limitation upon realising commercial potential. That may have been apparent even in the early sixteenth century, when some of the few surviving wills include bequests by private individuals towards the repair of roads in or leading to Manchester. Thus, Matthew Beck (d. 1520) gave 6s 8d to the 'mendyng of the payvment in Salford lane' and similar sums for 'the mendyng off Dob Lane' and 'the mendyng off Newton Lane'. Further evidence of such concern for highways in the Manchester area among the commercial fraternity is provided by, for example, the will of John Hanworth of Bury (1570) who left 20 shillings each for the repair of 'Salford streete' and 'the platting anenste Trafford', and ten shillings for 'the waye in Chetham Lane'.[15] These examples are all relatively close to Manchester itself, but a valuable indicator of the longer-distance traffic which the town generated is found in a bequest by Thomas Birch, merchant of Manchester (d. 1520). He left twelvepence to 'the mendyng off the lane on this syde the chapell off the frythe'.[16] That a Manchester businessman should leave money at such an early date for road repairs at Chapel-en-le-Frith, 25 miles away in the heart of the Peak District (and, perhaps significantly, on the ancient highway to London), is a sure sign of the town's developing regional status. It was this route which would have been used when, for example, Sir George Vernon of Haddon Hall had wine and other luxury goods delivered from Manchester in the late 1540s.[17]

By the reign of Charles I, over a century later, there was a very clear sense that some roads were of particular importance as inter-urban and inter-regional links. Thus in 1628 the inhabitants of Flixton, Eccles and Stretford parishes petitioned the justices because the route 'through the Towne of Barton upon Irwell over the Ryver of Irwell Being one of the most used high wayes leading to divers Markett Townes and out of Cheshire & other Countries [*sic*] into this County' had fallen into serious disrepair. It was used by people and goods in 'Cartes caridges on horse backe & afoote' but was dependent upon the ferry at Barton, which was also ruined and dangerous.[18] A rather more unusual example of Manchester being used as a reference point is in a petition from Westhoughton in January 1634. Richard Laythwaite sought redress because his wife and children were being terrorised by the performing bears owned by Alexander Ascroft of

Wigan. The latter persisted in bringing his 'verie curste beares' along the footpath past Laythwaite's house, rather than using the 'finne highe Rodde waye for Cartes horse and beasse Leadinge betweene Wigan and Manchester and other markets townes'.[19] Here the nearest market towns would have been Bolton and Leigh, but Manchester, though ten miles further away, was specified as the destination.

The year 1628 saw a series of petitions. That from Barton-upon-Irwell has already been mentioned, but in the same year the inhabitants of Openshaw, a small and thinly-populated township straddling the main road to Yorkshire, sought assistance because they had 'a great burden lying uppon us for the repaire of the high waies ... havinge for the space of two miles in lenght [sic] or there aboute of Causey to bee paved and mended And [it] being a way that is much traviled being the high way betwixt Ashton under Line and Manchester'. They asked for financial assistance from the hundred, since this road was used by so many outsiders, and their plea was accepted – the magistrates granted them a lump sum of £5 from the hundred rate. Although the sum was relatively small the principle was important, for it represented acceptance of the argument that the maintenance problems consequent upon the growth of Manchester should not be the sole responsibility of individual townships in the rural area outside the town.[20] Also in 1628, in a document of major historical interest, the inhabitants of Cheetham petitioned the justices. This, like Openshaw, was a township small in area and population (and hence low in rateable value) but standing on one of the main roads into the growing town. The wording of the petition first emphasises the long-distance nature of much of the traffic, and an appreciation of inter-regional flows, stating that there was 'a highway leadinge from the Towne of Manchester unto the Markett Townes of Rachdall Burie and Boulton and to most of the Markett Townes in the County of Yorke through the Towneshippe of Cheetam'. It then, significantly, claims that 'of late the same way is of farre greater use than heretofore' and, later, that there had been 'extraordinarie use' of the road. Such phraseology is not unique, but what follows is quite exceptional, for it is the first contemporary description of the impact of economic change, and gives a detailed list of the commodities carried by road. It states that the increased use of the road (now Cheetham Hill Road and Bury Old Road) was 'with Cariage of Coale, Turves, Cannell, timber, wooll, Slate flagges, Stounes and other thinges for the use of the said Towne of Manchester (divers Coale Mines beinge of late found neere unto the said high way)'.[21] Cheetham, like Openshaw, asked for the burden of upkeep to be alleviated by making it chargeable upon the whole of Manchester parish. The magistrates met the demand halfway, making the repairs the liability not only of Cheetham but also of the

The medieval king's highway from Blackburn to Bolton and Manchester, one of the key routes which focussed on the seventeenth-century town; this illustration shows the road at Hollinshead, where it begins to descend southwards from the watershed between the Darwen and Irwell catchments. Narrow and running between high banks as a hollow-way, it was the main road between the three towns until superseded by a new turnpike in 1805 (Alan Crosby)

townships of Manchester, Salford, Broughton and Crumpsall.

The most detailed petition from the pre-Civil War period was submitted in 1632, by the justices and other gentlemen of the hundred of Blackburn. They were technically petitioning themselves, but the intention was to make their case before a county audience. The petition referred to 'a very dangerous passage … over the river of Calder called Fenysford'. This was a ford, on what is now the main A680 road from Accrington to Clitheroe, about two miles south of Whalley. As was customary, the petition described the route in terms of origin and destination, but in this case the latter was far more distant than was normal. The ford, it said, lay between 'the towneshippes of Whalley and great Harwood [on the highway] Between the Burrough towne of Cliderow and the townes of Whalley Wiswell pendleton and other townshipes on the one side of the River and the townshipes of Manchester Bury and other markette townes & townshipes on the other side'. There is a clear sense that this road formed part of a great regional route, with Manchester as the crucial destination at the southern end. Furthermore, there is a unique attempt to quantify the traffic – unreliably, it is true, but the wish to do so again makes this petition exceptional: 'over which ford when the Water is little there is commonly 200 or 300 Loaden horses every daie passe over, besides great numbers of other passengers'. The volume of traffic and the erosion by the river had combined to make the ford 'of late yeares so worne and growne so rocky that, in short tyme, it is thought yt will become alltogether impassable'. There were already major difficulties: 'the River being every often (especially in the winter season) so great that there is no passage for man or horse and many attemptinge … to passe have been drowned, and almost daily some persons are here put in danger of theire lives, or have there Loades & carriages drowned or

Lost'.[22] The petitioners asked for a rate to be levied for the building of a bridge which, at an estimated £100, would be substantially more expensive than any other contemporary road project in the county.

The request was granted and a bridge, paid for by the hundred, was duly constructed. This petition tells us that not only was there an exceptional amount of traffic, but that Manchester and Bury were destinations. The usual procedure in petitions was to note the nearest market towns (which were Clitheroe or Whalley to the north and Blackburn or Haslingden to the south). Instead, towns eighteen and 30 miles distant were identified. Although we should not place too much weight on a single petition such as this, it is instructive to compare its evidence with the conclusions that Willan drew about the late-Elizabethan town: 'Manchester [had] a market area comparable with Preston's which had an inner zone extending from seven to twelve miles and a more irregular outer zone that could extend to twenty miles',[23] but that the town's trading area was very much wider. The presence of Manchester merchants in many of the country's trading centres and ports, and the detailed evidence of debts, location of stock and other items in inventories, emphasises this nationwide network. The documents relating to highways and bridges reflect the growing pressure that this ever-widening and intensifying trading role brought to bear upon the road system that focused on Manchester.

Most petitions presented in this period are more or less formulaic, with stock phrases which cannot be taken as reflecting the local circumstances. They normally record that a road or bridge impedes, or is dangerous to, his majesty's liege people, that the way runs between a rural community and the nearest market town or parish church, and that it is in very poor condition. However, the examples quoted here have a special importance because their wording departs from the standard formula, giving a distinctive and individual quality. It is apparent that in each case this is because the inclusion of more specific local detail was felt to be important, and we can therefore see these as more authentically reflecting contemporary circumstances. Manchester was, even before the Civil War, creating new patterns and networks of economic and commercial activity, a process which gathered pace rapidly during the second half of the seventeenth century.[24] The notion of an infrastructure network focussing on the town is not one that they would have identified in those terms, but it is clear that they were acutely aware of its existence. This research has used the Lancashire quarter sessions records, but in due course further stages will be undertaken, considering evidence in the comparable records for Cheshire, Derbyshire and the West Riding of Yorkshire, in the hope of gaining a broader view of Manchester's place in the perceptions of the people of the northern counties in the first half of the seventeenth century. Contemporaries were well aware of the changes which were taking place, seeing Manchester not only as the cause of their immediate practical problems of road and bridge upkeep, but also, more subtly, as the emergent regional capital.

Notes

1. Some of these issues are considered in more detail in Alan G. Crosby, 'The archaeology of Merseyside 1500–1750: an historical overview', *Journal of the Merseyside Archaeological Society*, 13 (forthcoming, 2007–8).
2. See Roger Swift (ed.), *Victorian Chester: essays in social history* (Liverpool, 1996).
3. Peter Seaman (ed.), *Norfolk Hearth Tax exemption certificates 1670–1674: Norwich, Great Yarmouth, King's Lynn and Thetford* (British Record Society / Norfolk Record Society, 2001), pp. xxxiii–xxxvi.
4. Hearth tax statistics are taken from Tom Arkell, 'Identifying regional variations from the hearth tax', *The Local Historian*, 33:3 (2003), pp. 148–74.
5. See, for example, the discussion in C. B. Phillips and J. H. Smith, *Lancashire and Cheshire from AD 1540* (London and New York, 1994), pp. 67–8.
6. David Hey, *Packmen, carriers and packhorse roads: trade and communications in North Derbyshire and South Yorkshire* (Leicester, 1980), esp. chap. 7.
7. To Buxton and Littlechester (Derby); Melandra (Glossop), Brough and Templeborough (Rotherham); Castleshaw and York; Ilkley and Aldborough; Ribchester and Carlisle; Wigan; and Northwich and Chester. The possibility of others (for example, to Wilderspool / Warrington) cannot be ruled out; see also M. C. Higham, 'The roads of Dark Age and medieval Lancashire', in Alan G. Crosby (ed.), *Leading the way: a history of Lancashire's roads* (Preston, 1998), chap. 2.
8. Alan G. Crosby, 'Roads of county, hundred and township, 1550–1850', in Crosby (ed.), *Leading the way*, chap. 3.
9. See, for example, Alan G. Crosby, 'Building bridges in Lonsdale', *Lancashire Local Historian*, 17 (2004), pp. 43–52, which considers the road along the Lune valley from Lancaster to Kirkby Lonsdale.
10. For a general discussion of the landscape of transport routes in the North West, see Alan G. Crosby, 'Moving through the landscape', in Angus J. L. Winchester and Alan G. Crosby, *England's landscapes: the North West* (London, 2006).
11. T. S. Willan, *Elizabethan Manchester*, Chetham Society, 3rd. ser., 27 (1980), discusses Manchester's wider commercial contacts during the sixteenth century, including links with Bristol and London (pp. 56, 124–9); and points out that the often-stated idea of Manchester and Lancashire as being 'isolated and economically backward' is completely untenable.
12. Lancashire Record Office [hereafter LRO], QSP.

13. LRO QSB 1/115/38.
14. LRO QSB 1/47/76; QSB 1/55/35; QSB 1/59/93.
15. LRO WCW, will of John Hanworth of Bury, 1570.
16. These will extracts are taken from G. J. Piccope (ed.), *Lancashire and Cheshire wills and inventories from the ecclesiastical court, Chester*, vol. ii [1483–1589], Chetham Society, old ser., 51 (1860).
17. Hey, *Packmen, carriers and packhorse roads*, pp. 187–8.
18. LRO QSB 1/43/55; see also Diana Winterbotham, 'The building of Barton Bridge', *Lancashire Local Historian*, 8 (1993), pp. 33–42.
19. LRO QSB 1/130/54.
20. LRO QSB 1/43/60.
21. LRO QSB 1/43/61.
22. LRO QSB 1/109/46.
23. Willan, *Elizabethan Manchester*, p. 79.
24. For some contextual analysis of this, see Dorian Gerhold, *Carriers and coachmasters: trade and travel before the turnpikes* (Chichester, 2005), esp. chap. 1, 'The carrying network'.

In the labyrinth: John Dee and Reformation Manchester*

Stephen Bowd

The labyrinth

On 8 September 1597 John Dee (1527–?1609), the warden of Christ's College in Manchester, wrote to his old friend Sir Edward Dyer at court about his difficult new life in the north of England. Dee told Dyer that he was overcome or 'enforced' by 'the most intricate, [c]umbersome, and (in manner) lamentable affayres & estate, of this defamed & disordred Colledge of Manchester'.[1] In particular, he complained that he was assigned maintenance for himself and his household by the college fellows, and that he was bound by college oath to apply to them in order to earn this 'right & dignitie'. This humiliation had cost him a great deal of time and effort since he had arrived in the town the previous year. Furthermore, Dee explained that his problems were compounded by 'tymes of very great dearth here' so that unless God in his providence had not 'stirred up some mens harte' to send him barrels of rye from Danzig, some cattle from Wales, and some fish from Hull he could not see how his household of eighteen could have lived on the daily stipend of 4s.[2] He added: 'So hard & thinne a dyet, never in all my life, did I, nay was I forced, so long, to tast[e].' Indeed, no servant of his had ever had 'so slender allowance, at their table.'

Yet all of this had not disturbed him inwardly so much as the 'Cares & Cumbers for the Colledge affaires' which had 'altered, yea bar[r]ed and stayed' his 'whole course of life' and deprived him of 'so many years contynued Joyes, <taken> in ... most estemed Studies and exercises.' On this matter, he concluded that it had pleased God to lead him *'per multas tribulationes'*. However, he now sought somewhat less divine aid: 'I know no one (as yet) of her Majesties most honourable privy Cownsaile, who, willingly <& cumfortably> will listen unto my {pitifull} Complaynt, & declaration, how this Colledge of Manchester, is allmost, become No Colledge, in any respect (I say) in any respect. for I can veryfie my wordes, so manifestly'. Failing the intervention of the Privy Council he added a last hope that God would give 'grace sufficient, & send me mighty help, (tempore opportuno) to ende them: Or els they will help to hasten my deliverance, from these and all other vayne, & earthly Actions humane.' Dee expressed his considerable exasperation with Mancunian affairs in the margin at the top of one page of the letter by writing: 'EX MANCESTRIANO LABYRINTHO.'[3]

Dee's letter throws light on a relatively neglected episode in the life of a man better known for his studies of alchemy and astrology, or for his 'conversations with angels' than for his clerical duties in an early modern Barchester. However, the precise nature of Dee's Mancunian labyrinth has long puzzled scholars and some have suggested that his esoteric studies and his reputation as a 'conjurer' lay at the root of his troubles.[4] Dee spent a lifetime searching for the keys with which he might unlock the secrets of harmony between religion and philosophy in the universe in the past, present and future. He devoted himself to study and writing, experimentation, prayer and contemplation, and the promotion of his ambitious intellectual and political schemes at various European courts. Dee believed in his capacity to grasp the wonders and secrets of the world and to arrange them in some meaningful and useful way. He concluded that some men could lift their eyes up from the distractions of a busy and corrupted world and perceive some of the order and harmony of a universe that had been breathed into life by God. By comprehending much of this harmony using mathematics, and later in his career the cabalistic, alchemical, or scriptural keys given to him by the angels, Dee expected to understand the hidden connections between the earth and the heavens and between all natural things. God would reveal to Dee the divine language that he had used to create the universe. Using this immensely powerful language he would then help to usher in the Last Days, which the angels told him were due in 1588.[5]

Dee's interests aroused hostile contemporary comments which he was at pains to rebuff throughout his life,[6] but he was by no means an isolated figure in Elizabethan England. Nicholas Clulee, Deborah Harkness and William Sherman have carefully investigated his publications, surviving manuscripts and marginal annotations, and they have pointed out where Dee's natural philosophy drew upon medieval sources, or they have set Dee back in the mainstream of intellectual life in the Renaissance. They have also situated Dee at court or in other public or political arenas, and they have shown how his library and his vast expertise in arts and sciences were put to good use by prominent figures from the queen downwards. Dee has been renamed an 'intelligencer', a 'retailer of special knowledge' and a 'Christian natural philosopher'. The idea that he invoked demons has been discarded in favour of a more thorough analysis of the Christian and humanist aspects of Dee's conversations with angels.[7]

Dee's arcane knowledge was certainly of use to the crown in 1558–9,

George Cruikshank, 'Doctor Dee, in conjunction with his seer Edward Kelley, exhibiting his magical skill to Guy Fawkes'. This engraving of John Dee in Manchester with the famous gunpowder plotter appears in William Harrison Ainsworth's novel *Guy Fawkes* (first published in serial form in 1840) and reflects the growing Victorian interest in clairvoyancy which Ainsworth exploited in this Gothic (and largely unreadable) tale. (By permission of the Sir Kenneth Greene Library, Manchester Metropolitan University)

Doctor Dee, in conjunction with his seer Edward Kelley, exhibiting his magical skill to Guy Fawkes.

when he used astrology to calculate a propitious day for Queen Elizabeth's coronation, and again in the 1580s when the ambitious Earl of Leicester encouraged his work on the 'British Empire' to support claims to English Protestant leadership in the Low Countries.[8] However, there were limits to the patronage Dee received: Elizabeth never proved to be a substantial sponsor for Dee's schemes and his proposal for calendar reform, which would have brought England in line with the continent almost two centuries before it finally adopted the Gregorian system, was blocked by the ecclesiastical hierarchy.[9] Moreover, Dee was quickly dropped by courtiers such as Leicester in response to changes in royal policy or political events more broadly and his schemes for Elizabethan imperialism met with indifference or hostility. Dee's attempts to find support on the continent also failed: when he arrived in Prague in 1584 he found Emperor Rudolf II more interested in the financial rewards of alchemy than the role of 'world emperor' assigned to him in Dee's mystical programme of renewal.[10]

After Dee returned to England in 1589 he was shocked to discover that in his absence much of his large library at Mortlake had been dispersed. He petitioned the crown for help and in 1592 he set out his hopes for future projects to Queen Elizabeth's commissioners. In particular, he asked for the mastership of the hospital of St. Cross in Winchester because he would 'faine retyre myself for some yeares ensuing from the multitude and haunt of my common friends, and other, who visit me'. Dee argued that at St Cross he would be close to the glasshouses of Sussex where he could oversee the manufacture of instruments needed in his work; he could also provide room and lodging for more learned men and assistants than at his Mortlake home; set up a printing press; and indeed communicate with the continent with greater freedom.[11] Dee was also lobbying for the positions of chancellor at St Paul's and provost of Eton, but after some delay, during which he angled for an invitation to the court of the landgrave of Hesse,[12] he was awarded the less lucrative post of warden of Christ's College in Manchester in distant Lancashire.[13] Queen Elizabeth's response to the Countess of Warwick, who had thanked her on Dee's behalf for the appointment, may fairly sum up Dee's own feelings: 'She [the queen] took it graciously: and was sorry that it was so far from hence: but that some better thing near hand shall be found for me'.[14]

Elizabethan Lancashire

As Christopher Haigh has shown, during the reign of Queen Elizabeth, efforts to impose political control and religious conformity on Lancashire and the north-west of England were hampered by history, geography and socio-economic factors.[15] The county was large, poor, thinly populated and badly served by roads or other methods of communication, with very few towns of any significance. Political authority was divided, absent or ineffective. The Council of the North never held any authority over the county because it was a county palatine and a part of the Duchy of Lancaster. The Duchy administration based in London never provided leadership in religious or political matters and its local officers were more concerned with raising revenues from the land. The palatinate organisation was similarly ineffective. In practice the earl of Derby guided local government with the aid of a handful of county clients.[16]

The religious life of the county was focused on chapels rather than parish churches which, given the size of parishes, were often distant from the communities they were supposed to serve. These large rural parishes provided lucrative benefices for pluralists who were usually non-resident, and to make matters worse the educational standard of resident clergy was generally inferior to that of the rest of the country. Episcopal control over much of the county was also ineffective due to the size and topography of the diocese, conflicting and competing ecclesiastical jurisdictions, and a series of indolent or conservative bishops of Chester. The cumulative result of all of this was to keep Lancashire fairly isolated from the mainstream of religious change in Reformation England and to maintain traditional patterns of belief which were elsewhere being challenged or overturned. This meant, for example, that there was a high level of charitable bequests to religious causes, and a high number of chantry foundations even in the 1540s.[17]

One of the principal beneficiaries of pious bequests and grants was the Collegiate Church of St Mary, St Denys and St George in Manchester. A college was founded there in 1421 by the lord and rector of the manor to supply the church with a warden to fulfil the duties of rector, and a resident community of chantry priests to pray for the souls of the lord's family members in purgatory. In the fifteenth and early sixteenth centuries the collegiate community was endowed with some fine buildings, including several chapels – it was noted in 1539 that the college church was 'almost thoroughowt doble ilyd *ex quadrato lapide durissimo*'[18] – but it was dissolved in the second wave of Protestant dissolutions in 1547 and the buildings were acquired by the earl of Derby. Although the college was refounded by Mary in 1553, dissolved again by Elizabeth I and refounded in 1578 as Christ's College, the buildings remained in hands of the earls of Derby (whose forebears were wardens between 1481 and 1506) while much of its land was acquired by the crown and then leased.

The refounded college in Mary's reign was distinguished by the Catholic fervour of its new personnel, and there is some evidence that traditional Catholicism survived and prospered in the area well into the reign of Elizabeth. For example, there are instances of Mancunians saving church images, 'shrines' and 'monuments of superstition' from destruction in the 1570s.[19] Many households doubtless continued to use old books to recite Latin prayers and to observe fasts and feast days. The homes of landowners and gentry also served as centres for traditional beliefs and practices. For example, the Blundells at Crosby Hall in south-west Lancashire provided one focus for networks of Catholics.[20] The 'northern court' of the earls of Derby was also largely conservative in outlook: the enthusiastic patronage of theatre companies by successive earls and countesses of Derby reflects the more general persistence in Lancashire of an attachment to traditional pursuits increasingly deplored by the more rigorous, or 'hotter', sort of Protestant.[21] In sum, the county was known in London for its religious backwardness – a place where the Catholics, whether 'Church papists' paying lip-service to new rites or recusants who refused to go to church at all, and the religiously uneducated or plain uninterested were believed to exist in dangerously large numbers.

Oliver Carter, a fellow of Christ's College, lamented in 1579 that his 'poore neighbours' had been 'over much seduced ... by ... Popish devises', and that the 'godlie Magistrates' were hindered in their attempts to spread the word since

> there be not onelie close and secret enemies, which wander abroad in corners, seducing the simple by wicked doctrine, sedicious & traiterous libells, and false tales, alienating their mindes by all meanes, from true religion unto superstition, but also the rabble of the Romishe merchantes with their masking wares, do so increase and multiplie, that unlesse redresse bee had in time, I do feare least great inconvenience and mischiefe will ensue thereof.

Carter saw in his neighbours 'such a readinesse to imbrace everie fonde idolatrous tradition invented by man, to accept the advise and counsell of everie ignorant, & lurking rebellious priest, to persist in their old doating customes, and heathenishe ceremonies'.[22] In his view the Catholic church was 'a cage of uncleane birdes [Rev 18:2] ... a Sinagogue of Sathan [Rev 2:9]' led by adulterers and 'coniurers' such as Sylvester II who gave his soul to the Devil.[23] Carter asserted that the Catholic church exceeded previous idolatrous churches:

> In outwarde pompe, in superfluous ornaments, in unnecessarie toyes, in vaine decking of ... Churches with gold and silver, and other precious and costly attire, in unprofitable rites, in furnishinge ... temples with abominable idols, in pleasing the eare, in delightinge the eye, in ringinge, in roaring, in toying, in trifling, in nodding, in becking, & in ducking, in all such heathenishe shewes, and sensles significations.[24]

There may have been some truth in Carter's accusations of proselytising Catholics: in 1584 twelve priests held in the Salford gaol were described as forming a 'college' on account of their continued organization and bold activities in receiving 'both exhortations and absolutions at their pleasure'. Six years later the bishop of Chester noted the 'lewde rebellious speeches and usage of the prisoners in the ffleete at Manchester',[25] while in 1598 the Member of Parliament for Lancashire wrote of 'some lewd priests' who were alleged to have practiced exorcism in order to gain converts to Catholicism.[26]

However, the note of alarm sounded by Carter and his contemporaries does not simply reflect their fears about the danger and extent of Catholicism or superstition, but also indicates the ways in which they were writing towards their own different or overlapping ends. The spirit of reformation in Lancashire coexisted with a wide variety of responses to unsettled religious times which could range from acceptance or resignation to passive or even active resistance. The passage to a reformed church and people was also shaped by local politics and tradition in the shape of Carter's 'godlie Magistrate'. It was a combination of these religious and secular cross-currents, the 'birthpangs of Protestant England', which severely buffeted Dee during his time as warden in Manchester.[27]

Magistracy and ministry in Manchester

Historians of early modern England are now divided over the origins, extent, and pace of the reformations which occurred during the reigns of Henry VIII, Edward VI and Elizabeth I.[28] Triumphalist accounts of the royal sponsorship of a nationalized church rolling back the frontiers of a defective Catholicism with growing popular approval have been revised. For example, Eamon Duffy has provided compelling evidence for the survival and continuity of 'traditional religion', which confirms many of the conclusions Christopher Haigh reached in his study of Lancashire.[29] The extent of the political and social engagement of the English Catholic community is also being reassessed with emphasis shifting from the influence of trained Tridentine priests from the continent to continuities in local belief and practice. Historians have also issued warnings about too casual a use of terms such as 'Puritan' and too ready an assumption that Puritans were always contentious and disruptive elements in English society, paving the way towards the civil wars of the mid seventeenth century.[30]

In response to Eamon Duffy, historians have shown how many, perhaps the majority, of people in sixteenth-century England were persuaded by traditional or communal elements in Protestantism to accept the new regime and even to find it personally satisfying, although confessional identities may have been fluid well into the seventeenth century. The startling diversity of beliefs underlying outward conformity which have been uncovered has led 'post-revisionist' historians to offer caution rather than confidence in marking the ontological or temporal boundaries of that great monolith of Whig history: 'The English Reformation'.[31] Dee's outward conformity similarly masked, or was mingled with, a notable spectrum of beliefs,[32] while Manchester itself provides an interesting case-study of the highly complex process of reform. As Alexandra Walsham has remarked, the bare bones of the relationship between English society and belief may be fleshed out by means of a 'painstaking reconstitution of communities, and of the networks of religious affiliation criss-crossing them.'[33]

The deanery of Manchester certainly exhibited some of the most obvious signs of religious change, if not complete conformity to the prescribed rites of the Church of England, in Elizabethan Lancashire. By the end of the century the ancient township of Manchester had grown into a marketing and regional centre of about 2,000 people well placed for trade and commerce in wool and linen with London (and thence to France), the West Riding, and via the ports of Chester and Liverpool, with Ireland.[34] The existence of these channels of communication with puritan centres such as London and Halifax allowed elements of religious reform to enter the town's bloodstream.[35]

There are hints in Dee's letter of 1597 to Dyer that these national and county-wide religious battles were also being fought out in the college. The stage was set for a series of tense confrontations over conformity in which Dee seems invariably to have been on the losing side. In rather acrimonious circumstances the fellows of the college refused to grant Dee £5 for the rent of a house.[36] Oliver Carter, who practiced as a solicitor to supplement his income, threatened to sue Dee, probably for unpaid wages.[37] Carter also seems to have fallen to discarding the 'popish rag' of the surplice, or at least to have voiced his disagreement once again with this and other aspects of Elizabethan conformity in church. Dee noted in his diary how Carter exhibited 'impudent and evident disobedience in the church'.[38] The following day he 'repented, and some pacification was made', but Carter was still causing disturbances in the college house three years later.[39]

It is likely that Dee's problems with Matthew Palmer, the new curate, also originated in Palmer's obstreperous nonconformity: Palmer caused Dee some 'troublesome days' in the spring of 1597.[40] A letter from Edward Glover and others described as 'inhabitants of Manchester and Salforde' to Dee on 5 April that year may help to illuminate the origins of these incidents. The writer describes: 'The uncharitable and malitious proceedinges of Mr. Palmer against our godlie and learned preacher, Mr. Heaton'. Palmer had been attacking Heaton – for unspecified reasons – from the pulpit and in private, and Dee was asked to call him to order or to remove him altogether.[41] Dee notes a further 'supplication exhibited by the parishioners' in his diary five days later. Perhaps the puritan Palmer regarded Heaton's administration of the sacraments insufficiently godly.[42]

On his return to Manchester from London in the summer of 1600 after an absence of about two years Dee mustered some diplomatic energy and rather than displaying his 'heady displeasure' with the fellows 'by reason of their manifold misusing of themselves against' him, he 'did with all lenity entertain them, and showed the most part of the things that I had brought to pass at London for the College good, &c.'[43] In this way he managed 'a certain blessed reconciliation' among the wayward fellows, he had an organ installed, and even obtained the resignation of Thomas Williamson, one of the fellows appointed in 1578. However, despite his best efforts, Dee noted on 11 September 1600 that: 'Commissioners from the Bishop of Chester authorised by the Bishop of Chester did call me before them in the church about 3 of the clock after noon, and did deliver to me certain petitions put up by the Fellows against me to answer – before the 18 of this month. I answered them all *ex tempore*, and yet they gave me leave to write at leisure.'[44]

Dee's position in the college was not helped by the absence of local political support. William Stanley, the sixth earl of Derby and who succeeded to the title in 1594, had houses at Knowsley and Lathom near Liverpool, and Alport Lodge (formerly a collegiate property) on Deansgate in Manchester. However, between 1594 and 1607 the family was embroiled in inheritance difficulties and debts, and lost control of the lieutenancy of the counties of Lancashire and Cheshire (although the earl was elected mayor of Liverpool in 1603).[45] As a result the collegiate patronage which the Stanleys had enjoyed earlier in the sixteenth century was materially diminished: Alport Lodge was sold in 1599 and the other college buildings in their possession were leased by 1600.[46]

It seems that on the occasion when the magistracy – in the form of the new lord of the manor of Manchester – and the ministry did unite in action, Dee was the victim. Sir Nicholas Mosley was a wealthy and ambitious man who served as lord mayor of London in 1599–1600 after two decades in the capital exporting cloth. In March 1596 Mosley and his son Rowland acquired the manor of Manchester from John Lacy of London for £3,500.[47] Around the same time both men acquired the manor of Cheetham and Cheetwood, and Rowland paid £8,000 to Sir Robert Cecil for the manors and lordships of Withington and Hough near Manchester.[48] Mosley's regime began with a drive to survey manorial land and to enclose commons land with a view to maximizing his revenues from both. He also moved to enhance his political authority by means of doses of sweetness and fear. He wined and dined the officers of the manorial court leet over which Mosley or his relatives presided, and he regularly attended the Manchester quarter sessions. He saw off complaining burgesses with legal finagling and repelled rioters with cudgels.[49] In 1602 the enraged burgesses of Manchester claimed that Mosley had worked 'to alter, overthrowe and chaunge all the auncient priviledges, usages and customs' such as common pasturage in 100 acres of Collyhurst, which had hitherto benefited the town as a place of recreation, shooting, and mustering troops, and as a location of cabins for plague victims.[50] In short, Mosley may not have been popular but he was surely influential.

Mosley's involvement in town affairs extended in the direction of religious matters, perhaps as part of an attempt to enforce civic unity at a moment when the influence of the Stanleys in the town was somewhat weakened. Like other urban gentry in the later sixteenth century Mosley may have felt that when the local magnates and institutional church failed to provide leadership in moral matters there was a danger that local order and government would break down.[51] Similar holy alliances were promoted or actually in place at Beverley, Bury St Edmunds, Colchester, Doncaster, Dorchester, Gloucester, Norwich and Salisbury at this time.[52] The court leet in Manchester very occasionally dealt with moral failings such as prostitution and sports, while the quarter sessions held in Mosley's presence at the turn of the century indicted, presented or punished recusants, absentees from church, adulterers, prostitutes, the parents of illegitimate children, an 'ape' baiter and the case of one man who was alleged to have said that 'he cared not for the bisshoppe of Chester and that hee had no King but God'.[53]

Mosley, like Cecil and others in authority, seems to have been keen to promote preaching and he was content to lend his name to support the new fellow of the college William Bourne in this regard. Bourne, who replaced Thomas Williamson, was a preacher from Cambridge, a close friend of Carter, and a recalcitrant rejector of the surplice.[54] His appearance on the scene seems to have rallied opposition to Warden Dee who had absented himself from the college for much longer than the three months usually allowed in any one year.[55] It was likely due to these absences that Dee was reported by the Chester visitation court as 'noe preacher' in October 1601 and again in November 1604.[56] In February 1603 Mosley (together with Edward Fleetwood and William Leigh, whose attack on astrologers in a funeral sermon given in 1602 may be an oblique reference to Dee[57]) wrote to Cecil to recommend that Bourne be made a fellow of the college. Mosley, Fleetwood and Leigh observed that there was only one preacher in the town, and added rather pointedly that Dee was 'no preacher' while Bourne was 'a learned preacher'.[58] On the face of it, Dee's critics seem to have won this battle: at the end of September 1603 a letter was sent to the warden to ensure the election of Bourne as a fellow of the college. On the same day Bourne was even granted the wardenship of the college in reversion after Dee.[59] However, new royal priorities and national loyalty may ultimately have asserted themselves over this local matter for when Dee died, Bourne was passed over in favour of a Scotsman.[60]

Christ's College

Given all of these divisions it is not surprising that, as Christopher Haigh has noted, '[t]he Elizabethan college [of Manchester] was not, as some have supposed, a powerful agency of religious change but a society of careless and quarrelsome clerics'.[61] The resources available to the college were not on the scale of those of many other collegiate establishments such as Beverley and Southwell, which supported 56 and 63 priests and clerks respectively before the Reformation.[62] Unlike Canterbury cathedral or Westminster abbey after the dissolutions, the college did not maintain its choral worship or, apparently, increase its educational provision in any way.[63] In 1600 Dee visited the school 'and found great imperfection in all and every of the scholars' to his 'great grief'.[64] Moreover, the fabric of the Collegiate Church was neglected and in decay.[65]

At the root of some of these problems lay an erosion of clerical incomes. English clergy, especially those in small urban parishes, were badly affected by rising prices and new taxes during the sixteenth century. Some clergy were victims of tithes commuted to money which lost its value through inflation, or they may have been reliant on personal tithes or tithes on lambs and wool rather than the 'great tithes' on more valuable crops which rectors commonly held. The civic authorities might supplement incomes quite generously, as at Beverley in the 1580s,[66] but the vicars of the collegiate churches in Warwick and Stratford-upon-Avon in 1586 by contrast were poorly remunerated by their town corporations.[67] There is no evidence that wealthy Mancunians were willing to help the fellows of Christ's College in a similar fashion. On the contrary, there is ample evidence that the licit and illicit dispersal of collegiate goods after the dissolution, as at Worcester's college of Christchurch (as the cathedral was renamed), enriched everyone but Christ's College.[68]

The college's troubles originated in the 1560s when long leases were granted by the fellows to local gentry on very favourable terms – even if these lands were already subject to leases. In 1571 Warden Herle was found to be creaming off most of the college's income to pay his own salary, forcing impoverished fellows into 'physic and surgery' or even inn-keeping, and he seems to have been involved in forgery.[69] Oliver Carter was appointed in an attempt to improve the calibre of the fellows but he sued Herle (as he would Dee) for unpaid wages and was himself stabbed by a disgruntled litigant of the college.

Warden Herle also sold new leases with heavy entrance fines and legal fees, and even let farms out with little regard for the existing tenants' welfare. Disastrously, he granted long-lease of the great tithes of Manchester to the queen, and this was subsequently assigned to courtiers and sub-let.[70] As an anonymous well-informed contemporary, perhaps Dee, put it c.1603–9:

> He [i.e. Herle] sould all the lands and tithes and all other commodities belonginge, a fewe onely except; and the house it selfe to the Earle of *Darby*, (in whose hands it is now,) and granted long leases of most or all the tithes, Colledge lands, and other sperituall livings to one *Killigreve*; and *Killigreve* granted them to the Queene; & shee to them that are now possessed of them to the utter overthrow of that famous rich Colledg [*sic*] so that he left nothing to the mentenance of such a port [*sic*] as in times past had their bene keept: Also the Queene called in the old foundation, and granted a new one, of a Warden, 4 Fellows, ij Parish-Curatts, 4 Musitians, ij Parish-clarkes, and 4 Queristers, alltho living be not left for them; an [*sic*] dedicated it to our Saviour Christe; so Hearle when he had done, resined it, and Doctor *Wooton* was installed in his place. Their is no Quiristers keept now.[71]

An investigation instituted by Lord Burghley found that the warden and fellows did not live together in the college, whose property had been sold to the earl of Derby, but in their own homes – the warden stayed at an inn when he visited Manchester. When the queen refounded the college in 1578 four new fellows were appointed, although they remained non-resident. Moreover, the owners of the tithe leases acquired from the queen were unwilling to pay higher rents to fund the college or renegotiate the terms of their leases at all. By the time Dee arrived on the scene the lessees were suing each other, the college and tithe-payers 'in a legal free-for-all' which was typical of the increasing urban litigation after c.1540 between landlords who had acquired ecclesiastical properties and embittered townsmen.[72]

To make matters worse, the last decade of the sixteenth century was marked by economic depression and social tensions, if not an outright 'crisis' in the towns.[73] As Dee found, three years of bad harvests coupled with a marked rise in the population had increased England's reliance on imported Polish rye, and at this time the trade routes to the Continent were somewhat disrupted. As a consequence, not only were many areas of the north affected by a subsistence crisis and famine, but Mancunian cloth exporters were now competing with London to gain a foothold in the domestic textiles market. This combination of an inadequate income and economic depression meant that Dee, who had lobbied hard for a post in order to settle his debts, recoup the loss of his library, and promote new projects, was often in debt during his Manchester sojourn. Dee borrowed at least £36 17s 4d, no doubt to pay for his accommodation, for wet nurses for his children, and other servants.[74] Not surprisingly, Dee energetically pursued his right to various tithes – especially those of corn, the price of which had increased fairly rapidly – in the expensive and notoriously lax diocesan consistory courts between 1596 and 1598.[75] It is therefore not surprising to find Dee complaining to Dyer about the 'hard & thinne a dyet' his household had to endure, or to discover that in 1602 his son Arthur was chasing dowries and displaying 'great greaf & discontentment for wante'.[76]

As the new warden Dee was also immediately embroiled in the disputes over leased college land since the warden and fellows of the college were lords of the manor of Newton, which bordered with Clayton demesne along the River Medlock in Manchester parish, and was the area that Warden Herle had gouged. Three interlinked areas of dispute were to affect Dee's personal position from the moment he arrived in Manchester:[77] the recovery of tithes from tenants on these and other college lands; the prevention of encroachments and intrusions on college lands; and the upkeep of the fabric of the church and the maintenance of the warden and fellows, which relied on the income from tenants. Dee and the fellows pursued their claims against tenants by informal means, and also in three formal forums: the manorial court of Newton, over which Dee presided within a couple of months of arriving; the court of Duchy Chamber in London; and the diocesan consistory court in Chester.[78]

The surviving records of the manorial court, usually held at Newton township, a few miles from the college, reveal that many of the men pursued for encroachments on college land were frequent offenders, and it seems as if this court was ineffective in recovering fines or in enforcing its decisions. This may help to explain why the college prosecuted Richard Heape in the duchy court in 1598 for 'tresspass and encroachments on the wastes called Newton Common or Newton Heath'.[79] Heape had been called before the manorial court as far back as 1584 for building a smithy on college land there, and in 1596 it was noted at the manorial court that the encroachment remained and that there had been 'no reformation' in this matter.[80] Dee may have tried to exert some informal pressure on tithe defaulters and intruders through meetings with their landlord Sir John Byron of Royton, but he seems to have had no luck here.[81] The warden and fellows proceeded against Heape and others regarding Newton Heath again in 1600: on 13 June that year a commission was formed to enquire on behalf of the wardens and fellows of the college regarding intrusions on the wastes of the manor of Newton by Heape and others. Depositions were taken at Newton on 1 September.[82] Finally, in November 1602 the warden and fellows of the college successfully proceeded against Richard Heape and others in the chancery court at Lancaster for unlawfully using Newton Heath.[83]

At the beginning of 1596 a commission for the College was drafted in the duchy office in London. It noted the 'veray & [sic] poore estate' of the collegiate lands and leases; a problem compounded by missing, detained or damaged documentation. It was therefore necessary to undertake a new thorough survey of the collegiate lands with a view to restoring the collegiate income.[84] Of particular concern were several disputes over the line of demarcation of the parish at Theale Moor, or 'Theylemore', near Moston.[85] It was probably with this and the other matters in view that in 1597 Dee and others at the behest of 'the higher powres' made an especially thorough Rogationtide perambulation of the bounds of the parish of Manchester, which took in Theale Moor as well as Newton Heath. This 'survey geometrical of the very circuits of Manchester parish' took several days to complete and it allowed Dee to inspect the stakes placed at its bounds and to determine where the college's parish boundary touched that of the rector of Prestwich's parish: the aim was to use this 'exact workmanship' to draw up 'a plat, or Charte', presumably to determine who had the right to the tithes there.[86] This provoked an 'unlawful assembly and rout' against the surveyors of the manor of Newton.[87]

On 20 May 1598 the commission again noted the 'great decay and poore estate of the foresaid Christs Colledg [sic] in Manchester', and directed special attention to discovering what belonged to the college and what had been detained. The six special commissioners – including Dee – were required to 'enquire, survey, search, and try out the yearly value quality and quantity of all the mannors lands' belonging to the college, and to call in documents and take statements from witnesses in order to do so. The '[r]ecord of survey made by our late dearly beloved Counsellor Walter Mildmay Knight (then our principall Auditor)' in 1548 was noted,[88] and presumably some use was made of the more recent surveys and maps, including one of 'Manchester town described and measured by Mr Christopher Saxton' under Dee's supervision, and another of 'the way to Stopford [Stockport]' undertaken by Dee's servants.[89] However, for better information, a jury of 20 'honest and sufficient gentlemen' made a perambulation on Theale Moor, viewed the boundary and gave a verdict favourable to the college. Moreover, interrogatories were made of five men regarding 'the lymytte and bounde of the parishe of Manchester uppon Theylemore'. In his diary Dee notes 'the Commission set upon in the Chapter House' on 3 July 1600 – probably in this matter.[90] All of this was certified in the

Duchy Chamber on 4 November 1600.[91] However, the case dragged on for several more years as the commissioners sought to deal with other Theale Moor defaulters such as James Asheton.[92] College lands at Dunham Massey in Cheshire were also a source of dispute with Sir George Booth between 1597 and 1604.[93]

Finis

It was probably with some sense of relief from these lengthy and tiresome affairs that Dee set out for London in November 1604 intending to stay in the city until the following Easter.[94] However, his absence from Manchester may have been prolonged by the outbreak of plague in the town during 1604–5 and rendered permanent by the death of his wife there.[95] Dee seems to have died in London on 26 March 1609 after a fairly long illness,[96] ignored by the new king and his court, satirised on the stage,[97] scorned by the well placed or well informed,[98] and unlamented in Manchester.[99]

By any standards it was a disappointing conclusion to his life. The post of warden had offered Dee few, if any, of the rewards he expected in return for his years of hard work. Faced with religious and political division and assaulted by personal attacks, Dee may have found the prospect of an eirenic exploration of the secrets of the universe and promises of a universal order ever more attractive, if increasingly illusory and impractical in such a hostile environment. Dee's natural philosophical investigations, including alchemy, and his conversations with angels required an 'experimental household' with private rooms, apparatus and assistants.[100] However, no warden's lodging was built until the seventeenth century, and Dee may only have been able to use Alport Lodge until 1599 when the earl of Derby sold it. Dee certainly had the use of some rooms at the college itself by 1600 since he mentions 'my dining-room' there on one occasion when he was entertaining visitors,[101] but a few months after the fellows withheld Dee's grant he hired 'the close', which may indicate that with the sale of Alport Lodge imminent he was forced to take inferior lodgings.[102] It is therefore tempting to draw the conclusion that Dee's normal investigations would have been severely curtailed and that his wife Jane would have found this northern household particularly difficult to manage. There is some evidence that Dee practised alchemy in the north and that he was consulted locally as a 'cunning man' in a bid to recover stolen property and identify a thief.[103] On the whole, though, it seems as if Dee's studies, while not entirely 'stayed', as he claimed in 1597, were directed into narrower, more local and antiquarian channels by material and geographical restrictions.[104]

Perhaps as a result of these restrictions on his 'most estemed Studies and exercises', Dee avoided the accusation of conjuring which was made against him at other times. In fact, most of Dee's trouble in Manchester stemmed from the fact that he was the representative of conformity in the sense that he was an appointee of the archbishop of Canterbury and followed, outwardly at least, the rites of the Church of England. The 'graven images' (Carter's 'sensles significations'), paraphernalia such as the surplice, and non-scriptural texts such the Book of Common Prayer introduced by the church were regarded with almost as much repugnance by the liturgical nonconformists as any semi-Catholic 'superstitious' words, symbols, objects, rituals and ancient books employed by Dee in his angelic conversations or alchemical investigations. Any attempt by Dee to impose the former on such men was bound to cause trouble.

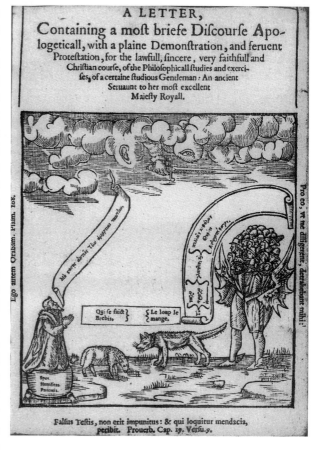

The Manchester Dee who aroused Carter's hostility was a practical warden keen to secure and augment his income through the courts and other semi-public arenas; an agent of conformity at odds with many of his colleagues over some key elements of worship; and a careful and energetic investigator of local history and topography. However, he was largely powerless to break the Gordian knot of religious, social, and personal difficulties that he found in the town and college. It probably did not help that although Dee was certainly not short of distinguished local visitors he was rejected or ignored by the royal court, probably as a consequence of his association with the disgraced Sir Walter Ralegh, and he was superseded by a younger generation with closer ties to the new king.[105] In sum, his natural and spiritual investigations signally failed to deliver the fruits and profits which they had initially promised, and Dee never found a path out of the labyrinth of the English Reformation as it was played out in the college of turbulent fellows in Manchester.

Finally, just as Dee's time in Manchester has not received the serious

John Dee, *A letter, containing a most briefe discourse apologeticall* (London, 1599), frontispiece. Dee defended himself against accusations of conjuring on many occasions throughout his life. In this frontispiece, probably designed by Dee himself, we see Dee kneeling on a cushion ('hope, humility and patience') in prayer ('O God impute not this sin unto them') while in the clouds float the ear, eye and hand of God wielding a sword over his enemies: the many-headed mob-monster with winged feet ('the swift sharp poison-tongued monster of many heads that devours men') and a wolf, which threatens to eat a sheep

attention it deserves until recently, so 'pre-industrial' Manchester has, in some ways, languished in the labyrinth of history. Unincorporated until 1838, the town's seigneurial government, its manorial courts and the dominance of the Stanleys or the Mosleys marked it out as something of an anachronism even in c.1600 as many comparable communities rushed to gain incorporation, or to take advantage of the dissolution of ecclesiastical lands and create an oligarchic civic culture. However, in this article I have attempted to show how an urban reformation also touched Manchester. Like many other towns, ecclesiastical lands tumbled from crown hands to the landed gentry and then to ambitious urban gentry such as the Mosleys.[106] The duchy or local manorial courts were the arenas for disputes over the ownership and use of land. Such disputes, as well as the open conflict of armed men on the mosses and moors around Manchester, reflect 'a virtual crisis of authority' which has also been identified elsewhere in England, especially during the crisis decade of the 1590s when plague and economic slump sharpened social and political conflicts.[107] The dominance of manorial forms of government perhaps stifled the development of robust self-governing institutions locally, but in seeking to promote their authority and autonomy after the Reformation some townsmen turned to the discipline and obedience embodied by Puritanism. It was this heady mixture of social, religious, and political authority which Dee encountered in the making in Manchester, and it was this same cocktail of assertive localism which surely fuelled the town's anti-royalist and anti-Derby stance into the 1640s and beyond.[108]

Notes

*   The Manchester European Research Institute, Manchester Metropolitan University generously supported the cost of research trips to London, Oxford and Cambridge. I am very grateful for the guidance I have received from the anonymous reader, Andrew Brown, Alex Craven, Craig Horner, Christopher Hunwick, Glyn Parry, Michael Powell, William Sherman, Alex Walsham and Tom Webster.

1. Dee to Dyer, Manchester, 8 Sep. 1597: B[ritish] L[ibrary], Harley MS 249, fos. 95r–105r. This letter largely consists of a guide to the reading of Dee's 1577 work *THALATTOKRATIA BRETTANIKI; Miscelanea quaedam extemporanea; De imperij Brytanici Iurisdictione, in Mari* [THE BRITISH SEA-SOVEREIGNTY; or an extemporaneous miscellany on the sea-jurisdiction of the British Empire]: Lisa Jardine and William Sherman, 'Pragmatic readers: knowledge transactions and scholarly services in late Elizabethan England', in Anthony Fletcher and Peter Roberts (eds.), *Religion, culture and society in early modern Britain: essays in honour of Patrick Collinson* (Cambridge, 1994), pp. 111–13.

2. On 27 June 1597 Dee noted in his diary: 'News came from Hull of 23 barrels of Dansk rye sent me from John Pontoys.' See also entries for 10 Aug., 5 Sep. 1596 (seventeen cattle were sent to Dee by Welsh relatives) and for 4, 7, and 20 July 1597. Dee's 'diary' for this period consists of annotations made in two printed astrological manuals (now Bodl[eian Library, Oxford], Ashmole 487 and 488). All references to Dee's diary in this article are to the modern-spelling edition of the text: Edward Fenton (ed.), *The diaries of John Dee* (Charlbury, 1998) [hereafter *dJD*]. I have compared this with the annotated text of the Manchester diary edited in six parts by John Eglington Bailey, 'Dr John Dee, warden of Manchester (1595 to 1608)', *Local Gleanings: an archaeological and historical magazine chiefly relating to Lancashire and Cheshire*, 1:1–6 (1879).

3. BL, Harley, MS 249, fos. 104v, 105r. <> = insertion between the lines, { } = marginal insertion.

4. Peter J. French, *John Dee: the world of an Elizabethan magus* (London, 1972), p. 7; Frances Yates, 'John Dee: Christian cabalist', in Frances Yates, *The occult philosophy in the Elizabethan Age* (1979; London, 2001), pp. 105–110; Charlotte Fell Smith, *John Dee (1527–1608)* (London, 1909), chaps. 21–3.

5. My outline of Dee's interests here is based on Deborah E. Harkness, *John Dee's conversations with angels: cabala, alchemy, and the end of nature* (Cambridge, 2000).

6. John Foxe (George Townsend [ed.]), *Acts and Monuments* (8 vols., repr. New York, 1965), vii, pp. 349, 641–4, 681, 756–7; *dJD*, 22 Feb. 1593. Dee's last four publications were concerned with rebutting just such a slander.

7. Nicholas H. Clulee, *John Dee's natural philosophy: between science and religion* (London, 1988); Harkness, *John Dee's*; William H. Sherman, *John Dee: the politics of reading and writing in the English Renaissance* (Amherst, 1995).

8. Glyn Parry, 'John Dee and the Elizabethan British Empire in its European context', *Historical Journal*, 49:3 (2006), pp. 643–75. I am grateful to Prof. Parry for letting me see this article before publication and for discussing his forthcoming book on Dee with me.

9. Robert Poole, *Time's alteration: calendar reform in early modern England* (London, 1998), chap. 5.

10. R. J. W. Evans, *Rudolf II and his world: a study in intellectual history, 1576–1612* (2nd. ed., London, 1997), pp. 218–28.

11. John Dee, 'The Compendious Rehearsall of John Dee … made unto two Honorable Commissioners … 1592', in James Crossley (ed.), *Autobiographical tracts of Dr John Dee, warden of the college of Manchester*, Chetham Society, old ser., 24 (1851), pp. 39–41.

12. Dee to Moritz of Hesse, Mortlake, 22 Jan. 1595, Murhardsche Bibliothek der Stadt Kassel und Landesbibliothek, 2° Ms. Chem. 19:2, fos. 114r–15v, 117v. Microfilm.

13. The wardenship was first mentioned to Dee by the archbishop of Canterbury on 3 Jan. 1595: *dJD*. The royal grant of the wardenship to Dee is dated 7 May 1595: M[anchester] C[athedral] A[rchives], MS 93. I am grateful to Dr Michael Powell for drawing my attention to this document.
14. *dJD*, 31 July 1595.
15. Christopher Haigh, *Reformation and resistance in Tudor Lancashire* (Cambridge, 1975), pt. 1.
16. *Ibid.*, pp. 104–5.
17. *Ibid.*, pp. 65–75.
18. Lucy Toulmin Smith (ed.), *The itinerary of John Leland in or about the years 1535–1543* (5 vols., London, 1964), iv, p. 6. One modern authority has commented, '[t]ogether the church and college buildings represent one of the largest and most complete examples of a late medieval collegiate foundation in the country': Clare Hartwell, *The history and architecture of Chetham's School and Library* (New Haven and London, 2004), p. 12.
19. Haigh, *Reformation and resistance*, pp. 203–5, 219–20. However, these instances may also reflect 'uncertainty about the succession' and a reluctance yet again 'to destroy expensive furnishings and fittings': Peter Marshall, *Reformation England 1480–1642* (London, 2003), p. 120.
20. Margaret Sena, 'William Blundell and the networks of Catholic dissent in post-Reformation England', chap. 4 in Alexandra Shepard and Phil Withington (eds.), *Communities in early modern England: networks, place, rhetoric* (Manchester and New York, 2000).
21. Patrick Collinson, *The religion of Protestants: the church in English society 1559 1625* (Oxford, 1982), pp. 205–6. Church ales and religious drama also persisted in Tewkesbury into the early seventeenth century due in part to a lack of strong noble or upper gentry leadership and episcopal inaction: Caroline Litzenberger, 'The coming of Protestantism to Elizabethan Tewkesbury', chap. 4 in Patrick Collinson and John Craig, *The Reformation in English towns, 1500–1640* (Basingstoke, 1998), here at pp. 86–8.
22. Oliver Carter, *An Answere ... unto certaine Popish Questions and Demandes* (London, 1579), 'The Epistle Dedicatorie' (to the fourth earl of Derby).
23. *Ibid.*, fos. 20r, 29r (sigs C4r, D5r).
24. *Ibid.*, fos. 34r-v (sig. E2r-v).
25. Haigh, *Reformation and resistance*, p. 257; Joseph Gillow, *Lord Burghley's map of Lancashire in 1590. With notes on the designated manorial lords, biographical and genealogical, and brief histories of their estates traced down to the present day* (London, 1907), p. 1; *Kenyon MSS.*, 14th report, appendix, pt. 4 (Historical Manuscripts Commission, 1894), pp. 603–4. For other cases of prisons as 'sites of evangelical and polemical activity' see Peter Lake and Michael Questier, 'Prisons, priests and people', chap. 8 in Nicholas Tyacke (ed.), *England's Long Reformation 1500–1800* (London,

1998).

. Haigh, *Reformation and resistance*, p. 291; Sir Richard Molyneux to Sir John Stanhope, Sestone, 13 June 1598, in *Salisbury MSS* (Historical Manuscripts Commission, 1899), viii, p. 213–4.

27. Patrick Collinson, *The birthpangs of Protestant England: religious and cultural change in the sixteenth and seventeenth centuries* (Basingstoke, 1988).

28. For an introduction to some of these issues see Christopher Haigh, 'The recent historiography of the English Reformation', chap. 1 in Christopher Haigh (ed.), *The English Reformation revised* (Cambridge, 1987).

29. Eamon Duffy, *The stripping of the altars: traditional religion in England, c.1400–c.1580* (New Haven and London, 1992). See also Christopher Haigh, 'The continuity of Catholicism in the English Reformation', chap. 9 in Haigh, *English Reformation*.

30. Collinson, *Religion of Protestants*. For some words of warning about the use of the terms 'Puritan' and 'Puritanism' in relation to popular culture see Christopher Durston and Jacqueline Eales (eds.), *The culture of English Puritanism, 1560–1700* (Basingstoke, 1996), intro.

31. A 'post-revisionist' synthesis which highlights the sheer variety of religious points of view is Marshall, *Reformation England*. See also Alexandra Walsham, 'The parochial roots of Laudianism revisited: Catholics, anti-Calvinists and "Parish Anglicans" in early Stuart England', *Journal of Ecclesiastical History*, 49 (1998), pp. 620–51. I am grateful to Dr Walsham for sending me an offprint of her article.

32. For evidence of Dee's conformity, such as disapproval of sabbath breaking, see *dJD*, 13 Jan. 1583; 21 May 1590; 13 Oct. 1592. On his rather less orthodox views see Clulee, *John Dee's*, pp. 207, 216–18, 221–2, 231–4; and Harkness, *John Dee's*, pp. 128–9, 149–56. Compare Elizabeth I's 'deeply idiosyncratic' Protestantism: Marshall, *Reformation England*, p. 119.

33. Walsham, 'Parochial Roots', p. 650.

34. T. S. Willan, *Elizabethan Manchester*, Chetham Society, 3rd ser., 27 (1980), pp. 39, 63; Norman Lowe, *The Lancashire textile industry in the sixteenth century*, Chetham Society, 3rd ser., 20 (1972).

35. On Halifax see William and Sarah Sheils, 'Textiles and reform: Halifax and its hinterland', chap. 7 in Collinson and Craig, *Reformation in English towns*. Similarly, in a study of religious change in Shrewsbury, Patrick Collinson has noted: 'Part of the story must be that the new religion was imported from London, in part exchange for … cloth'. See his 'The Shearmen's Tree and the preacher: the strange death of Merry England in Shrewsbury and beyond', chap. 12 in *ibid.*, here at p. 212. Mancunians were among the audience for a puritan sermon at Stourbridge Fair at the beginning of the seventeenth century: Collinson, *Religion of Protestants*, p. 146, n. 19.

MANCHESTER REGION HISTORY REVIEW

36. *dJD*, 14 Nov. 1597.

37. *Ibid.*, 22 Jan. 1597. A year later Dee came before the local justices of the peace to inform against two preachers for misusing his name to deceive a third party: *ibid.*, 19 Jan. 1598.

38. *Ibid.*, 25 Sep. 1597. Carter was presented for not wearing the surplice while administering the sacrament in 1592 and 1604: C[hester,] C[ounty] R[ecord] O[ffice], EDV 1/10, fo. 168r; EDV 1/13, fo. 64r. He was presented for non-residency in Oct. 1601: EDV 1/12b, fo. 110r.

39. *dJD*, 7 Nov. 1600. Dee mentions further 'Quarrels' on 18 Dec. 1600.

40. *Ibid.*, 11–12 Apr. 1597. Palmer expressed 'open enmity' before a visitor, Sir Edward Fitton on 27 May. Fitton 'told Palmer to his face that he had known him to be a mutinous man and a falsus &c.'

41. Edward Glover and nineteen others to Dee, Manchester and Salford, 5 Apr. 1597: *Kenyon MSS.*, p. 619. I have also consulted a contemporary copy of the letter: L[ancashire] R[ecord] O[ffice], DDKE/acc.7840, fol. 181v (pencil foliation).

42. Dee, who owed Heaton £5, may have been sympathetic to the maligned preacher since he accepted a curate on his recommendation, and lent him a biblical concordance and a book by crypto-Calvinist Christoph Pezel: *dJD*, 1 Aug. 1596; 5, 11 and 25 Feb. 1597.

43. 'We held our audit: I and the Fellows for the two years last past in my absence': *ibid.*, 31 July 1600.

44. I have found no record of this in the presentments listed in the diocese of Chester visitation court correction books for 1600–2: CCRO, EDV 1/12b, fos. 6r–30v (ex officio), fos. 103r–118v (Manchester parish).

45. On the difficulties of the 1590s, when the earls were forced to sell much of their land, see Barry Coward, *The Stanleys, Lords Stanley and Earls of Derby 1385–1672: the origins, wealth and power of a landowning family*, Chetham Society, 3rd ser., 30 (1983), chap. 4 and appendix A.

46. Alport Lodge was sold in Mar. 1599 to Sir Randle Brereton of Malpas: M[anchester,] C[entral] R[eference] L[ibrary,] [Manchester Archives and Local Studies], M377, box 6, no. 1. See also Hartwell, *History and architecture*, pp. 51, 53.

47. Willan, *Elizabethan Manchester*, pp. 8–9.

48. The impressive extent of Mosley's wealth and lands is revealed in his will of 1612 printed in John Booker, *A history of the ancient chapels of Didsbury and Chorlton*, Chetham Society, old ser., 42 (1857), pp. 131–40. The deeds relating to the Withington sale are in MCRL, Egerton MSS, M31/1/1/17–27. Cecil made a handsome profit from this sale: he had purchased the land from Sir William Hatton in July 1595 for only £2,660.

49. Willan, *Elizabethan Manchester*, pp. 9–17. For comparable examples of gentlemen exploiting tenants see Felicity Heal and Clive Holmes, *The gentry in England and Wales, 1500–1700* (Basingstoke, 1994), pp. 103–16,

123–25. On revolts in this period see Andy Wood, *Riot, rebellion and popular politics in early modern England* (Basingstoke, 2002).

50. Claim to the Duchy Court by the burgesses quoted in Willan, *Elizabethan Manchester*, p. 12.

51. I am indebted to Collinson, *Religion of Protestants*, pp. 149–53, for my argument here. See also Martin Ingram, 'Reformation of manners in early modern England', chap. 2 in Paul Griffiths, Adam Fox and Steve Hindle (eds.), *The experience of authority in early modern England* (Basingstoke, 1996).

52. Marshall, *Reformation England*, p. 139, n. 74; Collinson, *Religion of Protestants*, pp. 143, 158–64; Claire Cross, 'Religion in Doncaster from the Reformation to the Civil War', chap. 2 in Collinson and Craig, *Reformation in English*; and David Lamburn, 'Politics and religion in early modern Beverley', chap. 3 in *ibid*.

53. J. P. Earwaker (ed.), *The Court Leet records of the manor of Manchester* (12 vols., Manchester, 1884–90), ii, pp. 178, 239–40; James Tait (ed.), *Lancashire Quarter Sessions records*, vol. 1: *Quarter Sessions rolls, 1590–1606*, Chetham Society, new ser., 77 (1917), pp. 86, n. 1; 96, 98, 100–1, 298, among other instances.

54. On Williamson, see F. R. Raines (ed.), 'A visitation of the diocese of Chester by John, Archbishop of York, held in the chapter house of the collegiate and parish church of Manchester, 1590, with the archbishop's correspondence with the clergy' in *Chetham Miscellanies*, Chetham Society, old ser., 96 (1875), pp. 6–7, n. 7. He gave only one sermon as fellow of the college in 1601, perhaps because he held three benefices: CCRO, EDV 1/12b, fo. 110r; Christopher Haigh, 'Puritan evangelism in the reign of Elizabeth I', *English Historical Review*, 92 (1977), p. 35.

55. The foundation document of 1578 permits a maximum absence of three months per annum: S. Hibbert, 'History of the Collegiate Church of Manchester', in *History of the foundations in Manchester of Christ's College, Chetham's Hospital, and the Free Grammar School* (3 vols., Manchester, 1830), i, p. 93. Besides his absence from Manchester for much of the period between Mar. 1598 and June 1600, Dee was at Viscount Montague's house at Cowdray, West Sussex on 19 Sep. 1602; he was in London in July and Aug. 1604, and was preparing to return to the capital the following Nov.: Julian Roberts and Andrew G. Watson (eds.), *John Dee's library catalogue* (London, 1990), p. 156; Bodl., MS Ashmole 1488, fo. 21v [red ink], 224 [Ashmole's pagination]; MS Ashmole 1788, fo. 144r.

56. CCRO, Visitation Correction Book, EDV 1/12b, fo. 110r; EDV 1/13, fo. 64r.

57. Leigh wrote a letter on the corrupt state of religion and government in Lancashire on 15 Feb. 1603: *Salisbury MSS.*, xii, p. 643. His remarks on those who turn to astrology and ancient prophets such as Merlin to foretell the hour of doom can be found in *The Christians Watch: or, An*

Heavenly Instruction to all Christians, to expect with patience the happy day of their change by death or doome. Preached at Prestbury *Church in* Cheshire; *at the Funerals of the right worshipfull* Thomas Leigh *of* Adlington *Esquire, the 16. of* February Anno 1601 (London, 1605), sig. E3.

58. Sir Nicholas Mosley and others to Sir Robert Cecil, Manchester, 16 Feb. 1603: *Salisbury MSS.*, xii, p. 643. This letter is accompanied by another, dated the previous day at Wigan, which mentions '[h]aving latelie advertised yor [*sic*] Honor of the corrupte state of Religion and government in these parts' and assures Cecil of the good standing of Sir Edmund Trafford, the bearer of the letter: *The Palatine Notebook*, 1 (1881), pp. 45–8.

59. Mary A. E. Green (ed.), *Calendar of State Papers Domestic, 1603–1610* (London, 1857), pp. 41–2.

60. Arthur Scolfielde to Edmund Hopwood, 9 Apr. 1609, and letters of May and Aug. 1609, *Kenyon MSS.*, pp. 15–16; Green, *Calendar of State Papers*, 498–9. Note also the comment in a letter from John Langley to Edmund Hopwood, Preston, c.1609: 'Lett us praye for an honeste warden': LRO, DDKE/9/122/15.

61. Haigh, 'Puritan evangelism', p. 41.

62. Peter Cunich, 'The dissolution of the chantries', chap. 9 in Collinson and Craig, *Reformation in English towns*, here at p. 163.

63. Patrick Collinson, 'The Protestant cathedral, 1541–1660', chap. 4 in Patrick Collinson, Nigel Ramsay and Margaret Sparks (eds.), *A history of Canterbury Cathedral* (Oxford, 1995); C. S. Knighton, 'Economics and economies of a royal peculiar: Westminster Abbey, 1540–1640', chap. 2 in Rosemary O'Day and Felicity Heal (eds.), *Princes and paupers in the English Church 1500–1800* (Leicester, 1981).

64. *dJD*, 5 Aug. 1600. Admittedly, Dee's standards may have been far above the Elizabethan norm.

65. Both the chancel and church were in decay by 1578; and the chancel was liable to collapse in 1590: Haigh, 'Puritan evangelism', p. 44. The visitation court of Chester on 11 Oct. 1608 found against Dee and the fellows because the chancel was 'not in sufficient repaire': see CCRO, Visitation Correction Book, EDV 1/15, fo. 132v.

66. Lamburn, 'Politics and Religion', p. 67.

67. See Claire Cross, 'The incomes of provincial urban clergy, 1520–1645', in O'Day and Heal, *Princes and paupers*, pp. 65–89; and Michael L. Zell, 'Economic problems of the parochial clergy in the sixteenth century', in *ibid.*, pp. 19–43.

68. Diarmaid MacCulloch, 'Worcester: a cathedral city in the Reformation', chap. 5 in Collinson and Craig, *Reformation in English*, here at pp. 94–5.

69. Christopher L. Hunwick, 'Who shall reform the reformers? Corruption in the Elizabethan Collegiate Church of Manchester', *Transactions of the Lancashire and Cheshire Antiquarian Society*, 101 (2005), pp. 85–100. I

am grateful to Christopher Hunwick for sending me an offprint of his article.

70. A list of those who leased lands from the queen is given in the 1578 foundation document and includes names subsequently very familiar to Dee in the courts: Hugh Travis, Ralph Kemp, Adam Holland, John Byron, and Ralph Holden. See Hibbert, 'History of the Collegiate Church', i, pp. 94–5.

71. [London,] C[ollege] [of] A[rms], MS Lancaster C.37, fo. 169r.

72. Haigh, 'Puritan evangelism', p. 43. Material relating to these suits is in London, [The] N[ational] A[rchives]: P[ublic] R[ecord] O[ffice], E 133/6/905; E 134/32Eliz/Trin 4. Some nineteenth-century transcriptions of these manuscripts are in M[anchester,] C[hetham's] L[ibrary], Raines deeds and papers, miscellaneous rolls, bundles 190, 191. See also brief notices of plaintiffs in the court of duchy chamber in *Ducatus Lancastriae pars quarta. Calendar to the pleadings from the fourteenth year to the end of the reign of Queen Elizabeth* (3 vols., London, 1834), iii, pp. 64, 80, 106, 124, 237, 265, 286, 370, 401. Suits which came before the manorial court of Newton are given in H. T. Croften, *A history of Newton chapelry in the ancient parish of Manchester*, ii, part 1, Chetham Society, new ser., 53 (1904), pp. 47–52, 63–74, 126–30. An account of the tangled affair is given by Hibbert, 'History of the Collegiate Church', i, pp. 82–135. In general, see Robert Tittler, *The Reformation and the towns in England: politics and political culture, c.1540–1640* (Oxford, 1998), chap. 5. He does not mention Manchester but he does cite the case of Chester townsmen suing to gain the tithes of a collegiate church in 1596: *ibid.*, p. 81.

73. Peter Borsay, *The English urban renaissance: culture and society in the English provincial town, 1660–1770* (Oxford, 1989); Jonathan Barry, 'Provincial town culture, 1640–1780: urbane or civic?', in Joan H. Pittock and Andrew Wear (eds.), *Interpretation and cultural history* (Basingstoke, 1991), pp. 198–234; Tittler, *Reformation and the towns*, pp. 252, 340–1.

74. *dJD*, 11, 17, 25 Feb. 1597; 11 Mar. 1598; 20, 30 Dec. 1600; 19 Jan. 1601. See also Willan, *Elizabethan Manchester*, pp. 45, 89; G. J. Piccope, *Lancashire and Cheshire wills and inventories from the ecclesiastical court, Chester. The Third Portion*, Chetham Society, old ser., 54 (1861), p. 165.

75. The records of the consistory court at Chester reveal that Dee was the complainant in nine cases during 1596 and 1597: CCRO, Consistory Cause Papers, EDC 5/1596, nos. 31 (against Thomas Lowe), 32 (Thomas Travesse); EDC 5/1597, nos. 35 (Roger Sowle), 36 (John Booth), 37 (Thomas Goodyere), 38 (Robert Bourdman), 39 (Robert Brooke), 41 (George Birch), and 42 (Hugh Travers [sic]). Dee refers to Goodyere in his diary on 14 and 21 Mar. 1596. He also mentions his problems with the tithe-corns of Hulme and Crumpsall, 20–27 Aug., 30 Aug. 1596; and records that he 'stayed' his disputes with Birch, Goodyer, Traves, and one Baxter (not in the CCRO papers) in the Chester courts, 9 Feb. 1598.

All references to *dJD*. On the ineffectiveness, expense and unpopularity of the diocesan consistory court see Haigh, *Reformation and resistance*, p. 229.

76. Astrological casebook, Bodl., MS Ashmole 221, fo. 51v.

77. And even before he arrived: *dJD*, 12, 28 July 1595.

78. A group of men also met to view and discuss encroachments at the end of Sep. 1596. They reported to the Manchester court leet the following Apr. and June, but Dee is not mentioned on this occasion: *Court Leet*, ii, pp. 116, 124–5.

79. *Ducatus Lancastriae*, iii, p. 370, no. 12. In like fashion, Thomas Goodyer was regularly reprimanded for 'encroachments' by the Manchester court leet: see *Court Leet*, ii, *passim*.

80. Croften, *History of Newton*, pp. 60, 64, 68 (Heape fined for defaulting on an earlier fine), p. 72; *dJD*, 20 Apr. 1596.

81. *dJD*, 2 Apr., 10–14 July, 3 Sep. 1596.

82. NA: PRO, DL 4/42/9. See also the pleading of Dee and the fellows in the duchy court of Lancaster in 1600 against Ralph Sharplees otherwise Fogge for 'Wrongful Possession of a Tenement called Shonocrosse in the manor of Newton': *Ducatus Lancastriae*, iii, p. 456, no. 8.

83. MCA, MS 93.

84. The draft commission is in MCA, uncatalogued. I am grateful to the archivist Christopher Hunwick for drawing this newly discovered document to my attention and for providing me with a transcription. The commission's findings are in NA: PRO, DL 44/585.

85. NA: PRO, DL 44/585. There are extensive collegiate papers relating to disputes about the commoners' rights, enclosures, and tithes of Theale Moor in the sixteenth and seventeenth centuries deposited in Manchester: J[ohn] R[ylands] U[niversity] L[ibrary] [of] M[anchester], Clowes Deeds. College lands in Salford, some detained by Rafe Holden, were another source of dispute early in Dee's wardenship: see *dJD*, 7 May, 22 and 25 June, 10–14 July 1596; 12 Oct. 1597.

86. *dJD*, 4 May 1597; Dee to the rector of Prestwich, Manchester, 2 May 1597, MCL, Mun. C. 6.63.

87. *dJD*, 14–16 June 1597.

88. Sir Walter Mildmay was principal north auditor of the duchy of Lancaster between 1546 and 1589: Somerville, *History of the duchy*, i, p. 437.

89. Stephen Bowd, 'John Dee and Christopher Saxton's survey of Manchester (1596)', *Northern History*, 62 (2005), pp. 275–92.

90. *dJD*. Christopher Hunwick has recently discovered a record of the depositions of witnesses on this occasion. It is now in MCA, awaiting reference under the current cataloguing project. I am grateful to Christopher Hunwick for providing me with a transcription.

91. NA: PRO, DL 44/585.

92. James Asheton of Chadderton, farmer of tithes of Prestwich, was

in dispute with the college and at variance with James Chetham of Nuthurst: JRULM, Clowes Deeds, MSS 764, 762, 758. Dee and the fellows proceeded in the duchy court of Lancaster in 1600 against James Asheton for tithes of Theale Moor: *Ducatus Lancastriae*, iii, p. 456, no. 9. Dee mentions that 'the commission and jury did find the tithes of Nuthurst due to Manchester against Mr James Ashton of Chadderton', *dJD*, 4 Nov. 1600. In May 1601 publication of the findings of the commission called by Dee, Sir Edward Fitton, William Tatton, and the bishop of Chester into the boundaries of the waste between Manchester parish and Prestwich was stayed by Asheton: JRULM, Clowes Deeds, MS 461. Further material of 1600–4 relating to this dispute is in MCL, Raines Deeds and Papers, miscellaneous rolls, bundle 174.

93. *dJD*, 22 Apr., 23 June 1597, and 13 Oct. 1600. Three letters on this matter dating to Oct.-Nov. 1604 existed in a 'Register book' of instruments in the Manchester Collegiate Church archives in 1673. They are no longer extant but were noted and partially transcribed in the enclosure of a letter (from which I quote here) from H. Newcome to Elias Ashmole, Manchester, 11 Feb. 1673: Bodl., MS Ashmole 1788, fo. 144r. Also noted there are seven other leases, grants, and memoranda of 1597–1604 signed by Dee. Christopher Hunwick has informed me that these are no longer extant in the cathedral archive.

94. Interrogatories on the matter of Dee's dispute with James Asheton of Chadderton over Theale Moor took place on 8 Oct. 1604. Dee probably intended to present the findings to the Duchy chamber in London: MCL, Raines deeds and papers, miscellaneous rolls, bundle 174. Dee and the fellows of the college wrote to Sir George Booth, Manchester, 6 Nov. 1604: 'o[u]r Wardan is to goe towards London next weeke'; and same to same, Manchester, 10 Nov. 1604, requesting a postponement of business until next Easter since '[o]ur warden is to travill towardes London some day next week': Bodl., MS Ashmole 1788, fo. 144r.

95. It seems likely that he made this trip since Dee was found to be 'no preacher' by the Chester visitation court in Nov. 1604: see CCRO, Visitation Correction Book, EDV 1/13, fo. 64r. A confused local oral tradition about this sequence of events may lie behind a deleted sentence among the transcriptions of Dee material enclosed in the letter of 1673 from Henry Newcome of Manchester to his brother-in-law Elias Ashmole: 'Some old persons remember his wife living a widow in the coll[ege] house at Manchester and it may bee presumed did dye at Manchester': see Bodl., MS Ashmole 1788, fo. 144r. This letter is only partially printed in C. H. Josten (ed. and intro.), *Elias Ashmole (1617– 1692). His autobiographical and historical notes, his correspondence, and other contemporary sources relating to his life and work* (5 vols., Oxford, 1966), iv, pp. 1307–9. On Jane Dee's death see *The registers of the Cathedral Church of Manchester: christenings, burials, and weddings, 1573–1616* (Cambridge,

1908), p. 349. On the impact of plague in the area see T. S. Willan, 'Plague in perspective: the case of Manchester in 1605', *Transactions of the Historic Society of Lancashire and Cheshire*, 132 (1982), pp. 29–40.

96. John Pontois (who supplied Dee with grain in 1597, see n. 2 above) seems to have recorded the progress of Dee's last illness in Dee's diary: 15 Aug. 1608, 'Hor. 5. ½ p.m J. [illegible]'; 21 Aug. [death's head], 'H: 4. p.m.'; 26 Mar. 1609 'Jō [death's head] ?. Hor: 3. a.m.' See Bodl., MS Ashmole 488.

97. Ben Jonson, *The alchemist* (c.1610), act II, scene 2, lines 20–1.

98. John Chamberlain describes Dee as 'an old imposturinge jugler' in a letter to Dudley Carleton, London, 1 Mar. 1599: Norman Egbert McClure (ed. and intro.), *The letters of John Chamberlain* (2 vols., Philadelphia, 1939), i, p. 70.

99. Although note the generally favourable, if largely derivative, comments made by a local antiquarian cleric in *c.*1652–6: Richard Hollingworth, 'Mancuniensis or An history of the towne of Manchester & w[ha]t is most memorable', MCL, Mun. A. 6. 51, fos. 21r–22r.

100. Deborah Harkness, 'Managing an experimental household: the Dees of Mortlake and the practice of natural philosophy', *Isis*, 55 (1986), pp. 247–62.

101. *dJD*, 13 Oct. 1600.

102. *Ibid.*, 28 Jan. 1598.

103. *dJD*, 17 Dec. 1597; 1 Nov. 1600; Bodl., MS Bodley 485, fos. 176v, 179v; Bodl., MS Ashmole 1488, fo. 21v [red ink], 224 [Ashmole's pagination]; BL, Cotton MS, Appendix 46, part 2, fos. 231v, 232r. Microfiche.

104. See Bowd, 'John Dee', pp. 284–92.

105. For example, Dee dined with Ralegh soon after his return from Guiana, *dJD*, 9 Oct. 1595. The hostility of the earl of Salisbury (Sir Robert Cecil) towards Ralegh was marked, and may also have extended to Dee as was noted in an 'angelic conversation' of July 1607: BL, Cotton MS, Appendix 46, part 2, fo. 229r. Microfiche.

106. Compare the case of the rich and locally influential Whalley Abbey in east Lancashire, which passed to the crown in 1537 and was then purchased by local men in 1553: Michael Mullett, 'The Reformation in the parish of Whalley', chap. 6 in Robert Poole (ed.) *The Lancashire Witches: histories and stories* (Manchester, 2002), here at pp. 88–96.

107. On the role of Puritanism in consolidating 'oligarchic authority' in a town of comparable size under great socio-economic pressures see Peter Clark, '"The Ramouth-Gilead of the Good": urban change and political radicalism at Gloucester, 1540–1640', in Jonathan Barry (ed.), *The Tudor and Stuart town: a reader in English urban history, 1530–1688* (London, 1990), pp. 244–73, esp. 265–9.

108. See *ibid.*, pp. 272–3; Tittler, *Reformation and the towns*, esp. chaps 4, 5, 8, and conclusion.

Church or chapel? Restoration Presbyterianism in Manchester, 1660–1689

Catherine Nunn

During the period of national upheaval occasioned by the Civil Wars of 1642–50, the execution of the king in January 1649 and the period of the Commonwealth and Protectorate, Salford Hundred, into which Manchester fell, showed a marginally greater number of gentry families who supported the Parliamentary cause. Although some Mancunians did have Royalist sympathies, and suffered for their loyalty by having their property sequestrated, nevertheless the town gained the reputation for Parliamentarianism and it was during these years that Manchester became the heartland of Presbyterianism in the region.[1] Lancashire became one of the few moderately successful classical presbyteries in the country, Manchester being one of nine classes.[2] Based on the Scottish model of church government, it attempted to introduce a Presbyterian system as legislated for by parliament in 1646 and to complete the vision of a fully reformed church, which in the eyes of the Puritan faction, was incomplete.[3]

Manchester is particularly fortunate in that owing to the Chetham Society, a number of sources for these years has been preserved and published. An assessment of the changes on Mancunian life brought about by national events can therefore be attempted. The minutes of the Manchester classis as well as those for Bury have survived. There are the autobiographies of two of the region's leading Presbyterians, Adam Martindale and Henry Newcome, the latter a heavily abridged version of the manuscript *Autobiography* in the care of Chetham's Library. The manuscript of Newcome's diary for September 1661 to September 1663 (also published by the Chetham Society) is likewise to be found in its Library.[4] These sources chart the fortunes of English Presbyterianism in south Lancashire and north and east Cheshire in the 1640s and 50s, and in the case of Martindale and Newcome, the aftermath of the political upheaval of the period and their subsequent experiences.[5] This paper, however, considers the impact of these experiences in the longer term after the restoration of the monarchy and the Episcopal Church of England in 1660. How did those men, whose devout Puritanism had led them to attempt to complete their vision of the Reformation, adapt to the returning regime and its attempt to enforce conformity? In particular it will consider the fortunes of those of Presbyterian persuasion.

Following 20 years of warfare and political upheaval, most Presbyterians welcomed the restoration of the monarchy. Newcome had deplored the execution of Charles I. In his account of 1649 he had written:

> This January the 30th was his majesty Charles the First beheaded, which news came to us when I lived at Goosetree, and a general sadness it put upon us all. It dejected me much, I remember, the horridness of the fact, and much indisposed me for the service of the Sabbath next after the news came.[6]

After the collapse of the Protectorate, Manchester celebrated the return of the monarchy. On 24 May 1660, five days before the entry of Charles II into London, Henry Newcome preached a sermon at the Collegiate Church in Manchester entitled 'Usurpation defeated and David restored'. The biblical account in the second book of Samuel of David's return to his kingdom after the usurpation of his son Absalom was a theme popular in Restoration sermons. The parallel between this story and the Restoration of Charles II appeared to give authority to Presbyterian support for the monarchy.[7] The dedicatory epistle was addressed to Sir George Booth (later Lord Delamere), Sir Ralph Assheton of Middleton (MP for Lancashire) and Richard Holland, who had held a military rank in the Parliamentarian army and was governor of Manchester during the Royalist siege of the town led by Lord Strange in 1642. In it Newcome drew attention to the unstable nature of society in recent times:

> Neither are there any to whom I could more willingly

First page of the pamphlet, *The Manner of the Solemnity of the Kings Coronation at Manchester in Lancashire, April 23. 1661.* Reproduced with permission of Chetham's Library

THE
MANNER
OF THE
SOLEMNITY
OF THE
Kings Coronation
AT
MANCHESTER
in *Lancashire*, *April* 23. 1661.

Worthy Sir,

Itherto I perceive the actings of your Friends in this place, upon the day of his Majesties Coronation, hath not bin communicated by any Pen to a publick view, and least that silence might eclipse their loyall observing of that day, or you otherwise perswaded of it, be pleased to accept of this accompt and confidently engage myself for such a favour then yourselves, whom I have cause to be preferred in my thoughts, not only for your undeserved Respects upon occasion to myself, (which I would hereby with all-thankfulnesse acknowledge) but also for the Renowned Undertakings, Hazards and Sufferings you have undergone for the publique. It is gratefull to me, that I should by the Providence of God, Date this Epistle to such a sermon in this Moneth, which but a year since was the season of so many hazards, and dreadfully threatening dangers, to yourselves principally, and to many others with this poor Town of Manchester, which so willingly offered themselves with you in that cause of God you so signally engaged in.[8]

On 7 May 1661 William Heawood, the steward of Manchester's Court Leet, wrote to a relative describing the festivities held in Manchester on coronation day, 23 April. The local gentry, the warden and fellows of the Collegiate Church, together with the clergy, processed through the town 'with the Town-Musick playing before them on loud Instruments' towards the conduit, which ran with claret. Bonfires were lit in the streets, fireworks continued until midnight and the church bells rang day and night.[9] Newcome prayed for the king and hoped 'that the joy of the day might not be blemished by the open intemperance of one person, if it were God's will'.[10]

In common with many of his fellow Presbyterians, Newcome hoped that the king would deliver on his promise in his Declaration of Breda of May 1660, meaning liberty of conscience in matters of religion would be upheld and Presbyterianism might have some role within the restored Church of England.[11] English Presbyterianism differed from the Scottish model, in that it was less rigidly structured and was more individual.[12] A petition, subscribed by Sir George Booth, several eminent townsmen and over 400 of the townspeople of Manchester was presented to the king to have Newcome confirmed as a fellow of the Collegiate Church on its restoration to collegiate status in 1660. The king ordered that he be considered for the post. However, the appointments had already been made and Newcome missed his chance.[13]

The next two years saw an increasingly acrimonious level of debate between, on the one hand, those who were caught between duty, conscience and political expediency and wished to retain their Puritan stance in matters of liturgy and doctrine, and on the other, followers of the restored church, which became increasingly intractable in matters of conformity. The hopes that some role for Presbyterians might be found within the church were dashed when they found themselves categorized with Independents, Quakers and other sectarians as dissenters – a matter which they found hurtful and which called into doubt their loyalty to the throne. Newcome summed up their situation: 'The Royalists throw us among the fanatics because of piety. The fanatics throw us to them [the Royalists] because of our loyalty. These two extremes harden one another and hate us.' Despite the perception that the Restoration was universally welcomed, it is clear that there survived some scepticism as to monarchy and thus, government was wary of a possible radical threat to authority.[14]

The early years of the Restoration were therefore somewhat unsettled. An atmosphere of rumour and gossip contributed to a feverish expectation of plot and counter-plot, and the north west had its fair share of such scares.[15] During the next few years parliament enacted a raft of legislation designed to enforce conformity, which has become known as the Clarendon Code. The Act of Uniformity of 1662 required that all clergy should subscribe to the Thirty-Nine Articles, and that those who had been ordained by Presbyterian convention should submit to re-ordination, a matter that went against the conscience of many who subsequently lost their livings for non-compliance.[16] Some with Presbyterian ordination did, however, conform and were perhaps instrumental in establishing the Low Church tradition that eventually broadened the church's outlook.[17] It is at this point I want to consider the impact that rising dissent and the state's attempt to enforce conformity to the Church of England had on Manchester and the surrounding region.

Despite the attempt, reinforced by the Conventicle Acts of 1664 and 1670, ejected Presbyterians and other dissenters continued to preach and meet privately. Some were politically active, thereby risking imprisonment. John Harrison, for example, was a former member of the Manchester classis who had been ejected from Ashton-under-Lyne in 1662 and who proved to be a thorn in the flesh of both the outgoing and incoming regimes. In 1651 he had been imprisoned with other Manchester Presbyterians on suspicion of attempting a correspondence with the king in exile. He further drew attention to himself in the closing days of the Commonwealth when he was arrested and imprisoned for his part in Sir George Booth's ill-fated Cheshire rising. Something of a firebrand, he was imprisoned yet again in 1663 for preaching.[18] His death in 1670 meant he disappeared early from nonconformist activity.

Political action by nonconformists in Lancashire and Cheshire was greatly feared and, immediately following the Restoration, Roger Bradshaigh of Haigh near Wigan was knighted and appointed deputy lieutenant of Lancashire. Although an Episcopalian, Bradshaigh came from a prominent Lancashire Catholic family to whom he remained loyal.[19] Likewise, totally loyal to the crown, Bradshaigh saw it his duty to investigate any suggestion of disaffection and strongly opposed any dissenting activity.[20] The letter book that he kept from 1660–76 is illustrative of his zeal to monitor dissent. Despite Presbyterian support for the Restoration, Bradshaigh nevertheless mistrusted them. Local rumours of plots fuelled the suspicion that Presbyterians (the most moderate and tolerant of the various dissenting groups) were becoming radicalised. Local dissenting activities were monitored and the militia strengthened,[21] although the Militia Act of 1662–3 had posed the problem of attracting loyal and reliable people to serve in an area where conventicles were active.[22]

In June 1662, two months before the implementation of the Act of Uniformity, information was laid before Bradshaigh against one Margaret Smith of Westhoughton who it was reported had declared that: 'rather than that they Ministers (meaning Presbit[arian]s) would conforme they would resist; and if they weare forced to conforme there would be a rising.' She was reported of implicating 'My Lord Booth' amongst others, and went on to declare that 'most of the traynd Bands in Salford Hundred would be on there side'.[23] Later in March 1663/4 it was reported to the deputy lieutenant that Mr Mosley of Manchester had received anonymous letters making accusations against Lancashire Presbyterians. Although on this occasion the accusations were not taken seriously, Thomas Jolly (an Independent), Henry Newcome, John Angier and John Harrison, amongst others, were described as 'pretending Levies calling to the office of Ministers' and all were implicated for complicity in plots against parliament for failure to honour the Declaration of Breda.[24] Thomas Jolly was one who had already been accused of seditious preaching in 1661.[25] That no distinction appears to have been made between the Independent and the Presbyterians underlines that all dissenters were being categorized as troublemakers. Shortly afterwards, on May 21, Newcome boldly recorded: 'we had an account of the passing of the bill against conventicles, which was the second degree the waters rose in upon us'.[26] It is significant, however, that March 1663/4 saw the first concrete reports of a possible insurrection in the North.[27]

In August that year Lord Derby wrote to Major John Byrom and the constables of Manchester ordering the search of various houses in Manchester. Although the reasons for this are not clear, it is obvious that there was some fear of armed insurrection. The order ran:

> Theise are to will and require you upon sight hereof to search for and seize all Armes and Amunition which you find in the custodie or possession of John Leeds, Richard Ellor, Ralph Ridgeway of Manchester, and Henry Taylor of New Barne in the same county, the said persons being judged Dangerus to the peace of this Kingdom.[28]

In the three or four years following the Restoration and Venner's Fifth Monarchist rising in January 1661/2, there were regular rumours of radical activity in Lancashire and Cheshire. Local manifestations of discontent, and the numbers of active Presbyterians in the North West led to a request that Chester should be garrisoned.[29]

In an attempt to curb this dissenting activity, the Five Mile Act was passed in 1665. It was designed to prevent dissenting ministers from residing within five miles of their former cure, thereby diluting any influence they might have upon former parishioners. They were, nevertheless, very mobile. Adam Martindale, formerly minister at Rostherne in north Cheshire, moved to Manchester to teach mathematics at the Grammar School. As with all excluded clergy, Martindale was thrown back on his own resources to support his family. His first choice of career was as a physician but on reflection he decided that:

> I considered the time would be long, practice uncertaine, and above all, that the lives of men were not to be jested with, and bethought me of a lesse dangerous studie, viz. of some useful parts of the mathematickes.[30]

This, however, did not curb his enthusiasm for preaching. In 1668, Henry Newcome heard that certificates from the bishop were granted against Martindale and Edmund Jones, formerly minister at Eccles, for preaching at Gorton. Rumour had it that a third certificate was to be issued against Newcome, although nothing seems to have come of it.[31]

Although dissenters preached wherever they could, a favourite location was Cocky Chapel in the parish of Middleton. Although the Rector of Middleton preached there once a month, the place retained a reputation for nonconformity, and a meeting house was built so close to the chapel that it was reported 'the congregations may hear one another sing psalms'.[32] Nonconformist activity in and around Manchester was such that the episcopal returns for 1669 reported that in Manchester there were 'Frequent conventicles of nonconformists (which are the most numerous) others of Anabaptists, Quakers. The persons are Tradesmen and mostly women.' Conventicles were also identified at Gorton and Denton where a conventicle of 150 people was recorded, and at Bury it was recorded that there were meetings of 'Quakers to a great number, several other conventicles of Presbyterians, Independents Dippers and such like, of the best rank of the yeomanry'.[33] It is clear that people who had enjoyed a degree of religious self-determination during the Interregnum were expecting to continue in the same style, despite the pressure to conform.

These conventicles were obviously giving some cause for concern in parliament. Writing to Roger Kenyon of Peel Hall in Little Hulton on 3 March 1669, Roger Bradshaigh described a debate in the House of Commons regarding conventicles. It had been pointed out that there was no evidence that the various meetings in Manchester had produced 'insurrection, or that any treason, scisme, or any contrivance or disturbance to the government, had beene theare hatcht'. This did not convince Bradshaigh, who continued:

> This mayde my modestye moved to speake, and such instances, as I had formerly observed and in my memorye had retained, I layd open to the House, with the necessitie for a Bill of restraint, and what ways to meet their subtle evations.

After describing the remainder of the sitting, Bradshaigh closed his letter:

> Soe I would desire you, that you would gather mee what instances you can of insolencys, of scisme, of dangerous words spoken, or any other thing that hath happned, since the Act of Oblivion, worthy taking notice of, to object against them, and I shall not fayle to urge them when tyme serves. In the meantime, I pray, let the further examination of the business at Gorton Chappell bee taken; and send me word what you know of the chappell called Birch Chappell, and of their meetings. You shall not need to be named in anything.[34]

Throughout the later years of the seventeenth century the country as a whole was a hive of rumours of plots and counter-plots, and Manchester was no exception. Dissent, as we have seen, was considered seditious, and nonconformists of all persuasion were considered to be potential insurgents. Despite the apparently smooth transition back to monarchy, in some quarters at least, the radicalism of the Commonwealth and Protectorate survived.[35] 1666 seems to have been rife with reports. In his account of that July, Newcome recorded:

> We had sad discourses, (of what afterwards was the talk of the whole year,) viz., of the Papists arming, and the fear of commissionated massacre. How groundless soever the fears were, they had this influence on me at the time, as if they had been just fears.[36]

This fear of the return of an authoritarian Catholicism and the destabilising effect of militant sectarianism was felt countrywide. Following the outbreak of the fire in London in September 1666, rumours flew, blaming the Catholics on the one hand or the rigidly Puritan Fifth Monarchists on the other for starting the fire. Quakers argued that it was God's punishment for their persecution. Preachers of all persuasions were quick to ascribe the twin tragedies of the 1665 outbreak of plague, and the fire as a visitation of the wrath of God as punishment for a catalogue of sins and misdemeanours.[37]

The situation briefly became a little easier when in 1672 Charles II issued the Declaration of Indulgence. In Manchester former Presbyterian ministers, namely, Henry Newcome, Robert Eaton, Henry Finch (both of whom had been ejected from Walton-on-the-Hill), William Wilson and John Angier were licensed to preach in their houses. In addition, the houses of thirteen townspeople were licensed to hold meetings.[38] Likewise, in the townships surrounding Manchester, preachers were licensed in Gorton, Chorlton, Salford, Eccles, Blackley, Prestwich and Ashton-under-Lyne, amongst others.

Up to this point it is difficult to see what the personal viewpoint of conforming clergy might be other than from ecclesiastical records. Here the account left by Henry Newcome's eldest son, also Henry, is useful. The second of five children, he was born in Gawsworth in 1650 when Newcome senior was Presbyterian minister there. After his parents moved to Manchester in 1657, Henry junior was educated at Manchester Grammar School and St. Edmund's Hall, Oxford. In common with his younger brother, Peter, Henry junior conformed. He was ordained priest in June 1674 and appointed rector of Tattenhall in Cheshire. He had discussed conforming with his father, who, when satisfied that the son had made the decision as a matter of conscience, made no objection.[39] We know on what matters of doctrine the father and son differed. Newcome junior recorded:

> In August I began to deliberate about the subscriptions and oaths required ... gave m'father an account of them in a letter Aug. 20 and desired his objection in order to a fair debate and full resolution about 'em. The matter of our debate was, Reading the Apocrypha, surplices, cross in baptisme and baptismal regeneration, concerning which I gave such an account that he perceived I thought conformity lawful and thereupon left me to my liberty.[40]

Newcome senior was the son and grandson of Church of England clergy, as were many of his descendents. He was, in fact, the odd one out in an Anglican clerical dynasty. Despite differences over doctrine, and on occasions, lifestyle, the father was close to all his children. Both father and eldest son recorded their debates and discussions of contemporary events. One such was Newcome junior's record of his father's licence to preach as a dissenter:

> About the beginning of April came out licences for Dissenter's liberty upon the King's Declaration and my father setting up a meeting house at the college barn, I went in the afternoon to hear him, tho had I not been under his authority I should rather

have gone to the church, especially being sensible the design of the Declaration was to have assemblies and disjoin protestants for the advancing of the catholic cause and had I as well understood that state of the case, as I do now, my fault had been great as it somewhat extenuated my ignorance, and an opinion that I should please my father.[41]

Some Dissenters had, likewise, reservations about toleration. In typically robust style, Adam Martindale wrote:

And I did so little like an universall toleration, that I have oft said, and once writ, in answer to a booke, which Mr. Baxter, after, more largely answered in print, that if the King had offered me my libertie, upon condition that I would consent to Papists, Quakers, and all other wicked sects should have theirs also, I think I should never have agreed to it.[42]

Nevertheless, Martindale took the opportunity to obtain a license to preach in his former parish of Rostherne, where one Humphrey Peacocke's house was licensed as a meeting place.[43] This experiment in toleration, crucially for developments in the later 1670s and 1680s, permitted Catholics to practice their faith in the privacy of their own homes. However, this period of limited freedom was short-lived, and the declaration was withdrawn in March 1673. The cancellation hinged on the ever-present fear of Catholic revival. The king was perceived as tolerating both Protestant dissent and Roman Catholicism, as James II did subsequently. The composition of parliament was, however, more hard-line Anglican.[44] Philip Henry, the Presbyterian dissenter from Broad Oak on the borders of Cheshire and Flintshire recorded in his diary: 'March 10. Difference high between king and parliament touching papists, the king yielded, the laws against them should be put into execution.'[45] For conformists, to permit Protestant nonconformity was the thin end of the wedge that would encourage Catholic nonconformity.

Despite the withdrawal of the Declaration, Manchester dissenters continued to meet and preach illegally. During that short period of toleration, what is believed to have been the first ordination in England of nonconformist ministers took place on 29 October 1672, at Robert Eaton's house on Deansgate. This was a curious occasion, but one that I would argue underlines the solidarity needed amongst the various dissenting communities in the face of conformist disapproval. The ordinands were Joseph Dawson, a Presbyterian; Samuel Angier, nephew of John Angier of Denton and his assistant at the chapel at Denton; and John Jolly, an Independent. A committee of ministers comprising Oliver Heywood, John Angier, Henry Finch,

Robert Eaton and Henry Newcome, all former classis members or sympathizers, ordained them.[46] Here again we see Presbyterian beliefs were still strong, and whilst at the time seeking to find a role within the national church, they had not yet come to perceive themselves as being a separate denomination.

This fluid situation, where the dissenting community had not yet firmly separated into denominations, is juxtaposed with another element in the attempt to find a confessional role within a society where conformity was demanded. Despite his non-conformist activity Henry Newcome continued to hope that his doctrine might be accepted by the established church and he continued to attend services in the Episcopal Church. His son Henry considered that his father had technically conformed and recorded that in October 1685: 'my father, mother and sister were with me at the sacrament and complied in the gesture of kneeling'.[47] At this time, and in common with other dissenters, he appears to have been a partial or occasional conformist. John Angier at Denton, although never formally ejected, and in common with other Lancashire ministers such as John Tildsley, formerly minister at Deane, seems to have compromised with authority by permitting the occasional reading of the Book of Common Prayer. It was this partial conformity that drew criticism from separatist and conformist alike, who saw such behaviour as hypocritical and schismatic and an attempt to have the best of both worlds. It is this apparent hypocrisy that Samuel Butler satirized in his *Characters*, written between 1667 and 1669 in his character of the 'Hypocritical Nonconformist'.[48]

How then did Manchester dissenters support themselves and their families financially during uncertain times? Robert Eaton was appointed Lord Delamere's chaplain at Dunham Massey for three years following his ejection from Walton-on-the-Hill. As we have seen, Adam Martindale turned to the teaching of mathematics, and had also been appointed as chaplain to Delamere in 1670, an appointment that was to last until Delamere's death in 1684. Nathaniel Banne, who had been ejected from his parish in Caldecot in Rutlandshire, had returned to his native Salford, turned to medicine and practised as a physician in Manchester and the surrounding area until his death in 1714. There was some support from sympathetic gentry, as seen in the case of Delamere, and Newcome also records visiting and dining at Dunham. Formerly Sir George Booth, Delamere continued to give the support that he had shown to the Presbyterian community in the unsettled years of the Commonwealth and Protectorate. Sir Charles Houghton and his family at Houghton Tower, between Preston and Blackburn, likewise entertained dissenters. In his account for 1664 Martindale recorded:

After Christmasse, 1664, I was entertained at Hogton Tower to instruct the wise and virtuous Mr. Charles (now Sir Charles) Hogton, his brother Mr. Benjamin, and some others, where Sir Richard, my ladie, and indeed all the family, shewed me great respect.[49]

Following Sir Richard Houghton's death in early 1679, his son Charles, who succeeded his father to the baronetcy, also became Knight of the Shire for Lancashire in the parliaments of 1679–81 and again in 1688–9, both men having served as deputy lieutenants.[50] It is clear that the family's influential position gave moral support to the dissenting community. Newcome considered them to be old friends.[51]

It is obvious that the dissenting laity of the region were helping with financial support both with gifts and bequests. In her will made in 1682, Mary Partington of Stockport left bequests to 20 ministers, all known nonconformists, some being the men discussed in this paper, and she likewise left legacies to ten widows of ministers.[52] Five years previously, her daughter, also Mary, made similar provision, including £5 'to my reverend friend John Angier pastor of the congregation at Denton.'[53] The findings of the Episcopal return for 1669 discussed above, in which it was found that members of conventicles were frequently tradesmen and women, seem to be confirmed by wills and inventories of Manchester people. In 1680 James Clough, a prosperous chapman, left £5 apiece to Newcome and Eaton. His inventory totalled £2,761 11s 0¾d. He was obviously engaged in the textile trade, his house (probably in Millgate) having a warping chamber and a yarn chamber. He had the reeds and bobbins necessary for weaving, together with linen yarn and cloth. He appears to have been putting-out as he had 'yarne out at working' as well as 'yarne at the whiteing crofts' and finished goods 'dressed up for the market'.[54]

This connection with the Manchester textile trades is reflected in other Manchester wills. In 1675, Robert Flitcroft, a hosier, left bequests to Newcome, Eaton and Finch. These three men also received bequests of £5 apiece from Nicholas Dearnall (or Dernally) in 1677. Dearnall was obviously engaged in textile production, his inventory listing dressed and raw cloth as well as troughs, boilers and looms consistent with the cloth-working industry. His house in Manchester (probably in Millgate, as this is where he is listed as living in 1659 and 1666) was one of those licensed as a meeting place for dissenters in 1672, as were the houses of Caleb Broadhead and Michael Buxton, cloth worker and woollen draper, probably of Market Street Lane and Millgate respectively.[55] Dissenting ministers profited from bequests from other people engaged in textile production too numerous to list here, including John Clayton, a chapman who requested that Newcome should preach his funeral sermon. Clayton also left a pair of gloves apiece to Newcome, John Angier of Denton, Henry Finch and Jeremiah Scholes, the latter, on ejection from his living in Norton, Derbyshire, returning to his native Salford where he was licensed to preach in 1672.[56]

National politics were never far away, the fear of a Catholic revival having haunted the Church of England throughout the century and rising to hysterical proportions in the 1670s and 1680s. When on Easter Day 1672, the Duke of York, heir to the throne, failed to take Anglican Communion, it confirmed what many had suspected, that he had converted to Catholicism.[57] Foreign policy was also a bone of contention. Charles II's leaning towards Catholic France and the policies of Louis XIV posed the threat of absolutism and popery. Likewise the wars against Protestant Holland were deemed unwise. The Catholicism of the queen and of some of the courtiers, together with Charles' somewhat lukewarm Protestantism, swung public opinion further against Catholicism.[58] As we have seen, many conformists believed that to permit Protestant nonconformity would inevitably lead to permission for Catholic nonconformity. It was this fear of schism that lead Sir Peter Leicester, sitting as a Justice of the Peace at Knutsford, just a few miles south of Manchester, to address the jury. After referring to the history of the previous 30 years, and the trouble and upheavals of the Interregnum, he exhorted the jurors:

> And now at this present how many Jesuitical pamphlets are daily scattered among the people to ensnare weaker judgments, and to draw them to rise a new rebellion? And how many kind of sectaries have we now amongst us, and numerous parties of each sort? To wit Presbyterians, Anabaptists, Independents, Quakers and I know not what: all fed by the Jesuitical party now lurking in every part of our Kingdom.[59]

Although there had been a temporary shift in parliament's attention away from Protestant nonconformity, the Church of England was as opposed to Protestant dissent as it was to Rome, and Anglicans began to feel beset on all sides.[60] In late 1678 rumours circulated surrounding the so-called 'popish plot'. Fabricated by the unscrupulous Titus Oates, and in a show of political chicanery and trumped-up charges, it purported to prove that the intention was to overthrow Charles II and install the Duke of York as king.[61] These rumours of plots were charging the already inflamed atmosphere and heralded a sea change in English politics. In Manchester, Henry Newcome recorded with some anxiety the unsettling effect that rumour was having on society: 'October 3rd (Thursday.) We heard the first news of the horrid plot

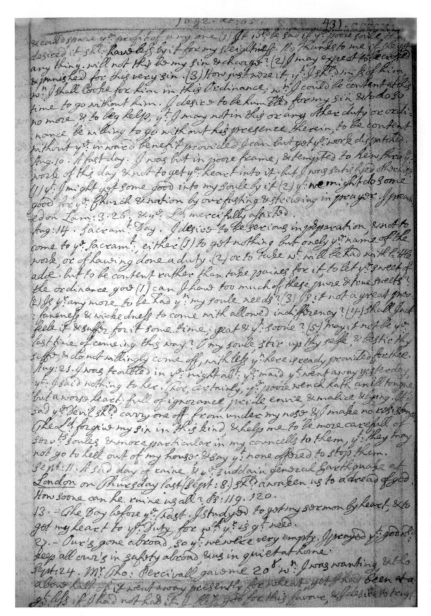

which hath since proved so deep and hellish, that hath caused so many thoughts of heart that it hath been a vexation to understand the report.' Anti-Catholic hysteria encouraged the emerging Whig faction to support an Act of Exclusion.[62]

During the next three or four years until 1682, parliament attempted to have the Duke of York excluded from the succession in favour of his Protestant daughter, Mary. The church feared that the political wrangling over religious differences would ultimately destroy its supremacy, and further encouraged some Presbyterians to hope that they might yet have a role within a national church.[63] A prime mover in the Exclusion Crisis was Henry Booth, the son of Lord Delamere, and like his father sympathetic to the Presbyterian cause. In an undated speech, but one that obviously refers to the Duke of York, Booth argued:

> Why is all this stir for a man that desireth the throne before his maj[esty] is dead he is in all the plot an one end, or another, who took evidence of London's fire, arbitrary power doth attend, and no religion like popery to sett it up. I will pay the duty of allegiance of an English man to any English prince, but popery and arbitrary power must be rooted out.[64]

The atmosphere surrounding confessional differences was becoming increasingly nervous. The quasi-royal progress of the Duke of Monmouth through Lancashire, Cheshire and Staffordshire in the autumn of 1682 only served to exacerbate the situation.[65] When in Manchester on 5 November 1682 Newcome heard a sermon on the Gunpowder Plot that drew parallels between nonconformist dissent and Catholicism, he commented: 'What a sad condition we are in, when men can bitterly preach against the Papists, and with the same breath against Dissenters, as those that hate Zion'.[66] This once again drew attention to dissenting conventicles. The Manchester churchwardens paid 'for two horses by Mr. Lightbowne's order for two of us to goe to Birch Chappell to break up an unlawfull Assembly;'[67] it was at Birch Chapel in Rusholme that Henry Finch preached at the invitation of the congregation.[68]

Yet again rumours of insurrection and plot reached Manchester. The discovery of the Rye House plot in June 1683 triggered a Tory-Anglican reaction against Whigs and nonconformists, and the (then)

Extract from the manuscript diary of Henry Newcome (bap. 1627, d. 1695): Chetham's Library, A2 140. Reproduced with the permission of the Library terms of abuse 'Whig' and 'Tory' entered the vocabulary of English politics.[69] On this occasion, Newcome became really frightened:

> The Doctor showed me a letter from the wardens about the plot, which did much trouble me, in that he says it was so horrid and so certain ... It is a sad and dangerous time. How may we be brought into trouble and danger, and know nothing ... But I am apt to tell my mind to some other at least, but this was such a thing that I durst not trust another with it; yet I was loath to trouble any friend in the world with it, but to keep silence was pain to me. (This was Mr. Ferguson's coming to me in disguise. I durst not discover him, nor own it to any that he had been with me. I only got him some direction for his way to Dunham, and he went from me quickly. I never told this to any person living till King William was crowned ...).[70]

Robert Ferguson, ejected from Godmersham, Kent in 1661, became notorious for his nonconformist activities and energetic participation in Whig politics. He was an active supporter of the Duke of Monmouth. A vociferous pamphleteer and conspirator, he earned himself the epithet 'the Plotter', although how he came within range of Newcome and Manchester is not clear. It is possible, however, that Henry Booth's central role in the attempt at exclusion might have warranted a meeting with Ferguson at Dunham.[71] However, once again the crisis passed, and the church bells were rung in Manchester on a thanksgiving day for the preservation of the king from 'the Horrid plot'.[72]

National politics intruded again in the lives of the Manchester dissenters in 1685. Charles II died in February and James II ascended to the throne. Following Monmouth's rebellion, the fear of insurrection flared and some dissenting ministers were arrested. Newcome recorded:

> June 16. The news was bad, of the Duke of Monmouth's landing etc. 17th Things look darkly on us. June 20th I was in the garden, and in that time they searched my house for arms. An unkind part, to set a mark thus upon me and some others ... June 24th I had intimation of some trouble like to come upon me, as to imprisonment ... 27th about five, Mr. Finch was seized; Mr. Eaton withdrawn. It troubled me and all expected my turn.[73]

A royal proclamation had been issued ordering all governors and sheriffs of the counties to arrest 'all disaffected and suspicious persons'.[74] The king certainly believed that any invasion would come through Cheshire, Lancashire or Scotland, and there was a general arrest and imprisonment of Whig gentry and nonconformist ministers as well as a crackdown on conventicles. In Manchester a gathering of

Quakers held in the house of the hosier Ralph Ridgway (and whose house had been searched for arms in 1664) was broken up and those attending fined five shillings apiece.[75] Once again a crisis was averted and the churchwardens of Manchester paid for the bells to be rung for the accession of James II and 'twice to the routing of the late Duk of Monmouth'.[76]

The accession of James II revived the vexed question of toleration. James claimed that his religious policies were merely that his co-religionists should be no worse treated than any other religious group, and that he had no intention of destroying the Church of England.[77] He also seems to have believed that if the penal laws against Catholics were lifted, there would be spontaneous conversions once the superiority of the Catholic Church was recognized. That he was also drafting Catholic officers into the army and replacing Protestant office holders with Catholics was seen as an attempt to enforce conversions.[78] English Catholics were, however, somewhat suspicious of James's tactics, who appeared to be out of touch with Catholic sentiment in the country as a whole, his brand of Catholicism being that of the Court and his Catholic courtiers. The general Catholic community, although not overwhelmingly large in numbers, nevertheless feared that James's policies might cause a Protestant backlash which would make matters worse for them.[79]

In an attempt to further his religious policies James turned to the nonconformists. Hoping to win them over, he issued his first Declaration of Indulgence in 1687. Later in the year he visited Chester and the clergy, conforming and nonconforming alike from across the region, descended on the town. Newcome junior recorded the almost festive atmosphere that surrounded the visit. He wrote: 'There came to my house Aug. 25 my fa[ther] Mo[ther] sisters. Neph[ew] James and Mr. Chorlton, my father's assistant, and the next day Judge Mosley, Mr. Finch and Mr. Worsley of the plat [Chapel], all to meet King James, who was expected the day after.'[80] The party remained in Chester until the king had returned from a visit to Holywell, when Newcome junior arranged for two of his parishioners, afflicted with scrofula, to be touched by the king. The centuries-old tradition of the monarch having the power to cure 'the Kings evil' had been cut back sharply by Charles I but revived by Charles II in an attempt to popularise the monarchy after the Restoration.[81] Neither Newcome nor his son were overly impressed by the king's tactics. The son, in his account of the visit somewhat tartly recorded:

> I stayed until the king returned from Holywell, and then with 9 or 10 clergymen more he [the bishop that is] introduced me to kiss the king's hand, who having first received the non-conformists

came towards us afterward, and with a disdainful smile said, 'Make way for the Church of England'.[82]

The father's account of the occasion was similarly terse. There was some debate amongst the party as to whether an address should be made to the king, something to which Newcome was averse: 'But it pleased God to order it that his majesty came by us, and stayed not; but put off his hat and passed on. And so there was nothing said, and all was well'.[83] Here again we can see a situation in which father and son were able to see the divisive nature of policy despite being of different doctrinal persuasion.

James's policies did him no good however, and the birth of the Prince of Wales on 10 June 1688 confirmed the possibility of a Catholic succession.[84] Manchester loyally rang the church bells for the child's birth and paid for a proclamation to pray for him.[85] However, the trial of the seven bishops for refusal to read the Declaration of Indulgence reinforced Protestant solidarity. When in August 1689 James was deemed by parliament to have abdicated by reason of his flight to France, and William and Mary were invited by parliament to take the throne,[86] Newcome recorded: 'We heard the news, amazing and surprising, of the general revolt of most of the great ones from King James'.[87] In Manchester the bells rang out for the proclamation of William of Orange as king and again for the coronation of William and Mary.[88] Political divisions, however, had hardened. Newcome recorded in May 1690, 'A poor miller at Knotmill, as I was coming home, cursed me, and bade the devil go with all Presbyterians', and his own political stance had become distinctly Whig in his opposition to 'the rampancy of toryism (which is enmity to all goodness).'[89] In May 1689 the Toleration Act was passed which granted limited rights of religious freedom for Protestant dissenters, provided they took an oath of allegiance, and abided by the rules laid down by the act. It is most likely that it was at this point the Presbyterians ceased to believe that they could have some role within a national church. Those whose heyday of Presbyterian ideals of reform had been in the 1640s and 1650s were now old men. The next generation would have had a different experience, never having known anything other than opposition.

Throughout the north west, dissenting congregations set about founding legally recognised chapels. Meeting houses were built throughout the Manchester area, including one in Pendleton for the Independent Thomas Jolly, one of Newcome's companions on the journey to Chester to see the king in 1687, and elder brother to John Jolly, who had been ordained in Robert Eaton's house in Deansgate in 1672;[90] Eaton was licensed at a barn in Pilkington to minister to the Presbyterian congregation he had drawn around himself.

Henry Finch's application to continue to preach at Birch chapel was challenged by the warden of the Collegiate Church, the legal owner of Birch chapel. He appears to have preached there, however, until 1697 when Thomas Birch, who had allowed Finch to preach, died and his son returned the chapel to the Collegiate Church. A Presbyterian meeting house was built for him at Platt in 1700.[91] In all about 25 persons were licensed to hold nonconformist meetings, either as ministers or in the homes of their congregations, including a Quaker meeting licensed in 'chamber at the upper end of the Smithy Door belonging to Ralph Ridgway in Manchester'.[92] This was undoubtedly the same Ralph Ridgway whose house was raided in 1664, and again when a meeting was broken up in 1686 as mentioned above. Henry Newcome was licensed to preach to his congregation in an outbuilding in Deansgate, the property of the heirs of Thomas Stockton, and at his house.[93] In old age he appears to have come to terms with the fact that his brand of Christianity would not be acceptable to the Church of England. In June 1693 land was bought in Plungeon's Meadow (now Cross Street) and a chapel was built for him. Newcome preached the sermon at the first service held there on 24 June 1694. There a nonconformist chapel, first Presbyterian and subsequently Unitarian, has stood to this day. Newcome did not long enjoy his freedom of religious expression; he died on 17 September 1695, aged 68, and was buried in Cross Street Chapel, where his remains, together with those of other Presbyterians and Unitarians, lay until 1996, when they were re-interred at Manchester's Southern Cemetery.[94]

Having placed this paper within the context of pre-industrial Manchester, it is nevertheless significant that many of the surviving records and commentaries on which this paper rests were published in the nineteenth century when nonconformist, liberal politics were so influential in the town.[95] N.H. Keeble has argued that modern nonconformity is rooted in seventeenth-century Presbyterian practices: not wearing the surplice, the omission of the sign of the cross on baptism and the liturgy, and the reception of the sacrament whilst sitting and the withholding it from the unworthy.[96] Although it was never their intention, it was the Presbyterian experiments in reform in the 1640s and 1650s, and the weakness of the system, which cleared the way for diversity of religious expression in the north west. In 1864, to mark the 200th anniversary of the Act of Uniformity, William Urwick, minister of Hatherlow Chapel, edited *Nonconformity in Cheshire*, a series of essays written by ministers of the various nonconformist denominations to chronicle the history of nonconformity in Cheshire. In 1869, Robert Halley wrote *Lancashire: its puritanism and nonconformity*, a definitive history of all shades of nonconformity in the county. The 1860s saw the development of Albert Square and the apogee of civic building, Manchester's town hall. It was at this time, on the corner of Albert Square and Southmill Street, that the Memorial Hall was built to commemorate the events of 1662.[97] Nineteenth-century Manchester nonconformity is firmly rooted in the events of the seventeenth century.

Notes

1. B. G. Blackwood, 'Parties and issues in the Civil War in Lancashire', *Transactions of the Historic Society of Lancashire and Cheshire* [hereafter *THSLC*], 132 (1983), p. 111; B. G. Blackwood, 'Parties and issues in the Civil War in Lancashire and East Anglia', in R. C. Richardson (ed.), *The English Civil War: local aspects* (Stroud, 1997), p. 278; R. N. Dore, *The Great Civil War (1642–46) in the Manchester area* (Manchester, 1971), pp. 9–19.

2. W. A. Shaw, *A history of the English church during the Civil War and under the Commonwealth, 1640–1660* (2 vols., London, 1890), ii, pp. 393–9.

3. Shaw, *History of the English Church*, ii, pp. 1–33.

4. Autobiography of Henry Newcome: Chetham's Library [hereafter CL] A3 123; Diary of Henry Newcome, Sep. 1661-Sep. 1663: CL A2 140; C. M. Nunn, *The ministry of Henry Newcome: Presbyterianism in south-east Cheshire, 1648–1662* (unpub. MPhil, University of Manchester, 1998), pp. 29–37.

5. R. Parkinson (ed.), *Life of Adam Martindale*, Chetham Society, old ser., 4 (1845; repr. 2001); R. Parkinson (ed.), *Autobiography of Henry Newcome*, Chetham Society, old ser., 26 and 27 (1852); T. Heywood (ed.), *The diary of Henry Newcome, from September 30, 1661 to September 29, 1663*, Chetham Society, old ser., 18 (1849); W. A. Shaw (ed.), *Minutes of the Manchester Classis*, Chetham Society, new ser., 20, 22 and 24 (1890, 1891); W. A. Shaw (ed.), *Minutes of the Bury Classis*, Chetham Society, new ser., 36 and 41 (1896, 1898).

6. Newcome, *Autobiography*, p. 13.

7. Henry Newcome, *Usurpation Defeated and David Restored* (London, 1660), *passim*.

8. Newcome, *Usurpation Defeated*, unpaginated.

9. J. P. Earwaker (ed.), *The Court Leet records of the manor of Manchester* (12 vols., Manchester, 1884–1890), iv, pp. 281–5.

10. Newcome, *Autobiography*, p. 120.

11. J. Spurr, *The Restoration Church of England, 1646–1689* (New Haven and London, 1991), pp. 29–30; Newcome, *Autobiography*, p. 120.

12. N. H. Keeble, *The literary culture of nonconformity in later seventeenth-century England* (Leicester, 1987), p. 8.

13. Newcome, *Autobiography*, pp. 314–24; C. M. Nunn, 'Henry Newcome (bap. 1627, d. 1695)', *Oxford Dictionary of National Biography* (60 vols.,

Oxford, 2004) [hereafter *ODNB*], xl, pp. 594–7; Nunn, *The ministry of Henry Newcome*, p. 136; Spurr, *Restoration Church of England*, pp. 29–42.

14. Newcome, *Diary*, p. 95; R. L. Graves, *Deliver us from evil: the radical underground in Britain, 1660–1663* (Oxford, 1986), p. 4.

15. Graves, *Deliver us from evil*, pp. 22–31.

16. Spurr, *Restoration Church of England*, pp. 42–61.

17. Nunn, *The ministry of Henry Newcome*, p. 157.

18. Newcome, *Diary*, p. 137; C. M. Nunn, 'John Harrison (1614–1670)', *ODNB*, xxv, pp. 509–10; A. G. Matthews, *Calamy revised* (Oxford, 1934), pp. 249–50.

19. B. Coward, 'The social and political position of the earls of Derby in later seventeenth-century Lancashire', *THSLC*, 132 (1983), p. 144; A. J. Hawkes, 'Sir Roger Bradhaigh of Haigh, knight and baronet, 1628–1684', Chetham Society, new ser., 109 (1945), p. 8.

20. Hawkes, 'Sir Roger Bradshaigh', p. 36.

21. Graves, *Deliver us from evil*, p. 101.

22. Graves, *Deliver us from evil*, p. 130.

23. 'Sir Roger Bradshaigh's Letter Book', *THSLC*, 63 (1911), p. 131.

24. 'Bradshaigh's Letter Book', p. 143; Nunn, 'John Harrison'.

25. Graves, *Deliver us from evil*, p. 25.

26. Newcome, *Autobiography*, p. 142.

27. Graves, *Deliver us from evil*, pp. 165–96.

28. 'Bradshaigh's Letter Book', p. 144.

29. Graves, *Deliver us from evil*, pp. 54, 65, 88, 101.

30. Parkinson, *Life of Adam Martindale*, p. 175.

31. Newcome, *Autobiography*, p. 171; Ernest Axon, 'John Jones and Edmund Jones, vicars of Eccles 1611–1662', *Transactions of the Lancashire and Cheshire Antiquarian Society*, 36 (1918), p. 74.

32. Francis Gastrell (F. R. Raines [ed.]), *Notita Cestriensis*, Chetham Society, old ser., 19 (1849), p. 105.

33. G. Lyon-Turner, *Original records of nonconformity* (3 vols., London, 1922), ii, p. 170.

34. Lancashire Record Office, Kenyon of Peel, DDKE/acc.7840 HMC/277.

35. Graves, *Deliver us from evil*, p. 227.

36. Newcome, *Autobiography*, p. 159.

37. Spurr, *Restoration Church of England*, p. 54; T. Harris, *Restoration: Charles II and his kingdoms* (London, 2005), p. 79.

38. Lyon-Turner, *Original records*, ii, pp. 678–9; E. M. E. Ramsay and A. J. Maddock (eds.), 'The churchwardens' accounts of Walton-on-the-Hill, Lancashire, 1627–1667', *Record Society of Lancashire and Cheshire*, 141 (2005), pp. ix–xii.

39. Nunn, 'Henry Newcome', pp. 594–7.

40. Manchester Central Library, Henry Newcome junior, Diary Ms. 922.3 N21, part 2, p. 4.

41. Newcome, junior, Diary, part 2, p. 11.

42. Parkinson, *Life of Adam Martindale*, p. 198.

43. Lyon-Turner, *Original records*, ii, p. 693.

44. D. Wykes, *A preface to Dryden* (London, 1977), pp. 74–6.

45. M. H. Lee (ed.), *Diaries and letters of Philip Henry* (London, 1882), p. 261.

46. O. Heywood (J. Horsefall Turner [ed.]), *Autobiographies, anecdotes and event books* (4 vols., Brighouse, 1882), iii, p. 115–6; R. Halley, *Lancashire: its puritanism and nonconformity* (Manchester, 1872), p. 412.

47. Newcome, junior, Diary, part 2, p. 70.

48. Samuel Butler (C. W. Davies [ed.]), *Characters* (Cleveland and London, 1970), p. 45; J. Spurr, 'Schism and the Restoration Church', *Historical Journal of Ecclesiastical History* [hereafter *HJEH*], 41 (1990), pp. 409–24.

49. Parkinson, *Life of Adam Martindale*, p. 177; J. D. Ramsbottom, 'Presbyterians and partial conformity in the Restoration Church of England', *HJEH*, 43 (1992), pp. 249–57.

50. D. P. Carter, 'The Lancashire militia, 1660–1688', *THSLC*, 132 (1983), p. 181; J. Croston (E. Baines [ed.]), *History of the County Palatine and Duchy of Lancaster* (4 vols., Manchester, 1891), iv, p. 184.

51. Halley, *Lancashire puritanism*, p. 155–6, 298–9; Newcome, *Autobiography*, pp. 218, 225–9, 233, 240–2, 273–4, 280.

52. Cheshire Record Office [hereafter CRO], will of Mary Partington, 1682.

53. CRO, will of Mary Partington, 1677.

54. Lancashire Record Office [hereafter LRO], will of James Clough, WCW 1680; J. P. Earwaker (ed.), *The constables' accounts of the manor of Manchester* (3 vols., Manchester, 1892), ii, pp. 198, 218, 244.

55. Lyon-Turner, *Original records*, ii, p. 678–9; LRO, wills of Nicholas Dearnall, WCW 1677; Caleb Broadhead, WCW 1683; Michael Buxton, WCW 1680; Earwaker, *The constables' accounts*, ii, pp. 168, 178, 187, 241, 250, 280.

56. LRO, will of John Clayton, WCW 1674; Lyon-Turner, *Original records*, ii, p. 679.

57. J. Miller, *James II* (New Haven and London, 2nd edn., 1989), pp. 59–62.

58. Wykes, *A preface to Dryden*, pp. 92–3.

59. Peter Leicester (E. M. Halcrow [ed.]), *Charges to the Grand Jury at Quarter Sessions 1660–1677*, Chetham Society, third ser., 5 (1953), p. 90.

60. Wykes, *A preface to Dryden*, pp. 77–9.

61. Harris, *Restoration*, pp. 136–7; Wykes, *A preface to Dryden*, pp. 94–5.

62. Newcome, *Autobiography*, p. 227; Wykes, *A preface to Dryden*, pp. 79–80.

63. Spurr, *Restoration Church of England*, pp. 77–80.

64. John Rylands University Library of Manchester, Ducie Muniments, D340b/XI/2.

65. F. H. Blackburne Daniell (ed.), *Calendar of State Papers Domestic, 1682* (London, 1932), pp. 406–11.

66. Newcome, *Autobiography*, p. 246.

67. E. Broxap (ed.), *Extracts from the Manchester churchwardens' accounts, 1664–1710*, Chetham Society, new ser., 80 (1921), p. 26.

68. Halley, *Lancashire puritanism*, p. 379.

69. Harris, *Restoration*, pp. 317–23; Wykes, *A preface to Dryden*, pp. 94–5.

70. Newcome, *Autobiography*, pp. 249–50.

71. Matthews, *Calamy revised*, pp. 193–4; M. Zook, 'Robert Ferguson (d. 1714)', *ODNB*, xix, pp. 365–67.

72. Broxap, *Manchester churchwardens' accounts*, p. 26.

73. Newcome, *Autobiography*, pp. 259–60.

74. F. Bickley and E. K. Timings (eds.), *Calendar of State Papers Domestic, 1685* (London, 1960), pp. 212–3.

75. Parkinson, *Life of Adam Martindale*, pp. 229, 234–5; J. B. Williams (M. Henry [ed.]), *The life of the Revd Philip Henry* (1698; Edinburgh, 1974) pp. 158–60; Bickley and Timings, *Calendar of State Papers Domestic, 1685*, p. 192; B. Nightingale, *The early stages of the Quaker Movement in Lancashire* (London, 1921), pp. 171–3.

76. Broxap, *Manchester churchwardens' accounts*, p. 26.

77. D. L. Smith, *A history of the modern British Isles, 1603–1707: the double crown* (Oxford, 1998), p. 275; W. A. Speck, *James II* (London, 2002), pp 52–5.

78. Smith, *History of modern British Isles*, pp. 276–80.

79. Wykes, *A preface to Dryden*, p. 86.

80. Newcome, junior, Diary, part 2, p. 81.

81. Smith, *History of the modern British Isles*, pp. 242, 351 n., 386.

82. Newcome, junior, Diary, part 2, p. 81.

83. Newcome, *Autobiography*, p. 265.

84. Smith, *History of the modern British Isles*, p. 269.

85. Broxap, *Manchester churchwardens' accounts*, p. 26.

86. Smith, *History of the modern British Isles*, pp. 269–70.

87. Newcome, *Autobiography*, p. 269.

88. Broxap, *Manchester churchwardens' accounts*, p. 27.

89. Newcome, *Autobiography*, p. 271.

90. LRO, record book of dissenting meetings, 1689–1852, QDV/4, p. 1.

91. Matthews, *Calamy revised*, pp. 195–6; J. Booker, *A history of the ancient chapel of Birch*, Chetham Society, old ser., 47 (1859), pp. 149–51.

92. LRO, record book of dissenting meetings, 1689–1852, QDV/4, pp. 1–10.

93. LRO, record book of dissenting meetings, 1689–1852, QDV/4, p. 3.

94. Nunn, 'Henry Newcome', pp. 594–7; Calendar for July and Aug. 1998, Cross Street Chapel, Manchester.

95. A. Kidd, *Manchester* (Keele, 2nd edn., 1996), pp. 63–8.

96. Keeble, *Literary culture*, pp. 6–7.

97. Kidd, *Manchester*, p. 138.

Manchester and its region: networks and boundaries in the eighteenth century

Jon Stobart

In the eighteenth century, Manchester was already widely recognised as the centre of a functional and cognitive region which was defined by the eponymous 'Manchester goods'.[1] These goods, and along with them recognition of the region, were carried by a network of Manchester Men as they visited fairs and retailers across the country. Defoe could write of 'the Manchester trade we all know', confident that his readers were familiar with the nature and importance of local manufactures. He was equally clear that this trade had its centre in Manchester, but spread deep into the surrounding countryside where, it was assumed, its impact was most profound.[2] The reality of this region was apparent to contemporary commentators then, and remains largely undisputed by historians and geographers today. However, this wide acceptance masks a lack of detailed understanding of the spatial extent of this region. Where did its boundaries lie, and what were the processes whereby it was created and recreated? Was it simply a product of a particular production system? Writing in the middle of the nineteenth century, Leon Faucher identified both creative forces and the broad spatial bounds of the Manchester region:

> Manchester, like an industrious spider, is placed in the centre of the web and sends forth roads and railways towards its auxiliaries ... which serve as outposts to the grand centre of industry ... An order sent from Liverpool in the morning is discussed by the merchants in the Manchester exchange at noon, and in the evening is distributed among the manufacturers in the environs. In less than eight days, the cotton spun at Manchester, Bolton, Oldham or Ashton, is woven in the sheds of Bolton, Stalybridge or Stockport; dyed and printed at Blackburn, Chorley or Preston, and finished, measured and packed at Manchester.[3]

It is tempting to simply project this region back in time and see it as part of the industrialisation which transformed south-east Lancashire from the seventeenth century onwards. But there are dangers in doing so. Firstly, regions are not absolute and immutable, but change through time. This truism is all too easily overlooked if we focus on the 'being' of regions rather than thinking of them as a process of 'becoming' – a problem which is exacerbated when we project later regional formations back in time.[4] Regions are, as Ansi Paasi argues, an historically contingent process as much as an end state, socio-economic constructions which are constantly remoulded by changing circumstances.[5] Manchester now appears the 'natural' centre of a regional textile economy, the seat of what Allen calls 'centred power'.[6] However, at the start of the eighteenth century, Bolton was the focus of much of the south Lancashire fustians trade, as well as an important manufacturing centre in its own right. As Cox noted in 1731, 'this town is the Staple Place for Fustians, which … are brought to this Market and Fair from all Parts of the Country'.[7] It was to Bolton that the Manchester chapmen travelled to purchase fustians 'in the grey' before finishing and selling them on to London merchants. It was the Bolton tradesmen who controlled the market and built warehouses to store the cloth and present it for sale, paralleling the activities of the Rochdale clothiers and those who organised the worsted trade in west Yorkshire.[8] Only gradually did Manchester assert its dominance over neighbouring towns, redrawing the spatiality of power relations and redefining the region in its own image. This mutability does not mean that regions were without material dimensions. Indeed, Massey has argued that past 'layers of investment' (which generally are taken to be economic, but could equally involve social capital or cultural institutions) help to shape the spatial interdependencies that mould regions. However, it does call into question attempts to define regions purely as material entities.[9]

This links to a second problem with Faucher's reading of the region around Manchester. It is essentially economic and material, defined by the spatial processes of industrial capitalism. As Langton, Gregory and others have argued, this is an important constituent of the region – what Paasi calls *territorial shape* – but it was the social and cultural dimensions which were central to how the region was felt and imagined. This was the *conceptual shape* of the region: the allegiances and alliances which brought together people in a collective spatial identity that transcended the local and parochial.[10] Significantly, this identity can be linked to both place and the connections between places. For Amin, 'the plural public sphere involved in the making of a region is spatially diffuse and geographically mobile'. Yet rootedness in the locality was also important in shaping socio-spatial groupings – especially in an age before hyper-mobility.[11]

In this paper, I draw on these conceptualisations of the region to explore three inter-related processes of regional formation: industrialisation, social interaction and cultural identification. In doing so, the intention is to shed some new light on the geography and nature of Manchester's region in the eighteenth century, how it was constructed and how this construction changed during this period.

A functional region: industrial capitalism

Jack Langton has argued that industrialisation produced a new kind of region. Industrial regions were characterised by the construction of fixed capital associated with particular industrial products. They were 'more specialised, more differentiated from each other and more internally unified'. Moreover, spatial differences fed into and were re-emphasised by cumulative and, more arguably, path-dependent investment and growth. The region thus became an internally reinforcing spatio-economic entity.[12] To what extent can such a functional region be seen around eighteenth-century Manchester?

From a distance, the specialism of the area is clear and coherent: the manufacture of fustians and, later, cotton textiles was concentrated here. These were the 'Manchester goods' sold across the country, a name which linked the town and the region in the popular imagination. However, the extent and coherence of the 'cotton districts' is less clear when we approach them more closely. The manufacture of fustians and other cotton-based textiles was initially concentrated in the districts north of Manchester, especially in the country between Bolton and Blackburn, and around Oldham. From there fustians diffused into the Manchester district, notably to the east and south of Manchester in Ashton-under-Lyne, Denton, Hulme and Chorlton Row as well as in the town itself (see Figure 1). However, both Manchester and its immediate surroundings were characterised by a heterogeneous mix of cloth types. It was the region's leading production area for linens and this, in turn, formed the most common cloth type in the district. Coarse woollens were also produced in some quantity, as was felt. But it was the manufacture of smallwares which distinguished this district from other parts of the textile-producing areas. Smallwares involved thread- and button-making, but principally comprised tape- and ribbon-weaving, trades which used the 'new' Dutch looms.[13]

Manchester also acted as a finishing and marketing centre for an equally wide range of textiles manufactured in the surrounding towns and villages. There were calenderers, cloth dressers, dyers, fustian dyers, fustian shearers, hot pressers, inkle calenderers, linen dyers, shearers, whitsters and woollen dyers. Manchester finishing trades received cloth from a broad area, including north-east Cheshire and central Lancashire. There was thus a hierarchical-spatial division of labour, with Manchester forming the key centre of control in the

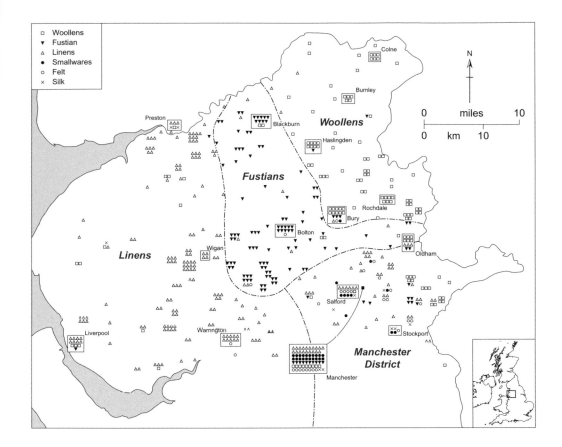

Figure 1:
Textile
production
in north-west
England,
1700–1760.
Source: probate
records, 1700–60

textile space economy, effectively integrating specialised production systems throughout the North West.[14] Part of the explanation for this clustering of finishing processes was the close relationship which existed between the various trades. As Wadsworth and Mann noted, 'much of the dyeing was done in Manchester, and it was customary for the dyer to send on the goods to the calenderer', almost invariably located in the town.[15] This close linking of rural manufacturers with Manchester finishers was the 'fact on which the growing tendency of the town to monopolise the marketing functions of the trade was largely based'.[16] Manchester housed scores of cloth merchants and a growing body of chapmen. Such men were central to the putting-out systems through which production was organised, and the marketing of cloth in London and elsewhere.[17]

All this implies an extensive region, with Manchester acting as a centre of control for textile production across eastern and central Lancashire. The regional space economy was thus drawn together through the flows of goods, credit and capital which centred on Manchester's warehouses, dye houses and Exchange (1729). However, the evidence of direct control suggests a far more constrained area of influence. In the early 1770s, the distribution of country manufacturers with warehouses in Manchester stretched little beyond Bury, Bolton, Leigh and Ashton-under-Lyne, with check manufacturers being found principally within Manchester parish: mostly in the townships east and north of the town (Figure 2).[18] Over the next 20 years, this distribution expanded towards Wigan and especially in north-east Cheshire, where Stockport and Dukinfield stood out. But the basic geography remained consistent. This constrained regional geography is confirmed by the business networks of those engaged in organising production, most particularly the Manchester linen drapers and merchants. The probate inventory of Joseph Jolley, a Manchester linen draper who died in 1735, recorded the names of a variety of people to whom he had put out work. There was £272 15s 6d of 'yarn at croft' in the hands of eight men; £178 15s 6d of yarn being woven by 40 men and two women; £15 10s 6d of 'yarn at winding' being worked by ten women and three men; £5 3s 7d (113lbs) of cotton at spinning; and £8 13s 4d of yarn at dyeing. In all, there was £1461 5s 2d in yarn and cloth and a production network involving well over 60 individuals.[19] It is impossible to trace the location of many of Jolley's contacts. Those who can be mapped with confidence lay within an area very similar to that defined by the distribution of country manufacturers: that is, a set of towns and villages within a six- to ten-mile annulus of Manchester. This is not to say that Manchester and its merchants held no sway over a more broadly defined region. Rather, I would argue that this influence was often affected through intermediate centres and merchants: towns such as Bolton and Blackburn, and men like Richard Lathom, with £124 5s 6d of yarn out at weavers, and Thomas Smalley, who was owed

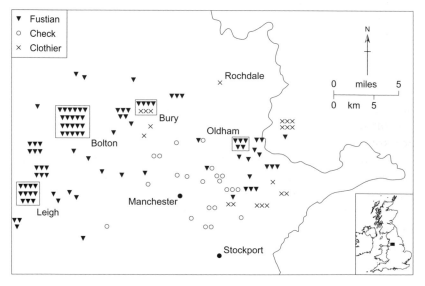

Figure 2:
Country manufacturers with Manchester warehouses, 1774. Source: Raffald, *Directory of Manchester and Salford* (1773).

£2 5s for yarn at spinning.[20] But these smaller centres were not wholly in the thrall of Manchester. Henry Escricke, the Bolton merchant, had close interaction with outworkers and small-scale manufacturers in Rochdale, Blackburn, Middleton, Oldham and Manchester itself. He also visited Liverpool and Lancaster to acquire raw cotton, and had dealings with merchants in Leeds, Bristol, Hull and London.

This has three important implications for the spatial characteristics of Manchester's industrial region. The first is that it might usefully be conceived in terms of an intensely linked core area, surrounded by a broader and less closely integrated, though spatially extensive, marginal zone. The second is that this marginal area comprised, at least in part, a series of nested smaller areas of influence. The third is that these nested centres enjoyed considerable autonomy, making the region open and porous: better conceived of as a condensation of networks rather than an homogenous bounded entity.[21]

An integrated region: transport and social networks

This reading of the region as core and periphery comprising myriad overlapping networks, nodes and linkages is supported by analysis of transport routes and services which served to weave together the regional space. Langton and Turnbull have both argued that canal construction and traffic were critical to regional integration and industrial transformation.[22] This is seen most vividly in the development of Liverpool and its relationship with the south-west Lancashire coal- and mid-Cheshire salt-fields.[23] Notwithstanding the early construction and commercial success of the Duke of Bridgewater's canal, which linked Manchester to Worsley and later to the Mersey at Preston Brook, other navigation schemes were slow to emerge in the area. By the 1790s, there was the 'Old Navigation', along the line of the Irwell and Mersey; the Ashton and Stockport Canal, and the Bolton and Bury Canal. In addition to large amounts of freight traffic, there were 'elegant passage boats' five days per week running to Preston Brook, and daily to Worsley on the Bridgewater Canal; they ran three times per week along the Old Navigation, every evening to Bolton, and on market days and Sundays between Ashton, Manchester and Stockport.[24]

Despite this, and the continued growth in canal traffic well into the 1840s, it is roads (and railways) that are highlighted in Faucher's sketch. Manchester had long been the focus of carrier and packhorse routes. By the 1730s, growing traffic was encouraging the establishment of turnpike trusts along many of the principal routes. As one petition argued:

the Towns of Manchester and Stockport are very large, and considerable Trading Towns, and send weekly great Quantities of Goods, Merchandizes, and Manufactures to Doncaster, in the County of York; which are carried from thence by Water to Hull, in order to be shipped to London, and foreign Parts; and bring back considerable Quantities of Flax, Yarn and other Commodities, which are manufactured in the said Towns of Manchester and Stockport.[25]

50 years later, Manchester was the centre of a web of turnpikes which connected it to neighbouring textile towns; led over the Pennines to Huddersfield, Halifax and Sheffield; across to Warrington and Liverpool, north to Preston and Lancaster, and, via Stockport and Macclesfield, down to London. The carrier services running along these routes and other roads linked Manchester to surrounding settlements, revealing an intense core of interaction encompassing an area bounded by Bolton, Rochdale, Oldham and Stockport. Just as telling was the orientation of these services, many of which linked Manchester to surrounding villages. Scholes's directory lists services to at least 24 villages, the majority to the east and north of the town (see Table 1). This distribution reflects that of the country manufacturers (see Figure 2), underlining the importance of roads in integrating the local textile economy. Wider links were apparent, however, with frequent services to Preston, Blackburn, Burnley, Macclesfield, Northwich and Warrington, and also to destinations beyond the region. These were predominantly in west Yorkshire, but also the east Midlands and especially London, which was served by 20 wagons per week.[26] Indeed, Manchester can be seen as a key node on a road transport system which integrated the region and tied it firmly into the wider national space economy.

Table 1: Carrier services from Manchester, 1797

No. of services per week	Places served
12 or more	Bolton (16), Bury (12), London (20), Oldham (12), Preston (14), Rochdale (12), Sheffield (12), Stockport (33)
9–11	Altrincham (9), Ashton-under-Lyne (9), Blackburn (9), Mottram (9), Northwich (9), Ratcliffe (9), Warrington (9)
6–8	Burnley (6), Chester (6), Haslingden (7), Gainsborough (6), Halifax (6), Huddersfield (6), Liverpool (6), Macclesfield (6), Norwich (6), Sowerby Bridge (7), Stalybridge (6)

Source: *Scholes's Manchester and Salford Directory* (1797).

Transport networks are tangible representations of spatial integration: they facilitated movement of goods, people, capital and knowledge, and have left us with measurable evidence of their importance. Social networks were just as important in giving territorial shape to the region, but are far more elusive. Diaries, account books, journals, letter books and so on provide us with detailed insights into individuals' social worlds. I have argued elsewhere that probate records can be very revealing of more general patterns of association and inter-connection, since executors and signatories to administration bonds would be drawn from the deceased's family or most intimate and trusted friends.[27] Taken together, these individual contacts constitute a comprehensive data set of inter-personal links which paint a picture of 'local country' – the occupational, religious, kinship and neighbourhood networks through which people lived their daily lives – and illustrate the spatial ties which bound together this nexus. The image of Manchester's social region thus (re)created closely resembles that of the economic region sketched earlier. There were clusters of social contacts in towns with which Manchester had especially close dealings – Bolton, Bury, and to a lesser extent Rochdale, Oldham and Ashton – and a more general concentration into the parishes immediately around the town (see Table 2). Indeed, it is telling that more than half the executors named by Manchester testators resided in rural locations – a reflection of the town's close contact with manufacturing in the surrounding countryside.[28] Beyond this was a much broader region more loosely connected to Manchester. This

Table 2:
Location of executors of Manchester testators, 1700–60

	Number of contacts	Prominent parishes
Salford Hundred (excluding Manchester)	92	Manchester (excluding Manchester town – 32), Bolton (12), Bury (12), Eccles (11), Middleton (5), Oldham (5), Prestwich (5), Rochdale (5)
West Derby Hundred	20	Warrington (6)
Blackburn Hundred	9	Blackburn (5)
Other Lancashire	3	
Cheshire	42	Chester (14), Sale (5)
Derbyshire, Yorkshire, Staffordshire	16	
London	9	
Other places	4	
Total	**195**	

Source: probate records, 1700–60

spread across the North West and out into neighbouring districts: west Yorkshire, Derbyshire and London standing out as places in which Manchester residents had close personal or familial connections. Again, this reflects the patterns of manufacture and trade, and underscores the importance of personal relationships to business in the eighteenth century.[29]

A cognitive region: cultural identification

What Paasi calls the 'territorial shape' of the region was becoming increasingly clear and coherent in the eighteenth century. Defined in terms of the distribution of industry, it was drawn together and given integrity through a series of inter-related business, capital and transport networks. Importantly, it was clearly *Manchester's* region: the networks of control and integration were focused on the town and its merchants, much as Allen argues for twentieth-century spatialities of power.[30] Whilst sometimes operating through intermediates, it is clear that Manchester was the heart of this regional economy: pumping the lifeblood of goods, capital and information to surrounding areas. Yet, as Langton makes clear, the formation of industrial regions was linked not just to spatial divisions of labour and the inter-connection of goods and people, but also to the emergence of a distinct cultural identity. This has two aspects: firstly, it depicts the region as a perceived space, imagined in particular ways by those within and beyond its boundaries. Secondly, it places emphasis on processes of cultural identification with space and with others within that space: a feeling of belonging to and identity with a particular geographical area. This links to more recent conceptions of the region as a 'territorially defined public sphere or public culture' – a collective spatial consciousness or identity which Paasi refers to as the 'cognitive region'.[31] Regional historians have taken a wide range of measures of this cultural dimension – reflecting, in part, the plurality of this public culture – including dialects, voting patterns, regional literature and popular protest. Here, I draw on just three to give a feel for the nature of this regional identity.

The first is the area covered by what is now one of the most famous analyses of north-west England in the eighteenth century: Aikin's *Description of the country from thirty to forty miles round Manchester* (1795). This was a representation of regional space, produced through the pages of a book, rather than the materiality of production or transport systems, or the mutuality of friendship networks.[32] Centring the description on Manchester is significant. It projected a conceived region, focused on the town, to a readership that was receptive to the idea that such regionalisation had some meaning. More significant, though, is the way in which this representation of space projected a particular regional geography to a wider public, and thus helped to create and recreate the region – and Manchester's centrality to the region – in the minds of those reading Aikin's description. In terms of its coverage, the book offers a general survey of Lancashire and Cheshire, plus Derbyshire, the West Riding and north Staffordshire. It thus defines a very broad region centred on Manchester; yet, in its more detailed 'Accounts of Particular Places', the coverage is more focused. Aikin offers the reader over 100 pages on Salford Hundred and nearly as many on West Derby, but devotes just ten pages on Amounderness and Leyland combined. Similarly, 40 pages are taken up with descriptions of Macclesfield Hundred, but just 30 pages to all the other Cheshire Hundreds. To an extent, this reflects a preoccupation with large towns, but it also suggests a more closely defined region around Manchester: one that echoes the industrial and social regions sketched above. More importantly, it implies that this was a region with resonance for the readership: Chester, Wrexham and the Potteries might be of interest, but clearly lay outside this more focused reading of region.

A different measure of the 'felt' region is given by the list of those subscribing to Aikin's book. This, of course, says much about the London and provincial connections of Aikin and his publisher, John Stockdale. However, those signing up to Aikin's project also reveal what we might term a 'community of interest': a set of people who felt some affinity with Manchester and with Aikin's attempts at regionalisation in north-west England – even if these sentiments were complicated by other motivations. In all, nearly 600 individuals and institutions subscribed to Aikin's book, including large numbers of rural and urban gentry, professionals and clergy, and several libraries. Subscribers were spread across the country and included at least 70 from London. However, the majority of subscribers came from an area broadly concomitant with that covered by the book. Around 100 were from Manchester itself and a further 50 from Liverpool, but the densest concentration was found in the manufacturing districts, especially to the east of the town: in Manchester parish and in neighbouring Oldham, Ashton and Stalybridge. This closely reflects the regions defined by industrial activity and social interaction, at least in its broad outline. But there were differences: Stockport and Rochdale stand out, as do the townships around Stockdale's 'home town' of Mottram in Longdendale, which itself provided eight subscribers (see Table 3). In contrast, the areas around Bolton and Leigh seem under-represented: two of the three subscribers in Bolton itself were libraries. Nonetheless, there is a strong spatial coincidence of this cognitive region with the functional region identified earlier.

The strength and integrity of both constructions was reinforced as the cultural was folded onto the economic.

Table 3: Location of subscribers to Aikin's *Description of the country from thirty to forty miles round Manchester* (1795)

	Number of subscribers	Prominent locations
Salford Hundred	149	Manchester (97), Rochdale (14), Manchester parish (18)
West Derby Hundred	71	Liverpool (54), Ormskirk (10)
Other Lancashire	5	
Cheshire	78	Stockport (26), Chester (9), Macclesfield (8), Mottram in Longdendale (8)
Yorkshire	28	Leeds (5), York (5)
Derbyshire	11	
London	67	
Other places	69	
Uncertain/unknown	112	
Total	**590**	

Source: John Aikin, *Description of the country from thirty to forty miles round Manchester* (1795): List of subscribers.

These elite spatial identities were echoed in the spatialisation of group solidarity amongst textile workers in north-west England. Wadsworth and Mann describe in some detail the spatial and social networking which underpinned the formation of early unions and combinations in the region, but it is the Luddite protests at the start of the nineteenth century which most clearly reveal the geography of shared experiences and identity amongst industrial workers. Stockport, which had a number of steam-powered weaving factories by the early nineteenth century, was the initial centre of Luddism in the North West. By February 1812, there were strong rumours of impending attacks on factories in the town. At a similar time, workers from Stockport moved to establish secret committees in other textile centres, including Bolton, Oldham, Eccles, Ashton and Manchester.[33] Protests included an attack on the Exchange in Manchester; others on factories and the homes of prominent industrialists; and a series of food riots. In all, some 33 incidents took place during March and April 1812. Their distribution reveals a common cause amongst the workers, from Bolton and Rochdale in the north to Macclesfield in the south, but with a particularly strong focus on Manchester and its immediate surroundings. The area covered again resembles that of the cotton/fustian districts identified earlier and, significantly, did not extend to the areas of handloom weaving further north in the county. Grievances there were expressed separately, most notably in the attacks on power looms in 1826 which were centred on Blackburn, not Manchester, and encompassed the emerging textile towns in the east Lancashire uplands.

We need to be careful of reading these disturbances in such spatially simplistic ways. Attacks in the 1760s and 1770s were very patchy and localised. Those in 1768 were focused on Hargreaves's homestead in Stanhill; the following year witnessed machine breaking in Bolton as well as in the Blackburn area, and in 1779 further incidents took place in the townships between Bolton and Wigan, and at Arkwright's mill at Birkacre. The somewhat disjointed nature of these disturbances perhaps reflects a lack of coherent geographical organisation amongst workers rather than the absence of common cause. Certainly, Hargreaves, Arkwright and their patented machines were the focus of widely felt grievances.[34] It is surely significant that, as the greater coherence of Luddite protests emerged a generation later, Manchester lay at the focus of events and drew on an area with an increasingly manifest common cultural identity. It acted as the focus for the economic, social and power networks that enfolded and defined the region, creating an identifiable (spatial) identity from everyday practices.

Conclusions

Whilst the foregoing analysis has moved through a wide range of ideas with almost indecent haste, two things are apparent. The first is that the boundaries of Manchester's region were remarkably coherent in terms of industry, transport, social interaction and cultural identity. This was, in Paasi's terms, a region with territorial and conceptual shape. It was also marked by the emergence of regional institutions. These included the Exchange, trade unions, and a range of learned and scientific societies. Many of these were based in Manchester, but drew their membership from both the town and the wider region, thus cementing the links between the two and underscoring Manchester's importance of the centre of power: shaping social and cultural life in north-west England. The gradual emergence of institutions reinforced the wider (national and international) recognition of the identity and coherence of the region as the 'cotton districts' wherein were manufactured 'Manchester goods'. For Paasi, these institutions and the process of naming are as revealing as patterns on the ground or in the imagination in establishing regional identities. They are an indication of how the economic and the symbolic aspects of regions became folded into one another. The cotton districts, with cottonopolis at their centre, were defined by their economy, but these names came to symbolise more than simply a product and a production system. They represented particular social, cultural and political values; values which resonated beyond the region in the early decades of the nineteenth century. The power wielded by Manchester during this period reflected this symbolic economic region, as the town drew authority from the region as well as the town itself.

The second point to make is that the industrial, social and cultural processes of regional formation were all affected through networks. They bound together the region through overlapping systems of interaction and gave it a vital internal coherence. In effect it was networks and the process of networking that effectively produced the region as a geographical, material and imagined space. Rather than drawing lines around the region and seeking to create a series of discrete spatial entities, we should focus on the lines that enmeshed and integrated the regional space. The region should be seen as Faucher saw it: a web, at the heart of which lay a spider industriously spinning together its constituent parts.

Notes

1. D. Gregory, '"A new and differing face in many places": three geographies of industrialisation', in R. A. Dodgshon and R. A. Butlin (eds.), *An historical geography of England and Wales* (London, 1990), p. 372; P. J. Corfield, *The impact of English towns* (Oxford, 1982), p. 22.
2. Daniel Defoe, *A tour through the whole island of Great Britain* (1724–26; London, 1971), p. 545.
3. Leon Faucher, *Manchester in 1844: its present condition and future prospects* (London, 1844), pp. 15–16.
4. See A. Gilbert, 'The new regional geography in English and French-speaking countries', *Progress in Human Geography*, 12 (1988), pp. 208–28; J. Allen, D. Massey, and A. Cochrane, *Rethinking the region* (London, 1998).
5. A. Paasi, 'The institutionalization of regions: a theoretical framework for understanding the emergence of regions and the constitution of regional identity', *Fennia*, 164 (1986), pp. 105–46. See also Gilbert, 'New regional geography'; Allen, Massey and Cochrane, *Rethinking the region*. For a fuller discussion of Paasi's work and the nature of regions and regional development, see J. Stobart, 'Regions, localities and industrialisation: evidence from the east midlands circa 1780–1840', *Environment and Planning A*, 33 (2001), pp. 1305–25.
6. J. Allen, 'Spatial assemblages of power: from domination to empowerment', in D. Massey, J. Allen and P. Sarre (eds.) *Human geography today* (Cambridge, 1999), p. 195.

7. T. Cox, *Magna Britainnia et Hibernia* (London, 1731).

8. E. Baines, *History, directory and gazetteer of the County Palatine of Lancaster*, 2 vols (1824–5; repr. Newton Abbot, 1968), i, p. 534; D. Gregory, *Regional transformation and industrial revolution: a geography of the Yorkshire woollen industry* (London, 1982).

9. See Allen, 'Spatial assemblages'; D. Massey, *Spatial divisions of labour* (Basingstoke, 1984).

10. Paasi, 'Institutionalization of regions'; J. Langton, 'The industrial revolution and the regional geography of England', *Transactions of the Institute of British Geographers*, 9:2 (1984); Gregory, *Regional transformation*.

11. A. Amin, 'Regions unbound: towards a new politics of place', *Geografiska Annaler 86B* (2004), p. 40; A. Everitt, 'Country, county and town: patterns of regional evolution in England', *Transactions of the Royal Historical Society*, 5th ser., 29 (1979), pp. 79–108.

12. Langton, 'The industrial revolution', p. 162. See also P. Krugman, *Development, geography and economic theory* (Cambridge, MA; 1995).

13. A. Wadsworth and J. de L. Mann, *The cotton trade and industrial Lancashire, 1600–1780* (Manchester, 1931), pp. 98 106; J Stobart, *The first industrial region: north-west England 1700–1760* (Manchester, 2004), pp. 72–5.

14. Stobart, *First industrial region*, pp. 77–80.

15. Wadsworth and Mann, *Cotton trade*, p. 253.

16. Wadsworth and Mann, *Cotton trade*, p. 252.

17. Stobart, *First industrial region*, pp. 81–9, 91–4.

18. E. Raffald, *Directory of Manchester and Salford* (1773; repr. Manchester, 1989). See also J. Aikin, *A description of the country from thirty to forty miles round Manchester* (London, 1795), p. 158.

19. In addition, Jolley was owed £1145 4s by a further 74 people, whilst he himself owed 28 debts totalling £1,043 5s. The precise nature of these two sets of debts is unclear: Lancashire Record Office [hereafter LRO], WCW, 1735, Joseph Jolley of Manchester.

20. LRO, WCW, 1753, Richard Lathom of Wigan; LRO, WCW, 1721, Thomas Smalley of Blackburn.

21. For more on this relational sense of place, see Gregory, 'Geographies of industrialisation'; Allen, Massey and Cochrane, *Rethinking the region*; D. Massey, 'Questions of locality', *Geography*, 78 (1993), pp. 142–9; Amin, 'Regions unbound'.

22. J. Langton, 'The industrial revolution'; G. Turnbull, 'Canals, coal and regional growth during the industrial revolution', *Economic History Review*, 40:4 (1987), pp. 537–60.

23. J. Langton, 'Liverpool and its hinterland in the late eighteenth century', in B. L. Anderson and P. Stoney (eds.), *Commerce, industry and transport: studies in economic change on Merseyside* (Liverpool, 1983), pp. 1–25.

24. *Scholes's Manchester and Salford Directory* (Manchester, 1797), pp. 183–6.

25. *Journals of the House of Commons*, 23 (1735), p. 575, quoted in E. Pawson, *Transport and economy: the turnpike roads of eighteenth-century Britain* (London, 1977), p. 143.

26. *Scholes's Directory*, pp. 190–4; Stobart, *First industrial region*, pp. 50–2, 189–90.

27. J. Stobart, 'Social and geographical contexts of property transmission in the eighteenth century', in J. Stobart and A. Owens (eds.), *Urban fortunes: property and inheritance in the town, 1700–1900* (Aldershot, 2000), pp. 110–12; Stobart, *First industrial region*, pp. 193–4.

28. Stobart, *First industrial region*, pp. 196–9.

29. See, *inter alia*, D. Hancock, *Citizens of the world: London merchants and the integration of the British Atlantic community, 1735–1785* (Cambridge, 1995); R. Pearson and D. Richardson, 'Business networking in the industrial revolution', *Economic History Review*, 54 (2001), pp. 657–79; J. Stobart, '"A settled little society of trading people?" The eighteenth-century retail community of an English county town', in B. Blondé, E. Briot, N. Coquery and L. Van Aert (eds.), *Retailers and consumer changes in early modern Europe* (Tours, 2005).

30. Allen, 'Spatial assemblages'.

31. Langton, 'The industrial revolution'; Amin, 'Regions unbound', p. 37; Paasi, 'Institutionalization of regions'.

32. On the representation of space, see: H. Lefebvre, *The production of space* (Oxford, 1991).

33. A. Charlesworth, D. Gilbert, A. Randall, and C. Wrigley, *Atlas of industrial protest in Britain, 1750–1990* (Basingstoke, 1996), pp. 42–3.

34. Charlesworth *et al.*, *Atlas of industrial protest*, pp. 18–22.

Lost in translation? Documents relating to the disturbances at Manchester, 1715

*Kazuhiko Kondo**

Manchester in the age of Defoe and Walpole has been described either as 'one of the greatest, if not really the greatest meer village in England ... which is greater and more populous than most cities', or as 'remarkably disaffected and that disaffection to be greatly supported by the members of the [collegiate church]'.[1] Antiquarian publications since the eighteenth century are informative but often laden with contemporary pride and prejudice. Recent historians of toryism and Jacobitism have made a remarkable contribution in uncovering the political and religious contentions and rivalry, and have revised the happy, whiggish vision of Manchester.[2] The aim of this article is, first, to explore historical documents relating to the disturbances at Manchester in the summer of 1715, which preceded the Jacobite risings of September to November of that year. They include materials of diverse characters, both well known and little known, published and unpublished, local, national and international, written in English and French. Secondly, the article aims to place the local history of Manchester in a wider, national and European context. In the process the government's serious interest in Manchester affairs will emerge.[3]

Manchester disturbances and the documents

5 May 1715 dawned in Manchester with a considerable number of disguised persons who proclaimed James Edward Stuart king.[4] Disguised in this case meant 'either masked or in women's apparel', and wearing oak leaves. This was the start of the early summer riots at and around Manchester with appropriated Stuart and Restoration symbolism adding to the festive atmosphere of the world turned upside down.[5] On 28 May, King George's birthday, a crowd defied the friends of government by putting out bonfires and breaking illuminated windows. On the 29th, Restoration Day, they distinguished themselves by dressing their hats and houses with oak branches, and became more unruly. Whitsuntide, 5 and 6 June, coincided with the annual Manchester fair,[6] and the mob rallied again, insulting all 'honest

men', that is, whigs and Presbyterians. During the night they broke all the windows of the Presbyterian meeting house (later called Cross Street Chapel), and set fire to several family pews. The disturbance culminated in the complete destruction of the Presbyterian chapel during the three nights from 9 to 11 June, the 10th being the Pretender's birthday. A drum beat was heard, together with cries of 'Down with the rump', and the pulpit and the clock in the chapel were dashed to pieces. (The symbolic meanings of demolishing the pulpit and the clock will be discussed below.) This, however, was not the end, but 'excursions' followed, with attacks on other dissenters' chapels in the countryside.[7]

St James's Post (SJP), a London newspaper, printed an account of the 'the high-flown mob' at Manchester on 20 June, and another London newspaper, The Flying-Post (TFP) printed the same account on 21 June, including a preface and long postscript. A tract, An Account of a Dreadful Mob at Manchester (ADM) appeared shortly thereafter.[8] The three accounts derive from the same sources: letters written by correspondents at Warrington and Leeds to the editors. As far as known sources can testify, the SJP appeared first with an 860-word letter of 11 June from Warrington; TFP and the five-page tract, ADM, printed the same with postscripts from Warrington of the 14th and Leeds of the 15th, adding another 480 words. More bibliographical research may confirm the unproven claim of the editor of TFP that 'the following account of the rebellion at Manchester, &c. was publish'd on Saturday night last [18 June] in a postscript to this paper, and is thought proper to be inserted again, for the farther information of the publick'.[9]

Apart from brief, independent prefaces, there are minor spelling and phrasing differences between the three publications. ADM, for example, uses the terms mob and riot, but not rebellion or rebel. It is cautious and suppresses such fearsome expressions as 'they threaten to dig up the graves of such dissenters as are buried about the chappel and expose their bodies' and insinuations of 'the tory faction' being in liaison with 'the great popish families' as printed in SJP and TFP. TFP is more sensational. It refers to the incidents as rebellion and calls the crowd rebels and a mob. In fact the article of 1,340 words in this newspaper is sandwiched between a rumoured report at the end of a page on European outrages relating to the digging up of the corpse of a Protestant captain at Berne by 'French papists', and information on page two about 'Popish emissaries' and other zealots in London and the provinces.

Cover of *An Account of a Dreadful Mob at Manchester* (Edinburgh, 1715)

AN
ACCOUNT
Of a Dreadful
M O B
AT
MANCHESTER
And other PLACES in
ENGLAND.

EDINBURGH,
Printed by JOHN MOSMAN, Junior, Anno DOM. 1715.

The character of *SJP* is ambiguous because it is not easily identified. It was published by J. Baker, who sold the *St James's Evening Post* on Tuesdays, Thursdays and Saturdays. The *SJP* we refer to was issued on Monday, 20 June, and the two newspapers were not the same.[10] The character of *TFP* was more straightforward. Edited by George Ridpath and other whig and Presbyterian journalists, it was an unequivocally whig newspaper, published three days a week – each week issuing some 4 to 5,000 copies.[11] The title page of our tract, *ADM*, cites the printer as John Mosman, junior, of Edinburgh. 62 items published or printed by John Mosman between 1695 and 1729 are held in the National Library of Scotland, 20 in the Bodleian Library and eighteen in the British Library. (Six items overlap in the three libraries.) Included among these are the Bible, sermons, tracts of the Kirk of Scotland and the SPCK, as well as secular books on English writing style, Scottish history, sovereignty, the royal family and the king's speeches; a Latin textbook, extracts of statutes relating to taxation, manufactures, fishery; and handbooks on geometry, bills of exchange, bookkeeping and the crafts of Edinburgh.[12] Mosman was apparently a typical eighteenth-century publisher in a Presbyterian mould.

The anonymous correspondents at Warrington and Leeds cannot be identified, but there is no mistaking their religious and political affiliation. They write of the crowd as a 'high-flown mob', stressing their Jacobite disposition and describing them with contempt as 'chiefly consist[ing] of poor workmen who could not long subsist without money, with which they are plentifully supplied'. The correspondents deplore the irresponsible magistrates, saying, 'a set of good justices … might have prevented all this'. They use the words chapel and meeting house but never Presbyterian, supplying plausible evidence of their own Presbyterianism. They are 'honest men' who support the Hanoverians and the whig government, 'the most loving, peaceable neighbours … that could possibly be'.[13] For instance, Jeremiah Aldred, a Presbyterian minister at Monton, was a witness to the special commission of the Court of Exchequer in December 1716 and delivered a sermon in 1716 at Manchester to commemorate the 'happy deliverance from the rebels'; and Charles Owen, Presbyterian minister at Warrington, delivered another the next year.[14] Either of them might well have written the letters. In addition, questions arise as to the triangular relationship between the correspondents at or near Warrington and Leeds; the editors of *SJP* and *TFP* in London; and John Mosman in Edinburgh. I have at present no evidence to testify to specific links between the three, but anti-Jacobite alarm among the government supporters of a Presbyterian disposition could easily have brought about such a collaboration.

Similar incidents in London, Oxford and other towns in the early summer of 1715 were reported in newspapers and state papers;[15] the rioting at Manchester was one among many. And it was after hearing the accounts of riots in the Midlands that the House of Commons decided on 1 July to draft 'a bill for preventing tumults and riotous assemblies, and for the more speedy and effectual punishing the rioters'. A committee to prepare and bring in the bill was formed of four MPs: Sir Edward Northey, attorney general; Nicholas Lechmere, solicitor general; Sir Joseph Jekyll and John Barrington. Jekyll was a government lawyer, soon to become master of the rolls. Barrington was a Utrecht-educated Presbyterian barrister. Prompted by such a strong collaboration of whig-Presbyterian lawyers, the Riot Act passed both houses swiftly, and was given royal assent on 20 July, to take effect on 1 August, the very beginning of the second regnal year of George I.[16]

The Court of Exchequer recorded depositions of witnesses at the special commissions organized in 1716 for several counties 'to inquire into any of the losses and damages which any of his majesties Protestant subjects have sustained' between George's accession and 1 August 1715. The commissions were organized to remedy the damages incurred by the friends of government before the Riot Act came into effect. The commissioners for Lancashire consisted of nine whiggish gentlemen and merchants of Manchester and its environs.[17] There are two extant versions of the depositions, one among the Hibbert-Ware papers at the John Rylands Library.[18] This document, with frequent additions and deletions, was vividly drawn from the lips of witnesses, but it is incomplete and some pages are missing. The other is among the special commissions series E178 at The National Archives.[19] The latter is a fair copy of the depositions on parchment written both in Latin and English.

The *Calendar of treasury books* also includes the summary return of 'losses and damages sustained by the king's subjects by reason of the tumultuous and rebellious proceedings in the several counties … in their buildings, houses and other real and personal estates'. These damages amounted to £5,234 9s for the eight counties excluding London. The damage done to the Manchester meeting house was assessed at £665 13s, being the maximum figure among the 28 chapels cited in the treasury books. Blackley (£40), Failsworth (£10), Monton (£200) and Pilkington (£24) and were other meeting houses in Lancashire where due reparation was made.[20]

What I wish to emphasize here is the highly-charged field of force of the Stuart-Hanoverian contention that relates not only to political and religious allegiances but also to the socio-cultural rift between two world-views with contingent symbolism of the period. The Riot Act included a proclamation to be read by a magistrate to the crowd, 'immediately to disperse themselves, and peaceably to depart to their habitations, or to their lawful business'.[21] The mob who destroyed the pulpit and the clock in the Presbyterian chapel at Manchester, 9–11 June, were assaulting the symbols of faith and methodical way of life. The proclamation espoused the Protestant ethic and the spirit of industrial capitalism, which promoted diligence, punctuality and a rational way of life, in opposition to traditional 'customs in common'.[22] And the timing of the riots and legislation coincided with the Jacobite-Hanoverian crisis of 1715. The government had reason to be serious. The people in the street knew that something provocative was necessary and effective to express their dissatisfaction with, and disaffection to, the new regime. The rift between government supporters and the disaffected was manifest and deep, but it did not necessarily mean that the disaffected were Jacobites.

The National Archives, SP35/3/68: Letter from Wyvill to Townshend, 25 June 1715

Wyvill and Townshend

Though the state papers domestic do not contain as many letters relating to the Manchester disturbances as to the London and Oxford incidents, there is an interesting letter among the official correspondence of the secretary of state. It is headed *Traduction de la lettre de Mr Wyvill à Mylord Townshend datée à Manchester le 25e juin 1715*. This apparently is a letter originally written in English and translated into French for some purpose. The English original is most probably lost. The text cites the cries of the crowd at Manchester saying *'on assomme la rump'* [down with the rump] three times and underlined, and ends with humble words, *'avec tous le respect et la vénération possible, Mylord, de votre grandeur, &c'*.[23]

Who is this Mr Wyvill? The *Oxford DNB* has no entry for a Wyvill flourishing in 1715, but the letter clarifies his identity. Translated back to English, it begins:

> My Lord, on Thursday between five & six o'clock in the morning I came for his

Majesty's service to the Market Place at Manchester with two companies of dragoons, one of which I made a guard, and placed the other between two inns very close. I kept them as close to me as possible because I did not want so small a number of brave dragoons set amongst many ill-intentioned people.

So this Wyvill was the loyal officer of the dragoons dispatched to Manchester on Thursday, 23 June, to suppress disturbances. It continues:

On the same day around seven or eight o'clock in the evening, they came from everywhere into the Market and encountered us as if to drive us off, crying 'Down with the Rump', and uttering other insolent words. I judged it prudent to keep us under arms until after midnight. Yesterday [Friday] around the same time, some of them holding big clubs defied two or three dragoons and dared to cry 'Down with the Rump' and to kill them. The guard having arrived, the scoundrels retired to a house and locked themselves within. But the doors were immediately broken open and we arrested five ... If you please, my Lord, let me know in what manner I should act according to the laws regarding these people, supposing they should venture to come again upon us or pull down houses.

At the first night [Thursday] the constable had, according to my request, the town crier tell people that it was banned to cry 'Down with the Rump'. It seems the number of the *canaille* yesterday decreased from before. The scelerat Wegstaffe told Colonel Killegrew, as I heard, that he was absent on the birthday of *Roy Jacques 3* [the Pretender]. I hope that the fury of some others will be smoothed down a little.[24]

The crowd's violence, as described in Wyvill's letter, was more tense and symbolic than physical. The Restoration cliché 'Down with the Rump' had been revived in the early eighteenth century almost as a flashback against the Hanoverians and whigs. To this, *TFP* adds a relevant piece of news:

We are tolerably easy and quiet since the arrival of that brave and loyal gentleman, Maj. Wyvil [sic], with two troops of horse, who came here on June 23[d], about six in the morning ...[25]

Lord Townshend wrote back to Wyvill on 28 June in English acknowledging Wyvill for his letter and advising him to 'regulate yourself' and act with 'prudence and zeal'.[26] A peculiar tract held at Manchester Central Library may be discussed in this context. The anonymous tract entitled *A True and Exact Copy of a Letter, from Major Wy_l to Lord C_b_m his New Colonel*, dated 'Manchester the 25th of June, 1715', is apparently

Cover of *A True and Exact Copy of a Letter from Major Wy_l* (n.p., 1715)

a transcript of a letter from Wyvill to Lord Cobham, colonel of the First Dragoons.[27] It is filled with Wyvill's bravadoes dealing with the 'mutineers' and 'the damn'd high church dogs'. The expression of the tract is stronger and more partisan than his letter to Lord Townshend of the same date. Wyvill stands by 'the honest Presbyterians' and says 'I call and teach all the dragoons to call the tories Jacobites':[28]

> By G_d my Lord let me have smart orders, and you shall see, how I will execute them. I have wrote to Lord Viscount To__nd to know, what I shall do with my prisoners, since we have no Justice of the Peace in this town, but one Mr Balladine a sad Church dog, who will certainly take the town's peoples's part against the brave dragoons.

Wyvill was eager to show his loyalty, and avoided even citing 'Down with the Rump', modifying the slogan into 'grumbling complaint'. He was also a hot-blooded officer, finishing his letter thus:

> I have likewise desir'd orders about burning and pulling down of houses[.] Your Lordship knows my character, I love action and am devoted to my superior.[29]

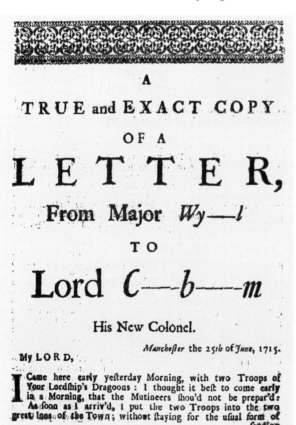

A

TRUE and EXACT COPY

OF A

LETTER,

From Major *Wy—l*

TO

Lord *C—-b—-m*

His New Colonel.

Manchester the 25th of *June*, 1715.

My LORD,

I Came here early yesterday Morning, with two Troops of Your Lordship's Dragoons : I thought it best to come early in a Morning, that the Mutineers shou'd not be prepar'd : As soon as I arriv'd, I put the two Troops into the two great Inns of the Town; without staying for the usual form of sending

This explains why Lord Townshend advised Wyvill to abide by the law and act with 'prudence and zeal'. Do the different tones of the two letters relate to the different recipients, secretary of state and colonel? Or did the translation change the tone at all? These queries must remain unanswered until we come across the English original of Wyvill's letter to Townshend.

Two other factual points remain unanswered about Wyvill's identity and the dates concerned. First, the army lists of officers in the war office papers describe John Wyvill as captain of the dragoons or horse guards, and he was only promoted to major in February 1723.[30] Yet, he is addressed – as a piece of flattery? – as major in *TFP* as well as in the tract *True and Exact Copy of a Letter*. Secondly,

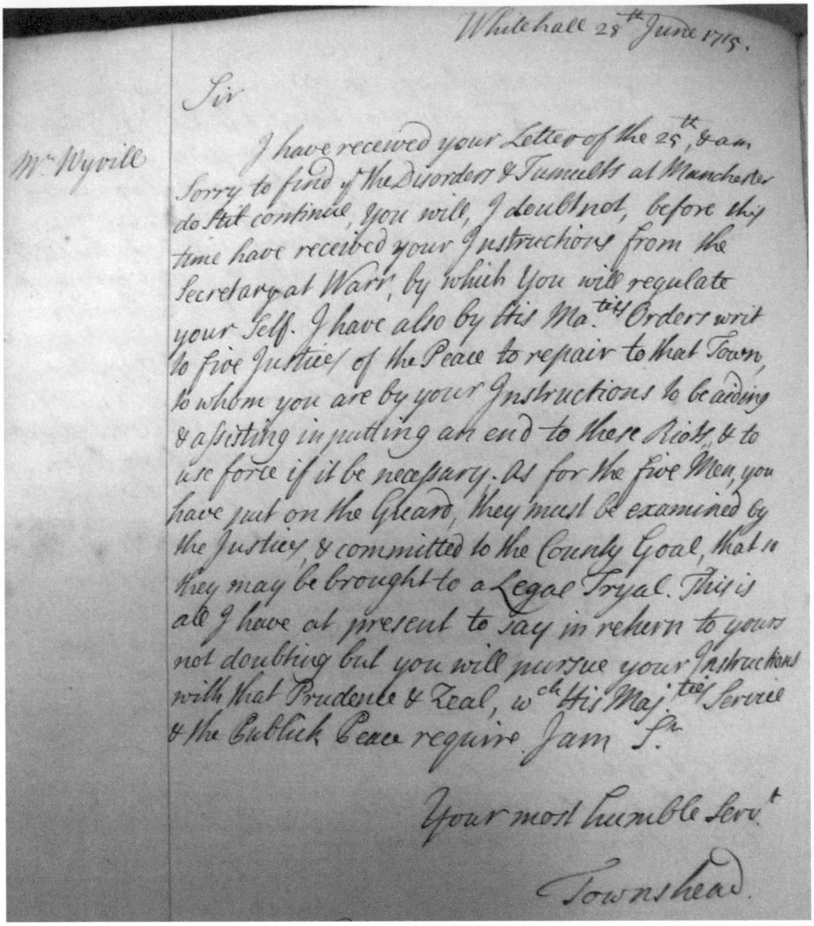

The handwritten letter reads:

> Whitehall 28th June 1715.
>
> Sir
>
> I have received your Letter of the 25th, & am sorry to find yt the Disorders & Tumults at Manchester do still continue, you will, I doubt not, before this time have received your Instructions from the Secretary at Warr, by which you will regulate your Self. I have also by His Maty Orders writt to five Justices of the Peace to repair to that Town, to whom you are by your Instructions to be aiding & assisting in putting an end to these Riots, & to use force if it be necessary. As for the five Men, you have put on the Gleam, they must be examined by the Justices, & committed to the County Goal, that so they may be brought to a Legal Tryal. This is all I have at present to say in return to yours not doubting but you will pursue your Instructions with that Prudence & Zeal, wch His Majties Service & the Publick Peace require. I am Sr.
>
> Your most humble Servt
>
> Townshead.

The National Archives, SP44/116: Townshend to Wyvill, 28 June 1715

as for dates, the birthday of the Pretender and the peak of violence occurred on 10, not 23, June. Did anything, apart from necessary transmission lag, prevent Wyvill from reaching Manchester earlier? Or, was 23 June important for some reason? In fact, after 14 June the site of disorder dispersed from Manchester to the outskirts of the town, and the mob marched in the countryside, from Blackley, Platt, Monton, Greenacres, Stand to Wigan, raiding dissenters' chapels.[31] In the tract Wyvill says, 'I thought it best to come early in a morning, that the mutineers shou'd not be prepar'd ... My sudden arrival and [seizing] those two inns, struck a great damp amongst the tories'. A letter of 30 June from Manchester is quoted in *TFP*: 'The reason of [Wyvill's] coming so early was to prevent an opposition he was threaten'd with from the rebels, had he come in the evening, as he was expected'. Another letter of the same date says, 'Since Major Wyvil arriv'd with 2 troops, which was on the 23d instant, the Jacobites have finish'd their Midsummer campaign'.[32] These may imply that serious disturbances were expected on the eve of St John the Baptist, midsummer's night. If that was the case, it would indeed have been sensible of Wyvill to arrive at Manchester in the early morning of the 23rd. His two letters of 25 June described skirmishes with the mob on Thursday night. He went on to ask Lord Townshend what to do with the arrested '*canaille*' and reported that the situation was calming down.[33]

With the benefit of hindsight, the peak of violence in Manchester had passed by late June. Wyvill's action might have been belated, but it was by no means so late as to render it useless. Three more letters followed – acknowledged by Lord Townshend on his own back to Wyvill on 5 July.[34] They described the situation at and around Manchester at a time when Parliament was informed of riots in Shrewsbury, Worcestershire and Staffordshire and had been debating the Riot Bill. *TFP* reports the arrival of Wyvill and its effects as late as 7 July.

However, a more significant question relates to why and for whom the letter was translated into French. John Wyvill apparently wrote the letter in English. Lord Townshend read it and judged it necessary to have a French translation made. For whom? Most probably for the king or his Hanoverian ministers, whose knowledge of written English was far from assured. French in the century of enlightenment was aptly the *lingua franca* among European statesmen and men of letters. In June and July Lord Townshend communicated to the king 'several accounts' of the disorders and officers' conduct at Manchester. On 19 June Lord Townshend wrote to Sir Ralph Assheton in Lancashire,

> The king has received several accounts that the tumultuous and disorderly proceedings at Manchester have not only continued there for many days without any check to the great terror and damage of many of his royal and dutiful subjects, but have also grown more daring and dangerous by spreading further into the neighbourhood. That these riotous people ... destroyed the meeting house at Manchester ... Hereupon his majesty being highly moved with these insolent, illegal & treasonable proceedings so destructive to all government ... has commanded me to signify his pleasure to you ... His majesty has an entire confidence that you do exert your utmost power & authority in suppressing all such treasonable riots.[35]

This was followed on 25 June by his letters of the same text to five other Lancashire JPs.[36] And on the 28th Townshend replied to Mr Wyvill: 'I have received your letter of the 25th, & am sorry to find that the disorders & tumults at Manchester do still continue'. Townshend advised Wyvill to 'regulate yourself' by the 'instructions from the secretary at war', and mentioned that 'by his majesty's orders [he had written] to five Justices of the Peace to repair to [Manchester], to whom you are … to aid & assist in putting an end to these riots'. The arrested five should 'be brought to a legal tryal'.[37] On 5 July Townshend wrote again to Wyvill:

> Since yours of the 25th June, I have received those of the 29th, 30th, and of the 2[d] instant, and have acquainted the king with your conduct in this matter, who is very well satisfyed with it.[38]

And finally in the under-secretary's letter book, Horace Walpole wrote to Mr Cracherode on July 14: 'the inclosed informations [sic] relating to the riots committed at Manchester having been laid last night before the committee of lords, I am directed by my Lord Townshend to transmit them to you, etc.'[39]

Thus the exchanges of information and instructions among the army officer at Manchester, Lancashire JPs, the secretary of state, his officials and the king in London can be traced. Though it is not yet possible to give any direct evidence to testify that Wyvill's letter was perused by the king himself, it is highly plausible that the French translation was among several accounts King George heard or read about the disturbances at and near Manchester while discussing state affairs with ministers. Such accounts would have helped him to form a clearer idea of the affair and the difficulties experienced by magistrates and military officers when dealing with the mob. Lord Townshend acted energetically on his majesty's orders, and the king was 'very well satisfied'. Furthermore, he would have been persuaded that new legislation (the Riot Act), as well as several orders and proclamations, was necessary to meet the nationwide disaffection and violence. And it proved effective. An ordinary letter from St James, London to Hanover on 13/2 August reads: 'All is calm in Scotland and in our provinces since *l'acte contre les emeutes* [the Riot Act] has been published'.[40]

The government's concerns and Manchester

Few of the papers and correspondence generated by George I survive either at Windsor Castle or at Kew. The *Hauptstaatsarchiv Hannover* holds some occasional correspondence of the king and a lot of ordinary business papers of the *deutsche Kanzlei*.[41] Without a collection of King George's substantial business papers and relevant correspondence, the evidence about the king's specific involvement in the Manchester affairs remain tantalizingly circumstantial. However, records of the cabinet council and committee of lords in the state papers during George I's reign include several entries for 'riots at Manchester'. There is no question as to the significance of the Manchester disturbances and the government's concerned response.[42] In fact the *Nouvelles ordinaires de Londres* of 28/17 June from St James to Hanover wrote that 'Some companies of dragoons were sent to Manchester where there have been renewed grand disorders of the Restoration day of Charles II, the pretender then having been proclaimed by some seditious people'.[43] The information about the *'grands desordres'* in the *Nouvelles* was thus brief, but it was accompanied by a copy of the *SJP* of 20 June. It printed a two-page account of the high-flown mob and the common cry of 'Down with the Rump' in Manchester, and it was deemed sufficient to ensure the Hanoverian ministers grasped the full impact of the seditious riots there.[44]

A remote market town in north England attracted the serious attention of government ministers and the king in the critical conjuncture. Apparently the secretary of state thought it necessary to update him in French translation at the height of the unrest. George I has conventionally been described as having been far more preoccupied with continental than British affairs, and as distanced from domestic politics because of his poor English and lack of interest.[45] The exchanges between Manchester, Westminster and Hanover emerging from the documents we have examined provide us with circumstantial yet convincing details not just about the disturbances at Manchester in 1715, but also about the involvement of the government and the king, and their interest in political, religious and Mancunian affairs.

Notes

* This is a revised version of my paper read at the Manchester Metropolitan University conference on early modern Manchester, 2 Apr. 2005. My thanks are due to Prof Harry Dickinson and Prof Bill Speck who both responded with enthusiasm to my incipient ideas in Tokyo, as well as to Prof Hiroyuki Ninomiya who helped me read French manuscripts of the period.

1. Daniel Defoe, *A Tour thro' the Whole Island of Great Britain* (2 vols, 1724–6; repr. 1927), ii, pp. 670–1; The National Archives [hereafter TNA], SP 36/32: Gibson to Newcastle, 29 June 1734.

2. Among the most important works are D. G. D. Isaac, 'Study of popular disturbances in Britain, 1714–54' (unpub. PhD thesis, Edinburgh University, 1953); Nicholas Rogers, 'Riot and popular Jacobitism in early Hanoverian England', in Eveline Cruickshanks (ed.), *Ideology and conspiracy* (Edinburgh, 1982), esp. pp. 74–8; P. K. Monod, *Jacobitism and the English people, 1688–1788* (Cambridge, 1989), pp. 182–5; J. D. Oates, 'Jacobitism and popular disturbances in northern England, 1714–1719', *Northern History*, 41 (2004), pp. 111–28. Daniel Szechi, *1715: The Great Jacobite Rebellion* (New Haven, CT; 2006), deals with the rebellion and not the nationwide disturbances before Sep. 1715.

3. My publications on contentious Manchester in the early eighteenth century include 'An account of a dreadful mob at Manchester, 1715' in H. Hasegawa (ed.), *Europe* (1985), pp. 241–82; 'The workhouse issue at Manchester: selected documents, 1729–35, I', *Bulletin of the Faculty of Letters, Nagoya University*, 33:98 (1987), pp. 1–96; 'The "mob" and the Riot Act of 1715', *Mita Gakkai Zasshi*, 86 (1993), pp. 197–213; and 'The church and politics in "disaffected" Manchester, 1718–31', *Historical Research*, 80 (2007), pp. 100–23, which contains a critical bibliography.

4. All the early eighteenth-century dates as they relate to Britain are in Old Style, though taken to start on 1 January. Where necessary – in the European context – both Old and New Styles are given.

5. As to the liminal symbolism of popular riots see M. M. Bakhtin, *Rabelais and his world* (Cambridge, MA; 1968); Christopher Hill, *The world turned upside down* (1972); Natalie Davis, *Society and culture in early modern France* (Stanford, 1975); Kazuhiko Kondo, *Tami no moral: culture and society in early modern England* (Tokyo, 1993).

6. William Owen, *An Authentic Account Publish'd by the King's Authority, of All the Fairs in England and Wales* (1756), pp. 48–50.

7. The quotes are from the tracts and newspapers as mentioned in n. 8.

8. *St James's Post*, 20 June 1715; *The Flying-Post: or the Post-master*, 21 June 1715; *An Account of a Dreadful Mob at Manchester and other Places in England* (Edinburgh, 1715). The two surviving copies of the last are in the British Library (BL) and the National Library of Scotland (NLS), and available in the Eighteenth Century Collections Online (ECCO), although the ECCO copy, alas, has indecipherable lines. Refer to the full transcript in Kondo, 'Account of a dreadful mob', which contains a critical comparison of *TFP* and *ADM*. Also relevant are [anon,] *A True and Exact Copy of a Letter, from Major Wy_l to Lord C_b_m* (1715); [anon,] *The History of All the Mobs, Tumults and Insurrections ...* (1715, available in ECCO). The latter (pp. 56–7) contains a two-page account of 'the insurrection at Manchester' but provides little original news.

9. *TFP*, 21 June 1715. Historians of the London newspaper may be reminded here of Henry Snyder's remark on the *Postscript to the Flying Post* published by George Ridpath, which Snyder assumes to have disappeared after 1712: H. L. Snyder, 'The circulation of newspapers in the reign of Queen Anne', *The Library*, 5th ser., 23 (1968), pp. 206–35, at p. 210. A discovery of the *Postscript to TFP* would revise Snyder's assumption.

10. *SJP*, 20 June 1715, p. 3. The Burney collection at the BL has both *St James's Evening Post* and *SJP*, but it lacks *SJP* for June 1715. I used a copy at Hanover, for which see n. 40 below.

11. Snyder, 'Circulation of newspapers', pp. 210, 225; J. A. Downie, *Robert Harley and the press* (Cambridge, 1979). Other editors included John Salisbury and William Hurt.

12. Results of online searches of the NLS, the Bodleian and the BL. The

ECCO has proved less helpful for Mosman, and there is no entry for him in the *Oxford Dictionary of National Biography*, online edn. (Oxford, 2004).

13. In Bishop Gastrell's survey of his diocese (1714–25) the large parish of Manchester counted 2,763 families, and those of dissenters (mainly Presbyterians) counted 422 (15.3 per cent), more than double the national average of 6.2 per cent: F. Gastrell (F. R. Raines [comp.]), *Notitia cestriensis, or historical notices of the diocese of Chester* (2 vols in 4 parts, 1845–50), ii, part 2, pp. 57–67; Michael Watts, *The dissenters* (Oxford, 1978), pp. 270, 509.

14. Jeremiah Aldred, *The History of Saul and David … in a Thanksgiving Sermon Preach'd at Manchester, November 14, 1716 …* (1716); for his witness see TNA, E178/6905: Lancashire, 3 Geo I; Charles Owen, *De Jure Divino Woe: Exemplify'd in the Remarkable Punishment of Persecutors, False-teachers, and Rebels: A Thanksgiving Sermon Preach'd at Manchester, November 14, 1717 …* (1717). Other sermons delivered at the Manchester chapel included those of Joseph Mottershead (1718) and Joshua Jones (1719).

15. These have been dealt with by Isaac, Rogers, Kondo, Monod and Oates with telling accounts of the disorder and colourful street performances as well as their political discourse. See n. 2 above. *History of All the Mobs …* is a tract clearly to justify and publicise the legislation of the Riot Act of July 1715.

16. *Commons Journals*, 18, pp. 194–232; 1 George I, stat.2, c.5.

17. They were John Levor, esq; George Cheetham [sic], esq; James Chetham, esq; Samuel Hallowes, esq; Thomas Horton, esq; Charles Worsley, gent; John Andrews, gent; Hugh Parr, gent; James Bayley, merchant: PRO, *Calendar of treasury books*, 30, part 2, p. 424 (27 Aug. 1716); TNA, E178/6905: Lancashire, 3 Geo I (Dec. 1716).

18. John Rylands University Library of Manchester (Deansgate), English MS 1031, ff. 155–60. An incomplete transcript of this is in *The Palatine notebook*, 2 (1882), pp. 241–4.

19. TNA, E178/6905: Lancashire, 3 Geo I.

20. PRO, *Calendar of treasury books*, 31, part 2, pp. 141, 184–9 (Feb./Mar. 1717).

21. 1 George I, stat.2, c.5.

22. Max Weber, *The Protestant ethic and the spirit of capitalism* (1930); E. P. Thompson, *Customs in common* (1991).

23. TNA, SP35/3/68: Wyvill to Townshend, 25 June 1715. I follow the large, pencilled number given at the head of each dossier. The folio number is stamped 162.

24. *Ibid*. For Captain Henry Killigrew see Charles Dalton, *George the First's army 1714–1727*, i (1910), p. 106. The 'scelerat Wegstaffe' may refer to the nonjuring bishop Thomas Wagstaffe (1645–1712) or one of his relatives: *Oxford Dictionary of National Biography*.

25. *TFP*, 7 July 1715.
26. TNA, SP44/116: Townshend to Wyvill, 28 June 1715.
27. This 3-paged tract lacks date and place of publication, but was most plausibly printed in the summer of 1715. For Lord Cobham's regiment of dragoons commissioned on 13 June 1715 see Dalton, *George the First's army*, i, p. 106.
28. *A True and Exact Copy of a Letter*, pp. 1–2.
29. *Ibid*, p. 3.
30. TNA, WO64/3, WO64/8/8: Army lists; Dalton, *George the First's Army*, i, pp. 101, 106, 188; ii (1912), p. 196.
31. *TFP*, 14 July 1715; TNA, E178/6905.
32. *True and Exact Copy*, pp. 1–2; *TFP*, 7 and 14 July 1715.
33. TNA, SP35/3/68.
34. TNA, SP44/116. The three letters of Wyvill do not survive in the state papers.
35. SP44/116: Townshend to Assheton, 19 June 1715.
36. SP44/116: Townshend to Mawdesley, etc., 25 June; Townshend to Wyvill, 5 July 1715. The five JPs are Robert Mawdesley, esq.; Bertie Entwisle, esq.; Jonathan Case, esq.; Edward Norris, esq.; Ambrose Pudsey, esq.
37. SP44/116: Townshend to Wyvill, 28 June 1715.
38. SP44/116: Townshend to Wyvill, 5 July 1715.
39. SP44/147: Under-secretaries' letter book. Horace Walpole (1678–1757), brother of Sir Robert and minister to the Hague, later in 1715. Records of the cabinet council and committee of lords in the state papers during the reign of George I are listed in *List and Index Society*, 224 (1987), with several entries for 'riots at Manchester'.
40. Niedersächsisches Landesarchiv, Hauptstaatsarchiv Hannover [NSLA], Cal. Br. 24, Nr. 1713, f. 172ᵛ (my translation): Nouvelles de Londres.
41. Documents held at NSLA are consulted. For more extensive argument, see K. Kondo, 'The Manchester disturbances and George I in 1715', in David Bates and Kazuhiko Kondo (eds.), *Migration and identity in British history: proceedings of the 5th Anglo-Japanese conference of historians* (2007).
42. Records of the cabinet council and committee of lords during the reign of George I are listed in *List and Index Society*, 224 (1987).
43. NSLA, Cal. Br. 24, Nr. 1713, f. 144ᵛ (my translation).
44. Cal. Br. 24, Nr. 1713, ff. 146–7.
45. Those definitive works disavowing the myth about George I include John Beattie, *The English court in the reign of George I* (1967); Ragnhild Hatton, *George I: elector and king* (1978; 2nd ed., 2001); G. C. Gibbs, 'George I (1660–1727)', *Oxford Dictionary of National Biography*.

'What have I to do with the ship?': John Byrom and eighteenth-century Manchester politics, with new verse attributions

Timothy Underhill

> We are not of the man's humour, who being on board a ship at sea, and a storm arising, and being desired to work a little, for that the ship was in danger of being sunk, replied, 'What have I to do with the ship? I am but a passenger.' We look upon ourselves embarked in the *good ship Manchester*, and whenever we apprehend her in the least danger, are ready to work as hard as if we were never so considerable sharers in her cargo. We profess a love and service to the fellow inhabitants of our country, although we should not have a foot of land in it, not measuring our affection for our brethren by our's or their acres, but by justice, kindness, and liberty.
>
> (Byrom to an unknown correspondent, c.30 December 1730)[1]

Introduction: 're-Mancunianizing' Byrom

Although a once-strong 'folk memory' of John Byrom in his home town faded many decades ago, he is not invisible in its centre today. The half-timbers of his sixteenth-century birthplace, long since the peripatetic Old Wellington Inn, have been made prominent in the redevelopment of Manchester's Cathedral Triangle area, the pub retaining its plaque about him not far from the bar (Figure 1). While Byrom's memorial stone in the Cathedral's Jesus Chapel is often obscured through daily activity, he can be seen kneeling in a post-Blitz stained-glass panel in the East Window, bearing a scroll of his famous Christmas hymn 'Christians awake', just three panels away from Christ in Majesty himself (Figure 2). It might seem churlish to complain of this recognition in an age when poets are seldom accorded such local tributes; after all, in Byrom's case there is a fitting resonance to their conception within programmes of local regeneration – which is not to deny that Byrom would have been deeply shocked by the stained glass. Nevertheless, for me they function as unintended symbols of partial or mis-interpretation: of Byrom as appropriated and tamed

establishment hymn writer, and of a Byrom who, through later acts of translation, became shaped and distorted. (Compare Figure 3.[2])

For the modern biographer seeking a lapidary descriptor, 'polymath' might be the most appropriate for Byrom: medic turned stenographer, he was a Fellow of the Royal Society, a linguist, theological scholar, teacher, bibliophile, diarist, and a prolific poet, whose output included one of the most popular secular song lyrics of the earlier eighteenth century – 'My time, O ye muses'. He mixed with some of the most famous figures in eighteenth-century English cultural life – including classicist Richard Bentley, mystic and controversialist William Law, evangelists Charles and John Wesley and John Newton, physician George Cheyne, printer and novelist Samuel Richardson, and philosopher David Hartley – and, no less interesting and important, a host of lesser-known clergymen, writers, dissidents, gentry, freethinkers, scholars, eccentrics and other individuals for whom valuable biographical evidence is furnished by his journals and correspondence. At 138 words, his obituary notice in the *Manchester Mercury* significantly exceeded all previously published there. This in itself would seem clear indication of his status among the town's 'principal inhabitants',[3] the men who constituted Manchester's rich trading elite, the ranks into which he was born, scion of a dynasty of linen and silk merchants and property magnates. But separating him from this group was the fact that he did not occupy any clearly defined profession, rank or civic office; and for much of his life did not hold personal property. (While he had some early medical training, the

Figure 1:
Old Wellington Inn, Manchester, 2007

Figure 2:
Stained glass panel (c.1950; repaired post-1996) in the East Window, Manchester Cathedral. With thanks to Christopher Hunwick and Manchester Cathedral Archives

'Dr' often prefixed to his name did not indicate that he held an MD, but functioned rather as a quasi-courtesy title and badge of learning, helping to distinguish him from other family members.) Manchester could be proud of (probably) its first obituarised creative writer and intellectual, but from a local perspective it is not apparent from the *Mercury* notice what Byrom actually *did* there to merit such local fame outside the 'learned World' for whom his 'Accomplishments in the literary Way [were] too well known [...] to need enumerating'.[4] Nearly 250 years after the notice, a sense of Byrom as Mancunian is hardly any sharper in a potentially more influential type of obituary: his entry in the newly revised *DNB*, which even mislocates his place of birth and death.[5]

An underlying rationale for my paper is that further study of Byrom and his networks of acquaintance and kinship needs to attempt more recovery and re-assessment of his Manchester life, to engage with Byrom as 'Loncashire mon',[6] redressing ways in which he may have become de-Mancunianized and, through that, de-politicised. This might seem perverse given that the Chetham Society's misleadingly-titled *Private journal and literary remains* has long been found a rich mine of detail about some areas of pre-Cottonopolis life — not least by modern scholars engaged in reconstructing the ecclesiastical underpinnings of the town's contending ideologies and factions.[7] Even in more general accounts, the idea of Byrom as political animal is well worn, after all. Yet consider, for example, a spectrum of summary verdicts on his Jacobitism, ranging from 'the Mouth and Master tool of the [Jacobite] Faction in the Neighbourhood of *Manchester*' to 'mildly Jacobite', with various shades – such as 'ardent Jacobite', 'strong Jacobite tendencies', 'one of the most consistent and honest of English Jacobites', 'cautious supporter', 'stern old Jacobite', 'happy-natured countryman Jacobite', 'slightly cautious Jacobite', 'Jacobite sympathizer'[8] – between the extremes. My point is that we have not got much closer to understanding, let alone defining, the nature of Byrom's own Jacobitism, nor to the ways it displayed or exercised itself in Manchester. What implications or inferences are there in the phrase sometimes applied to him, 'Manchester Jacobite' (or, for that matter, 'Manchester poet') and how is that to be distinguished from, say, 'Bristol Jacobite'? Can we define what sort of a Jacobite Byrom was, and what made him one?

What follows hardly pretends to be a comprehensive solution to such questions – it offers simply some relatively short overviews of selected areas of Byrom's Manchester political life for further investigation in arriving at such a solution. What connects them is that they are part of a wider attempt to establish the Byrom canon more accurately. As a first step to re-Mancunianizing Byrom we need to

Figure 3: Christmas greetings postcard, c.1910, published by Reckie & Heaviside, Stockport

consider the sources on which assumptions about him, both old and new, have been based – not just the 'content' of such sources, but their material nature too.

Texts and 'translation'

Rich mine it may be, but as textual authority, *Remains* needs cautious use. Its shortcomings stem from its being the product of a hands-off, pragmatic approach by its little more than nominal editor Richard Parkinson, with original manuscripts – many in shorthand – sometimes hastily or inaccurately transcribed, and, more significantly, subjected to far from clear processes of abridgement, and with some startling lacunae. Had its editorial process and scope been better conceived and managed *ab initio*, *Remains* would have afforded readers more information about Byrom's home town. Without denying their abiding interest in local history, Parkinson's Chetham Society circle – above all James Crossley and F. R. Raines who between them wrote the bulk of *Remains*'s footnotes – hoped, somewhat in vain, that their edition might generate supra-regional interest in Byrom. This agenda seems to have led to their making some local material less of a priority than, say, London material. For example, an editorial note referring to unprinted journal entries of late 1724 frustrates us with its brisk summary: 'Mr. Byrom in Manchester, attends a few poor patients; no events of particular interest.'[9] A similarly tantalising case was that of a cache of letters written to Byrom rediscovered in 1850, deemed to 'add considerably to the information already obtained in reference to Manchester at the time that Byrom lived'[10] but, though known to the editorial team, never incorporated.

Similar decisions for exclusion lay behind the posthumous publication of Byrom's verse, and here political considerations were at work. The first printed collection was published in Manchester ten years after Byrom's death by Joseph Harrop, and parts of volume one reveal a poet attuned to contemporary politics. But as well as creating a misleading divide between Byrom's secular and religious work, the act of assembling and editing it for a posthumous readership had still tended to downplay elements of its regional contexts, and in so doing de-politicised elements of it. In order to maximise this readership, such processes were inevitable when much of Byrom's output was coterie writing, and as such heavily context-dependent. As the first editor of his poems conceded, 'many of them were written rather for private, than for Public perusal';[11] so in the translation from manuscript to print of material which had originally been aimed at a specific reader or readers, it is not surprising that material aspects such as the epistolary circumstances of poems, the identities of their recipients and the contexts of their circulation, became obscured, falsified or lost. One of the team involved in sifting materials for the edition acknowledged the difficulties with such parochial subject matter – and was not reluctant to criticise its shortcomings: 'Tedious & flat in many Parts'! Commenting on what appears to have been a provisional short-list for inclusion s/he advised that 'our Friend shines least in these controversial Pieces where he is answering Pamphlets'.[12] Such an outlook may explain the edition's rejection of 'minor' pieces such as (or like) Byrom's awkward anapaests on a contested Manchester Collegiate Church fellowship election, or similarly torturous verse about Manchester Grammar School's corn-grinding monopoly,[13] even if it does not entirely account for the exclusion of the densely footnoted 430-line *An epistle to a friend occasioned by a sermon intituled, The false claims to martyrdom consider'd ...* (Ironically, sections of the latter evince some of the most polished handling of iambic couplets to be found in all of Byrom's verse.) However, subjective aesthetic values were just one consideration behind editorial decisions. Seized on by Rochdale Presbyterian Josiah Owen as Jacobite propaganda, the *Epistle*'s publication and the hostility it provoked were episodes in a bitter controversy flaring up in Manchester in the aftermath of the '45 rebellion; the risk of re-opening old wounds and offending the sensibilities of friends and relatives of the poem's targets by reprinting it less than 30 years later was too great a one to take. Such considerations probably obliged the editor of the *Miscellaneous Poems* to own that

> At a Time when Party-Disputes are so happily subsided, it may *seem* to want an Apology, that, in the following Collection, some few Pieces are inserted, which *appear* to be tinctured with a

Party-Spirit – A small Attention however will convince the warmest Partizan, that what Mr. *Byrom* has written of this Cast was intended to soften the Asperity, and prevent the Mischiefs of an over-heated Zeal. Since this was the Author's chief Motive for writing, it is imagined no other Apology will be necessary for the Publication of such Pieces.[14]

Even 30 years later, Alexander Chalmers, who by handsome representation in his influential *English poets* series did more than anyone to bring Byrom's verse to a wider early nineteenth-century audience, could feel uncomfortable about the local political dimension. He omitted not only Byrom's political Lancashire dialect verse ('unintelligible to readers') but also 'some pieces [...] which are offensively tinctured with political prejudices and deservedly forgotten.'[15] (The second edition of Byrom's poems, published by James Nichols at Leeds in 1814, printed footnote verse 'translations' of the dialect pieces in standard English, as well as making some substitutions for colloquialism or dialecticism in others, without any clear textual sanction.)

Hence an editorial approach apparently keen to downplay any controversy seems to have dictated not just rejection of some pieces but the titling of some of those that were included in the 1773 *Miscellaneous poems*. For example, take the two short pieces about acts of public utterance, linked as presumed companions entitled 'An Admonition Against Swearing. Addressed to an Officer in the Army' and 'To the Same, Extempore. Intended to Allay the Violence of Party Spirit.' The first of these – a pious plea not to take God's name in vain – had previously appeared in print in a local anthology the year after Byrom's death under the title 'Spoke extempore at BUXTON WELLS by the late Dr. Byrom, to an Officer who swore much in vindication of the Duke of CUMBERLAND's behaviour in Scotland'.[16] Its title in *Miscellaneous poems* removes any hint of political context; whereas in the anthology its title – again, not Byrom's own – pushes such a context to the fore. Since the anthology was published by Manchester whig propagandist Robert Whitworth – who had been an active opponent of the tory-Jacobite journalism of Byrom's circle in the 1740s – the earlier title might, furthermore, have been a deliberately provocative way to re-emphasise Byrom's Jacobitism publicly, making life awkward for the Byrom family thereby.

The second of the apparent companion pieces was Byrom's far better known 'God bless the King' epigram:

> God bless the King, I mean the Faith's Defender;
> God bless – no Harm in blessing – the Pretender;
> But who Pretender is, or who is King,
> God bless us all – that's quite another Thing.[17]

Any idea that such lines had been, in the words of their new title, 'intended to allay the violence of party spirit', though, was not so much naive as it was disingenuous. It is high time, in my view, to jettison a standard reading of this epigram as epitomising the stance of an equivocating Byrom who held a 'scepticism about politics'.[18] For its pretence of equivocation is simply that – pretence. Whether voiced in an insouciant or a knowing tone, its mask of bemusement should be seen as actually highly political: provocatively Jacobite in highlighting that there might be any question of doubt over the line of succession. I have become dissatisfied with views of this epigram, and similar writing by Byrom, as exemplifying some sort of 'balanced' or calculatedly cautious stance. This is not to deny something of an ecumenical, bridge-building spirit we find in him, the strong sense of a man seeking a way out of dispute by encouraging disputants to get things in proportion and to seek common ground. But much of Byrom's writing does far more than 'appear to be tinctured' with politics. More than some sort of secondary witness discourse, to be assessed against the 'real world', it participates in that world, functioning as a means of articulating problems and furthering debate. More than just tuned to the world of politics, it is engaged in it.

Before looking at more examples of Byrom's writing, I turn to consider the medium in which so much was originally penned, the teaching and use of which gave Byrom a quasi-public role in Manchester.

The 'excellent Mancunian hand'

Political scruples had a key bearing on Byrom's prevarication over a career, a prevarication that seems to have vexed his family in the 1720s. Fuelled by extensive undergraduate reading of materials from both sides of the allegiance controversy argument, his grave and principled concerns over taking the oaths of allegiance had compromised what might otherwise have been an obvious path to a college fellowship and clerical living, and partly prevented Byrom securing the post of Chetham's librarian at this time. He also seems to have dithered over practising medicine in Manchester, an occupation he considered racked by 'party slavery'[19] there. His family looked askance at a very different career plan which was to become a sort of raison d'être: the promotion of a system of shorthand, styled by one of its users, the Manchester nonjuror Thomas Deacon, as '{the most exactly beautiful, regular, useful, excellent Mancunian hand}',[20] and praised by another, the London medic and philosopher David Hartley, as 'the most perfect invention that I have ever known from a single person'.[21]

The fundamentals of the system were invented between the late 1710s and early 1720s, and Byrom initially attempted to launch it through subscription in Manchester in the early 1720s. Terms were fairly standard for a subscription venture at that time: half a guinea deposit and half a guinea on receipt of a printed manual. But the project was soon dropped in place of teaching the system for five guineas a head. Outside the Manchester area, Byrom's key pupil bases were London and Cambridge, and the majority of his clients were drawn from the inns of court or the university colleges. A second, more metropolitan-based subscription campaign was mounted in the late 1730s and revived in the 1740s, but it was not until four years after Byrom's death that a printed manual appeared, published by Joseph Harrop as *The universal English short-hand* (Manchester, 1767). Without denying shorthand's very practical and vocational uses, the very high teaching fee reflects the fact that Byrom's services were aimed at a monied elite. Combined with his social connections, shorthand tuition gave Byrom routes into a metropolitan social, intellectual and political life he might otherwise have forfeited or been denied.

The potential this gave him for making contacts, and in so doing representing the interests of his fellow countrymen when he was in the capital, was soon recognised. This is especially well revealed by activities during the dispute over the Manchester Workhouse Bill during 1729–31, the sole area in Byrom's involvement with Manchester politics to have received modern scholarly attention. In work unravelling this complex episode, Kazuhiko Kondo suggests that because Manchester was still an unincorporated town, the envisaged nature of a statutory trust for a new workhouse may have been bound up with wider plans for transfers of initiative and power from Manchester's old established tory masters to new whigs and Presbyterians.[22] The centrality of religious affiliation in eighteenth-century Manchester public affairs is underlined by the way that those who organised a subscription deed for the workhouse planned its being ostensibly non-partisan overall; nominated trustees were to be divided equally between whig Anglicans, tory Anglicans (including Byrom's uncle and father-in-law Joseph[23]) and Presbyterians. However, Byrom and others believed that it was inevitable that succession arrangements would result in a self-selecting and self-perpetuating board formed by an alliance of low churchmen and dissenters, a 'stagnating pool'.[24] Alarmed by the implications of this potential new oligarchy, Byrom worked for several months with the lawyers George Kenyon and Thomas Pigot to mount a strenuous and ultimately successful campaign against the Bill, joining in the organizing of a petition against it and canvassing parliamentary support for their cause. Not only did shorthand give Byrom opportunities for movement in circles where he might be able to raise support (such as those of the opposition whigs and peers to whom he was trying to promote shorthand at the time); on a more mundane but no less important level it facilitated transcription and circulation of documents, papers and, above all, speeches.

The power of the stenographer to capture and hence 'own' others' words meant that in what might be argued to be still fundamentally an 'oral society'[25] (as opposed to the 'print culture' so often assumed to have entirely supplanted it long before), one in which debates and sermons had crucial functions of governance, stenographers could be treated with suspicion if not downright hostility. Byrom was told 'I had been like to have been taken into custody' for taking down speeches in a House of Commons gallery in March 1729, and during a Commons committee's examination concerning the workhouse affair in February 1731 he found 'the liberty of shorthand men' under attack when he was rebuked for writing in the session because of its being 'disorderly': 'Not write in the cause of one's country in a matter of open trial!', he spluttered in a letter to his wife, 'but I'll have one more trial for it. We shall certainly overcome such low descending animals at last, the Gothic enemies of liberty and shorthand, which I hope will still flourish in Manchester'.[26] Shorthand was likewise an instrument of both intelligence-gathering and intelligence dissemination during disputes over the course of three decades connected with Samuel Peploe: Byrom claimed (albeit with some exaggeration) that he had 'the honour [...] of having taken down all the Bishop's sermons, speeches, depositions private and public, and of sending them up and down town and country'.[27]

The impression given by some biographical accounts that ultimately shorthand was not much more than a hobby-horsical sideline for Byrom, largely abandoned when he succeeded his elder brother Edward in 1740, needs to be challenged. Not only was Byrom teaching shorthand in the region well into his older age, possibly as late as 1761,[28] he seems also to have held a quasi-public, almost journalistic, role as a stenographer, albeit more of a self-appointed than a professional, paid one. For example, in 1757, in the context of events surrounding the Shude Hill food rioting, Tim Bobbin noticed '*Byromah*, the psalmist, whose pen is the pen of a ready writer' as a respected town elder and 'scribe' recording the words of fellow shorthander '*Clatonijah* [i.e. John Clayton] the Priest'.[29]

While this was shorthand's 'public' side, any manuscript written in Byrom's system before its printing by Harrop should still be seen as coterie writing, the product of a scribal network or scribal community. Taking this further, it may also be seen as secret writing, however mundane the content might actually have been, because it employed a script system known only to the initiated or leaked by them to others; pupils and subscribers were enjoined to keep it a closely guarded secret. Shorthand's association with the hidden and the subversive was long established when Byrom launched his method. Even though it was effectively a type of substitution cipher rather than a more complex code, we know that some who were not initiates found it hard to crack when they made attempts to do so. And it is hard not to suppose that Byrom, whose fears of politically motivated interception of longhand letters surface in undergraduate correspondence, and whose family thereafter seems to have been implicated in an allegation of treasonable correspondence,[30] would not initially have seen shorthand as a potential medium for securing privacy in communication. Of course, given that the number of Byromite shorthanders increased in the 1730s and the fact that the system was spread further by those who in turn taught it – usually, but not always, with Byrom's permission – the potential for clandestine use inevitably declined. Moreover, apart from resorting to the stock arguments from absence (or even

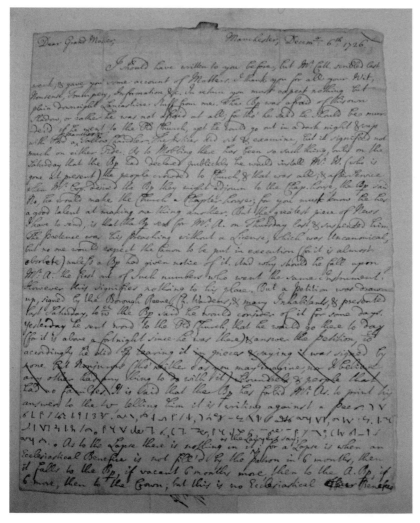

Figure 4: Letter from Thomas Deacon to Byrom, December 1726. Chetham's Library MS A.6.87 /3

common sense), actually *proving* that shorthand was used for secrecy is a hugely daunting task. So this makes one document pertaining to Mancunian ecclesiastical politics all the more valuable a survival: a letter of 6 December 1726 addressed to the shorthand 'Grand Master' by Thomas Deacon, where shorthand intervention in the longhand was certainly used a means of disguise (Figure 4).[31] The next section explores this letter's context: Byrom's involvement in one episode in the protracted disputes between Samuel Peploe and the high-flying fellowship of Manchester's Collegiate Church.

A curious *Collection*

There is much in Byrom's *Remains* – albeit often of a fragmentary or anecdotal nature – to support Stephen Baskerville's observation that the Collegiate Church came to constitute 'a ritual forum in which local partisans could carry on their ideological battles'.[32] Appointed bishop of Chester in January 1726, Peploe could hardly have been a less likely figure to secure the trust and cooperation of the Church's fellows, for his ascent of the preferment ladder was managed to strengthen whig interest in the region and destabilise the clerical toryism that had flourished under his predecessors. Byrom seems to have been on terms of perfectly civil acquaintance with the Peploe family until around the mid-1720s. (This was not simply because Peploe's son was reported to have had a 'design to learn my shorthand'.[33]) Moreover, one might even infer he was not entirely unsympathetic to Peploe's situation during protracted disputes over his right to the wardenship (which, controversially, he came to hold *in commendam* as bishop). Either Byrom did not initially seem to have fully read the signs of any party machinations there, or, more likely, felt that a strict whig *v.* tory binarism was far too simplistic an interpretative model; on Peploe's elevation to the bishopric he told his wife that while there was something 'very uncommon in't' when the news was confirmed, 'to make a whig or tory providence on't might lead one too far'.[34] But he moved firmly into the anti-Peploe camp following Peploe's monocratic action in suspending Richard Assheton as Collegiate Church chaplain and in attempting to install his own candidate, Thomas Whittaker, in Assheton's place. This was without the statutory consent of the fellows, and, furthermore, flew in the face of widespread opposition from local clergy and laypeople, causing some public disorder.[35] A petition in support of Assheton gained 341 signatories (including Byrom's uncle and father-in law Joseph), but Peploe's response was, according to Deacon, 'tearing it in pieces and saying it was signed by none but nonjurors [...] scoundrels and people that had no families'.[36]

The Assheton affair prompted a rather clumsily printed farrago of a 20-side quarto pamphlet entitled *A collection of curious papers* (Figure 5). Its 'curiosity' value for us today derives mainly from its mischievous combination of the ludicrous with the malicious. The pamphlet opens with Peploe's 'Reasons' for finding Assheton to be disaffected to the Hanoverian regime and objections to his behaviour as a chaplain. The second and third papers ('Further Reasons' and 'More Reasons') then parody the first, deploying a satirical technique that we find in some of Byrom's post-'45 verse: attempting to undermine the potential gravity of a key charge by simply swamping it in a wider context of the absurd or banal, by so doing attempting to imply false logic to Peploe's reasoning. For example, the third paper mimics Peploe's criticisms of Assheton's refusal to give pulpit recognition to the Hanoverian succession 'till of late when he durst not do otherwise' with its attendant imputation of Assheton's seditious preaching:

> tho' the sign of his Majesty King George hangs up in the very town where [Assheton] officiates as Chaplain, yet he never has been there to drink his health; this is the more remarkable because it is a house of good entertainment, and kept by a very good Protestant. [...] [I]n all his sermons it is his constant custom never to say any word of St. George and the Dragon, not even upon the 23d of April; and this, as is reasonably believed, for no other reason but because the Saint is his Majesty's namesake.[37]

Likewise with tongue firmly in cheek, the pamphlet's fourth 'paper' pretends to be an answer by a Peploe supporter, demonstrating with irony and sarcasm the inconsistency and groundlessness of Peploe's original charges, therefore 'we may boldly pronounce that they could not be the work of that Learned, Judicious, *Sincere* and Charitable Prelate'. The fifth paper argues that it should be Peploe, not Assheton, who is 'justly suspected of disaffection' to the Church and the Hanoverian succession, as well as outlining instances of Peploe's failure to conform to ecclesiastical rubrics and asserting that his behaviour and manners are ill-suited to the dignity of his office. If less entertaining, this section has more moment than the rest of the pamphlet, being an arch exposé from a tory-Jacobite perspective of the inconsistencies and contradictions inherent in whiggish appropriation of hereditary-right ideology. In incorporating claimed quotations from an unprinted Peploe sermon on 1 August 1726 – here Byrom's reference to having taken down many of Peploe's public speeches comes to mind – it emphasises Peploe as above all the political propagandist, and to the sensibilities of the Manchester clergy an outrageously erastian one:

> as is credibly reported by several who heard him, he used these words or words to this effect in his sermon upon the first of August.

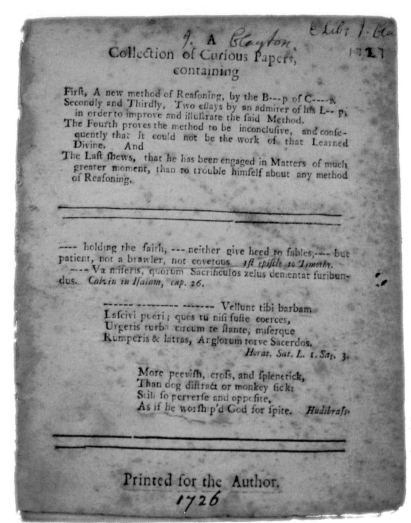

Figure 5:
John Clayton's
copy of *A
collection of
curious papers.*
Chetham's
Library
C.7.10 (51)

"And I make no doubt, had our Saviour and his Apostles lived under such a King (meaning King George) they would have paid ready duty and obedience to him, and perhaps have left us more and stronger directions to acknowledge such Government."[38]

A collection's publication history is obscure, but I incline towards its having been printed in 1726/7, perhaps in Leeds, rather than 'London [1726?]' as proposed by the *English Short Title Catalogue* (ESTC), where it is still unattributed.[39] Deacon's letter quoted earlier is important for pointing to Byrom's close authorial involvement with it. The shorthand in Figure 4 reads:

{We are resolved to have the three papers you know of come out some way or other, but Mr Cattell is desirous of having your categorical consent first, which therefore I desire you to send by the first post to him or me. We need fear nothing as to law; and as to suspicions, we need not feel them as long as we are safe; and therefore let us have your consent immediately.}

A second shorthand section in the letter masks some incendiary language, Deacon hoping that through the pamphlet '{we will blow [Peploe] up, mortify him, and break his heart}'. Together with a letter from Byrom to Deacon the following May, Deacon's shorthand implicates both himself and Byrom in its authorship by an anti-Peploe 'triumvirate', its third member being another shorthander, Thomas Cattell, a Collegiate Church fellow, who was later active in raising subscriptions for Byrom's system as well as teaching it.[40] Further external evidence for Byrom's involvement comes from a hitherto unexplored shorthand notebook of Byrom's lifelong friend Ralph Leycester, squire of Toft, near Knutsford, the self-styled 'Dean Rural' of a convivial fraternity of shorthanders in the Manchester region which held a club at Altrincham. Their penchant for quasi-masonic terminology (with Byrom as 'Grand Master' of shorthand) emphasises the strongly associational basis of much of Byrom's teaching, and the group might be seen as an unusual relation of better known eighteenth-century mock-masonic brotherhoods. (Whig Leycester's presence is just one reason it would be entirely wrong to define the Lancashire-Cheshire shorthanders as a tory-Jacobite grouping.) Drafting or transcribing a letter to Byrom

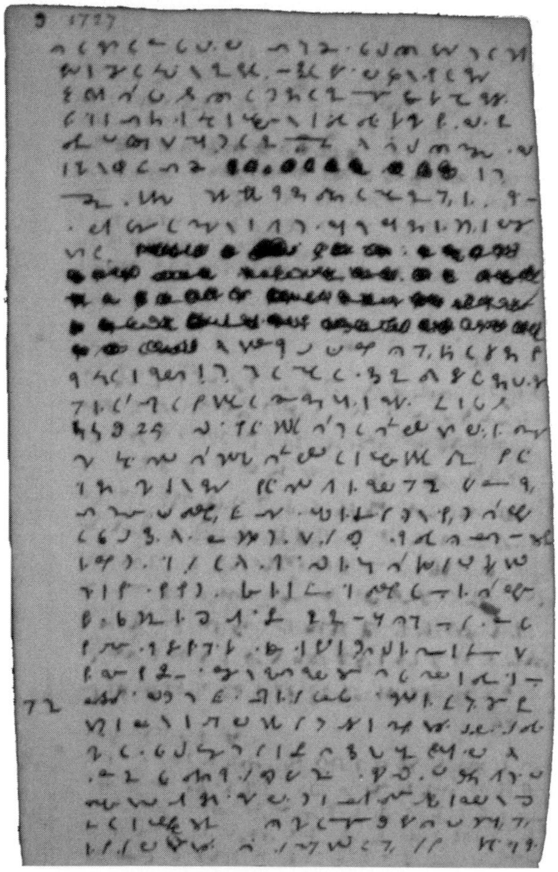

Figures 6a and b: Shorthand diary entries for April, June and July 1727 by Ralph Leycester. Manchester Central Library MS 923.9.Le

in the course of his late-April 1727 diarising, Leycester mentioned *A collection*'s distribution in the region (Figures 6a and b). As someone who regularly came into contact with Peploe in 1720s legal and gentry circles in Chester, he had mixed views about it:

{Some of the book I do not much admire but that part wherein the style and reasoning of his Lordship is exposed with a great deal of humour did divert Mr Dean Rural much and made him and his sisters shake their sides heartily though at the same time it aroused the indignation of the old lady their mother [...] If I am not much mistaken I know the author of this same book [*ten shorthand outlines inked out*]. The Bishop suspects you to be the man.} [41]

For the modern reader for whom grappling with the density of the pamphlet's allusion (not all of it recoverable) may be hard going, Leycester's testimony that at least some of it succeeded in making its audience laugh is reassuring. But even if there was a comic intent, and even if 'the disaffection of Shorthand against him' [42] seems to have been a thinly veiled secret, maybe an open one, [43] Peploe's influence and litigious track record made extreme caution over printing *A collection* imperative. Other correspondence in shorthand about the Peploe-Assheton controversy was more obviously masked than in Deacon's letter. After writing to Deacon in shorthand in a letter of May 1727 about his fears that his London acquaintance would be quick to suspect him of its sole authorship, Byrom signed off in longhand, 'I can't write this *Spectator* out'. [44] This was an ingenious and cunning screen, a pretence that the preceding shorthand of the letter had simply been an innocuous exercise in transcribing an Addison or Steele essay from the eighteenth-century's most famous periodical. The ruse was all the more believable since *Spectator* transcription was something encouraged as regular practice amongst Byrom's shorthand circle. In reality the letter clearly pointed to 'More Reasons ...' – the section that amused Leycester and his sisters – as being Byrom's work. The following month Deacon wrote Byrom a more comic 'screen' letter about the pamphlet's dispersal in 'swarms' amongst 'us Manchesterians', feigning bafflement about the author, and mentioning the unfounded suspicions that 'one Longimanus' amongst others had a part in it. Once again Peploe was said to display a physical response to subversive print matter: on receiving an intercepted batch of copies, he 'sacrificed 'em to his just resentment'.[45]

Byrom is not known to have been directly involved with organising the original petitioning, but 'being a Manchester man',[46] he was enjoined by Deacon to present another petition on the matter, this time signed by 214 names (appended by 'etc. etc') that reads like a roll call of the region's leading clergy, gentry and merchant classes, to the Archbishop of York (guided by the nonjuror and scholar George Harbin, a brother-in-law of Collegiate Church fellow John Copley) and to assist the archbishop with any queries about it. Byrom followed the Assheton case in London, taking down shorthand about it with his friend the Manchester lawyer Joseph Clowes ('Alderman' of the Altrincham shorthanders) when it came up in the Court of the King's Bench. In the meantime the fellows pursued Peploe's candidate Whittaker through the courts, requiring him to produce a licence to officiate and to prove why this should not be revoked, and also raised legal objections over Peploe's right of visitation.[47] Wrangling continued over who was to occupy the chaplaincies and Peploe vetoed another chaplaincy election by the fellows, that of Adam Bankes, again on political grounds. This episode is likely to have been the context of a lost poem by Byrom for which we have only the title – 'The Ghost of Adam Banks' – rejected from inclusion in *Miscellaneous poems* because, one of his editorial team opined, it 'flaggs a little in the two last pages'.[48] Eventually Assheton and Bankes's installations proceeded in the summer of 1728 but any implication of conciliation and compromise was superficial, as metropolitan legal authorities worked towards granting rights of visitation in the king and Peploe came to be in a position whereby it was easier for him to urge ministerial intervention in Collegiate Church affairs thereafter. Byrom's *Remains* continues over the following two decades to be a source of reference to further tension over Manchester visitations, fellows' appointments and allegations of seditious preaching.

'Skilful management of signs': 'secret views' and 'publick news'

Peploe was influential in the anti-Jacobite crackdown in Manchester both during and after its occupation for several months by government forces; and in the aftermath of the incursion in the town by forces of the Young Pretender Charles Edward Stuart in the course of his progress to, and retreat from, Derby in late 1745. Hoping that 'some examples will be made at Manchester of this detestable Rebellion where some Particular Persons are as insolent as ever in their behaviour towards the friends of the Government',[49] Peploe had approached the Duke of Newcastle for funding

> to carry on a discovery which is begun of certain Persons behavior before & at the time of the Pretenders army being at Manchester, such I mean as did not openly joyn, but abetted their Cause, and made their Court to the Prince, as they calld him. I find there are some Locks which will open more easily when the key is a little oyld.[50]

Whether Peploe had Byrom in his sights as one of these 'certain Persons' is not known, but its strong possibility is suggested by an extraordinary entry in the diary of Byrom's daughter Elizabeth ('Beppy') about how her father, together with Deacon, 'was fetched prisoner' to kiss the Young Pretender's hand, whereas she, Cattell and John Clayton (who 'said grace for him') 'did it without'.[51] The episode has sometimes been cited as exemplifying circumspection on Byrom's part – as such, it might fit with a reference to how he and acquaintances had previously consulted 'how to keep themselves out of any scrape, and yet behave civilly'.[52] But, as with the 'God bless the king' epigram, equating deliberated caution (through mock-imprisonment) with some sort of aloofness, indecision or misgiving is unconvincing to me.

Outside the evidence of Beppy's diary, we know relatively little about Byrom's movements at this time. Lack of a regular journal after the mid-1740s is one reason there is less evidence of shorthand use in public matters after 1745 than for the 1720s and 30s. But that this continued is suggested by Beppy's mention of her father's recording of Thomas Lewthwaite's anti-Jacobite sermonising at St Ann's in November 1745; Byrom's own reference to sending the 'case' of Jacobite prisoner Charles Deacon in shorthand to Manchester; and a tantalising reference to extensive though 'disjointed' shorthand notes of the treason trial of the Manchester constables at Lancaster Assizes which surfaced in the papers of Byrom's nineteenth-century descendant.[53] Shorthand also comes to mind when reading Byrom's witty 'A genuine Dialogue, between a Gentlewoman at Derby and her Maid Jenny in the Beginning of 1745', printed in the tory-Jacobite periodical *Adams's Weekly Courant* (and thereafter gaining wider circulation as a popular broadside, as did another Jacobite poem by Byrom 'The Bellman and the Captain', one overlooked by or excluded from the *Miscellaneous poems*). Jenny's mistress attacks her Jacobitism in lines that have to be seen as well as heard:

> *Mrs.* Good! this is you that did not call him K—g;
>   And is not P— e, ye Minx, the self-same Thing?

Jen. *You are so hasty, Madam! with your Snarles —*
      Wou'd you have me call the Gentleman plain Ch—s?
Mrs. P— *Ch*—s again! – speak out your Treason Tales;
      His R—l H—s, *Ch*—s, the P— of *W—s!*[54]

The pointed comic irrelevance of abbreviated forms in a supposedly spoken dialogue coexists with conveying a whispered sibilance about the 'secret views' (in contrast with 'publick news') of Jenny, and later those of her subsequently converted mistress. Redolent of the way that shorthand outlines omit vowels, the verse evokes the world of Jacobitical acronym-making, as manifested in inscriptions and not-so cryptic toasts, all part of what the whig journalists on Whitworth's *Manchester Magazine* attacked as local Jacobites' 'Skilful Management of Signs'.[55]

The nature of this 'Management' was a prominent theme in the rival journalism of Robert Whitworth's whiggish, pro-Peploe *Manchester Magazine* and Elizabeth Adams's tory-Jacobite *Chester Courant / Adams's Weekly Courant*, which in reviving the rhetoric of seventeenth-century allegiance controversy debates, also revisited broader themes of usurpation and tyranny behind the anti-Peploe pamphleteering. Byrom's involvement with *Courant* journalism has long been known to specialists, and one significant feature of Adolphus William Ward's Chetham Society edition of Byrom's poetry was expansion of the canon with fourteen pieces of *Courant* verse which had not appeared in *Miscellaneous poems*.[56] Ward's attributions mainly relied on a copy of *Manchester Vindicated* (the 1749 anthology published by Adams which reprinted much of this journalism) containing papers annotated 'B' and 'T' (assumed to be for Byrom and Thyer respectively) by an unknown hand; unfortunately his attribution methodology was highly inconsistent and selective. The evidence available dictates a far more conservative inclusion policy, leading me to argue that some of Ward's 'new' poems need to be rejected from the Byrom canon, and some relegated to a state of attribution limbo pending further proof.[57]

To make amends for this I want here to reclaim for the canon two overlooked *Courant* pieces. The first responds to a paragraph in the *Manchester Magazine* of 22 September 1746, about Deacon's defiant obeisance to the heads of two members of the Jacobite Manchester Regiment (one of these his eldest son's), eventually impaled on spikes outside Manchester Exchange after their execution in London. This act, and the consequent persecution of Deacon, embroiled Byrom in vituperative local disputation over issues of political martyrdom and familial piety. These hitherto unattributed lines are one early piece of the jigsaw:

The Reply of a *Quaker* to a Friend, who had told him the Story of Dr. *D–n*'s pulling off his Hat to the Heads, as related in Whitworth's Paper

> Doffing the Hat I hold no Sign of Grace,
> Saving in Pray'r, which was perhaps the Case:
> But yet, my Friend, I hope it may be said,
> I'd rather see a Hat off than a Head.[58]

The verse cited as 'To doff the hat I own^s no Sign of Grace' in the list mentioned earlier of Byrom pieces for possible inclusion in *Miscellaneous poems*, must surely correspond to this, or a scribal variant of it.[59] In its wider journalistic context, Byrom is of course not presenting his personal voice, the target being partly the bluffness of Quaker plain speaking, yet the grim humour is more than peculiarly unsettling, to later sensibilities, tasteless, even sick – a presumed reason for its being passed over.

The second poem, printed in the *Courant* as 'Phillis and Thraso', was definitely excluded entirely on subjective taste grounds. Even though it was annotated 'B' in Ward's copy (something he used as evidence to claim other poems for the canon), he had 'no hesitation in rejecting' it for being a 'coarse mock-ballad'.[60] In fact it can be identified as another poem cited in the manuscript list of Byrom pieces, 'The Defenceless Maid and Licentious Soldier'. This title fits with its introduction within the preceding *Courant* article as 'Verses […] made upon *the Eleventh of* June, on Occasion of a Rencounter that really happene'd the Day before betwixt a *defenceless Maid*, and a *licentious Soldier*.' The poem belongs to a series of *Manchester Vindicated* papers about wearing political symbols such as oak boughs or white roses, activities seemingly harmless, but in reality provocative enough to cause real physical violence, or function as a pretext for it. Here Thraso (a stock name for a braggart soldier), minion of the Duke of Cumberland, objects to Mancunian Phillis's wearing of Jacobite white roses on the Pretender's birthday:

Phillis and Thraso

I.

> PHILLIS, to deck her snowy Breast,
>   The Rival-Flow'rs around display'd;
> THRASO, to grace his warlike Crest,
>   Of Orange-Knots a huge Cockade.
> That Reds, and Whites, and nothing else
> Should set the Beaux against the Belles!

II.

Yet so it was; for Yesterday
    THRASO met PHILLIS with her Posies,
And thus began th'ungentle Fray,
    Miss, I must *execute* those Roses.
Then made, but fruitless made, a Snatch,
Repuls'd with pertinacious Scratch.

III.

Surpriz'd at such a sharp Rebuke,
    He cast about his cautious Eyes,
Invoking VICT'RY and THE DUKE,
    And once again attack'd the Prize:
Again is taught to apprehend,
How guardian Thorns the Rose defend.

IV.

Force being twice in vain apply'd,
    He condescended then to Reason;
Ye *Jacobitish B—ch*, he cry'd,
    In open Street, the Love of Treason
With your White Roses to proclaim!
Go Home, ye Rebel Slut, for Shame.

V.

Go you abroad to *Flanders* yonder,
    And show your Valour there, Sir Knight;
What Bus'ness have you here, I wonder,
    With Peoples Roses, Red or White?
Go you Abroad, for Shame, says PHILLIS,
And from the FRENCHMEN pluck their Lillies.

VI.

Lillies! says THRASO, Lillies too!
    The Wench, I find, would be a Wit,
Had she Command of Words enoo,
    And on the right one chanc'd to hit;
For pity, once, I'll set her clear:
The Laurels, you would say, my Dear.

VII.

No, but I would not, Sir, – you know
    What Laurels are no more than I;
Upon your Head they'll never grow,
    My Word for that, Friend, and good-bye;
HE THAT OF ROSES ROBS A WENCH,
WILL NE'ER PLUCK LAURELS FROM THE FRENCH.[61]

'The Good Old Times'?

My reason for highlighting these poems, minor as they are, is to emphasise how Byrom's *Courant* writing is anything but the stereotype of nostalgic Jacobite 'Charlie o'er the Waterism'. Rather it is rooted in the experiences of an edgy, violent Manchester where Habeas Corpus was suspended, and where the rebel heads rotted away for *years* as grim warning to the populace of the consequences of sedition. It was at a far remove from the Manchester of the '45 popularized by Harrison Ainsworth's novel *The Good Old Times* (1873), where Byrom and his daughter featured prominently in a world where men might become Jacobites on no firmer ideological grounds than desire to gain their sweethearts' favours.[62] Ainsworth, an intimate of the Chetham Society circle, acknowledged *Remains* – especially the Elizabeth Byrom diary section – as influential on his plot, but towards its unconvincing close committed the travesty of depicting the Byroms forswearing Jacobitism and converting to Hanoverianism after an act of clemency by Cumberland! A historiographical climate in which such distortions might not immediately be laughed out of court – and one where they could even influence subsequent popular, local-historical accounts of Byrom – lasted long into the twentieth century. The historical establishment's long-standing marginalisation of Jacobitism, with its assumed associations with the deluded, eccentric, irrelevant, reactionary, and right-wing, hardly made Byrom and his circle hot property. However, even if the place of Jacobitism within English eighteenth-century culture and society is still contested, the scholarship of the past two decades has put to rest notions of it as a doomed and an elite movement. To undermine simplistic assumptions about whig progressiveness versus Jacobite reaction, we need only contrast Peploe's views on the 'Occasion for the poor', their being 'necessary' to the 'Beauty and Comforts of Publick Bodies of Men', with Byrom's challenging of 'subordination that was necessary to be amongst people'; 'I contended for an equality, and for the poor people [...] I am too forward I doubt upon such occasions'.[63] Samuel Bamford was to claim it was the ascendancy of the 'rebel blood' of his Mancunian Jacobite ancestry that made him 'born a radical'.[64] In Byrom's desire that the 'consent of the people'[65] should hold sway against encroachment of whig corporations in Manchester, or in his sympathies for those dispossessed and persecuted by government forces there after the '45, we might find ideological strands that accord with more radical aspects of Jacobitism. Outrageous though it would once have been to the 'court end'[66] of the town inhabited by later generations of the increasingly powerful Byrom family, and perhaps provocative to some historians today, I want to conclude by merely raising the possibility that in time a 're-Mancunianized' Byrom and his eighteenth-century circle might even be accorded a new public visibility in a re-drawn map of 'radical Manchester'.[67]

Notes

1. Quoted in J. Aikin, *A description of the country from thirty to forty miles round Manchester* (London, 1795), pp. 215–6.
2. This card perpetuates the myth that Byrom wrote 'Christians awake' at Kersal Cell.
3. For discussion of this class/role terminology see Craig Horner, '"Proper Persons to Deal with": identification and attitudes of middling society in Manchester, c.1730–c.1760' (unpub. PhD, Manchester Metropolitan University, 2001), chap. 4.
4. *Manchester Mercury*, no. 645, Tues. 4 Oct. 1763.
5. J. R. Watson, 'Byrom, John (1692–1763)', *Oxford dictionary of national biography* (60 vols, Oxford, 2004) [hereafter *ODNB*], ix, pp. 341–3, http://www.oxforddnb.com/view/article/4278. The myth that Byrom was born at Kersal Cell, Broughton was put to rest by W. H. Thomson, *John Byrom's birthplace, Manchester* (Manchester, 1954). For more on the Byrom family see Thomson, *The Byroms of Manchester* (3 vols, Manchester, 1959–68). Leslie Stephen's original DNB article was more instructive than Watson's about Byrom's local politics. For a very different Byrom see Joy Hancox, *The queen's chameleon* (London, 1994).
6. Richard Parkinson (ed.), *The private journal and literary remains of John Byrom* [hereafter cited as *Remains*] (2 vols in 4 parts, Manchester, 1854–7), i, p. 563.
7. See for example Horner, '"Proper Persons"'; Kazuhiko Kondo, 'The church and politics in "disaffected" Manchester, 1718–31', *Historical Research*, 80 (2007), pp. 100–23; Stephen Baskerville, 'The management of the tory interest in Lancashire and Cheshire, 1714–47' (unpub. DPhil, University of Oxford, 1976).
8. Josiah Owen, *Jacobite & nonjuring principles, freely examin'd …* (Manchester, 1747), p. 5; Watson, 'Byrom, John', p. 342; Francis Espinasse, *Lancashire worthies* (London, 1874), p. 226; John Hoyles, *The edges of Augustanism* (The Hague, 1972), p. 81; Paul Kléber Monod, *Jacobitism and the English people, 1688–1788* (Cambridge, 1989), p. 5; John Gascoigne, *Cambridge in the age of the enlightenment* (Cambridge, 1989), p. 170; Josiah Rose, *Leigh in the eighteenth century* (Leigh, [1872]), p. 93; Hoole Jackson, 'Happy Jacobite of rural Lancashire', *Country Life*, 30 May 1963, p. 1277; Gordon Rupp, *Religion in England, 1689–1791* (Oxford, 1986), p. 210; Simon Brett (ed.), *The Faber book of diaries* (London, 1987), p. 175. I have chosen a typical cross-section of general/popular and academic citations.
9. *Remains*, i, p. 79.
10. Unsigned notice of Chetham Society AGM (by John Harland?) in *Manchester Guardian*, no. 2209, 9 Mar. 1850, p. 7.

11. John Byrom, *Miscellaneous poems* (Manchester, 1773) i, p. i.

12. Chetham's Library, MS A.4.122 (15), p. 1.

13. Chetham's Library, MS A.4.83; John Rylands Library: Thomson Collection [Box 4 (uncatalogued)]. These poems were later printed with many inaccuracies in Adolphus William Ward's Chetham Society edition, *The poems of John Byrom* (3 vols in 5 parts, Manchester, 1894–1913), i, pp. 550–3; iii, pp. 60–5. Ward misinterpreted the context of the latter.

14. Byrom, *Miscellaneous poems*, i, p. ii.

15. Alexander Chalmers (ed.), *The works of the English poets* (31 vols, London, 1810), xv, p. 182.

16. *The polite miscellany* (Manchester, 1764), p. 79.

17. Byrom, *Miscellaneous poems*, i, p. 342.

18. Watson, 'Byrom, John', p. 342.

19. *Remains*, i, p. 267.

20. Chetham's Library: MS A.6.87(*)/[1]; transcribed in Timothy Underhill, 'John Byrom (1692–1763): sources & shorthand' (unpub. PhD, University of Cambridge, 2001), Appendix A.1. Quotations of my transcriptions of shorthand manuscripts are placed within curly brackets { }, in order to emphasise that any shorthand transcription should be recognised as provisional. I have not found a more appropriate solution to the very clearly formed consonantal shorthand outline {mnknn}. Assuming my interpretation 'Muncunian' to be correct, it is noteworthy that the adjective is being used nearly two hundred years before the current *OED*'s earliest citation.

21. David Hartley to John Lister, 26 Sep. 1741: West Yorkshire Archives Calderdale (Halifax), MS SH/7/HL//26.

22. See Kazuhiko Kondo, 'The workhouse issue at Manchester: selected documents, 1729–35. Part one', *Kenkyu Ronshu: Bulletin of the Faculty of Letters, Nagoya University*, 33 (1987), pp. 1–96; Kondo, 'The church and politics'.

23. Byrom's wife Elizabeth was also his cousin, the daughter of Joseph Byrom.

24. *Remains*, i, p. 484.

25. John Feather, 'The power of print: word and image in eighteenth-century England', in Jeremy Black (ed.), *Culture and society in Britain, 1660–1800* (Manchester and New York, 1997), p. 60.

26. *Remains*, i, pp. 468–9.

27. *Remains*, i, p. 261.

28. See Underhill, 'John Byrom', Appendix A.14.

29. [Tim Bobbin [i.e. John Collier]], *Truth in a mask: or, the Shude-Hill fight* (Amsterdam [=Manchester?], 1757), p. 26.

30. See F. R. Raines (Frank Renaud [ed.]), *The fellows of the Collegiate Church of Manchester* (2 vols, Manchester, 1891), i, pp. 208–9.

31. Chetham's Library, MS A.6.87/3; *Remains*, i, pp. 231–4.

32. Stephen W. Baskerville, 'Peploe, Samuel (bap. 1667, d. 1752)', *ODNB*, xliii, p. 631, http://www.oxforddnb.com/view/article/21897.

33. *Remains*, i, p. 179.

34. *Remains*, i, p. 195.

35. Lancashire Record Office [hereafter LRO], DDKe/2/7/45–51; W. H. Thomson, *Previously unpublished Byromiana relating to John Byrom* (Manchester, 1954), pp. 18–22; *Remains*, i, p. 249.

36. Chetham's Library, MS A.6.87/3; this is crossed through in the manuscript. See *Remains*, i, pp. 231–4, 236, 248–51, 261–2, 265–6, 272; *The case of Mr. Richard Assheton and Mr. Adam Bankes*... [1726], n.p.; 'John Hartley, J. P., of Strangeways Hall and his fellow townsmen', *Palatine Note-Book*, 3 (1883), pp. 37–42; 'The petition of the townsmen of Manchester', *Palatine Note-Book*, 3 (1883), pp. 95–7; Raines, *Fellows*, ii, pp. 216–25.

37. *A collection*, pp. 3–5.

38. *A collection*, pp. 6, 15.

39. *Remains*, i, p. 262 suggests a Leeds imprint. In John Clayton's copy (Chetham's Library C.7.10 [51]) the annotation '1726' (by a different hand) underneath 'Printed for the Author', presumably reflects old style dating; '1727' adjoins Clayton's signature. References by Leycester and Deacon show the pamphlet was being circulated in Apr.-June 1727.

40. *Remains*, i, pp. 261–2 (mentioning the 'triumvirate'). According to Deacon 'the Bishop had forbid Mr. A. to print his answer to the {Reasons}' (i.e. Peploe's own Reasons) (Chetham's Library, MS A.6.87/3), but I take this to be distinct from the papers in *A collection*. It might be the 'book ... about the Bishop' sent to Cambridge in June 1727 mentioned by Byrom in a letter to his wife: 'Mr. Ashton against the Bishop, very severe upon him' (*Remains*, i, p. 265). Another possibility is that this was actually a reference to *A collection*, deliberately feigning naivety as to its authorship.

41. Manchester Central Library, MS 923.9.Le: 25 Apr. 1727 (my transcription). I remain hopeful that future documentary forensics will reveal the short-hand outlines deleted by Leycester here and elsewhere in the notebook.

42. *Remains*, i, p. 261.

43. Cf. *Remains*, i, pp. 272, 278.

44. *Remains*, i, p. 262.

45. *Remains*, i, pp. 265–6. 'Longimanus' seems designed as a pun on the reverse of 'shorthand'; perhaps a reference to Byrom's well-above average height was intended.

46. Deacon to Byrom, 21 Dec. 1726, quoted in Raines, *Fellows*, ii, p. 221. A draft of the main body text of the petition has surfaced in a tranche of the Kenyon papers in LRO, uncatalogued at the time of writing: DDKe/53/1. I am indebted to Christopher Hunwick for bringing these materials to my attention.

47. See Manchester Central Library, MS M39/2/5/7–10; *Remains*, i, pp. 250–1, 290–1, 293–4; LRO: DDKe/53/1.

48. Chetham's Library, MS A.4.122 (15).

49. Peploe to Newcastle, 14 July 1746: British Library, MS Add. 32707: 411–12.

50. Peploe to Newcastle, 29 Jan. 1746, quoted in Beatrice Stott, 'The informations laid against certain townsmen of Manchester in 1746', *Transactions of the Lancashire and Cheshire Antiquarian Society* [hereafter *TLCAS*], 45 (1925), pp. 26–7.

51. *Remains*, ii, p. 394.

52. *Remains*, ii, p. 392.

53. *Remains*, ii, pp. 386, 440, 491n.

54. Byrom, *Miscellaneous poems*, i, p. 174.

55. *Manchester vindicated* (Chester, 1749), p. 240 (reprinting, *Courant* 23 June 1747). The Byrom family's set of wine glasses engraved with 'Down with the Rump' in shorthand seems to date from a later decade: Thomson, *Byroms*, iii, pp. 56–7.

56. Ward (ed.), *Poems*, ii, pp. 295–331; Edmund Ogden, 'Robert Thyer. Chetham's librarian, 1742–1763', *TLCAS*, 41 (1924), pp. 131–2; O. M. Tyndale, '"Manchester Vindicated" and the later nonjurors', *TLCAS*, 53 (1938), pp. 119–30. See also Craig Horner, '"That Great Fountain of Truth, Good Manners and what not": competing for the hearts and minds of newspaper readers in Manchester, 1730–60', *TLCAS*, 72 (2001), pp. 51–70.

57. Underhill, 'John Byrom', pp. 53–5. I am engaged in a fuller attribution study of *Manchester vindicated*, although it is unlikely that Byrom's contribution can be precisely ascertained.

58. *Manchester vindicated*, p. 3 (reprinting, *Courant* 21 Oct. 1746).

59. Chetham's Library, MS A.122.15: 3. A nineteenth-century attribution list also assigns the issue where the epigram appeared – and likewise the issue containing 'Phillis and Thraso' – to Byrom (Chetham's Library, MS E.3.6[7]).

60. Ward (ed.), *Poems*, i, p. 316n.

61. *Manchester vindicated*, pp. 251–2 (reprinting, *Courant* 21 July 1747); cf. p. 241.

62. Later editions appeared under the title *The Manchester rebels of the fatal '45*.

63. Samuel Peploe, *A sermon preach'd at the anniversary meeting of the children educated in the charity schools* … (London, 1730), p. 13; *Remains*, i, p. 490.

64. Samuel Bamford, *Early days* (London, 1849), p. 22.

65. *Remains*, i, p. 483.

66. Leo H. Grindon, *Manchester banks and bankers* (Manchester and London, 1877), p. 24.

67. Weighted towards post-Cottonopolis Manchester, a current 'radical Manchester' tourist trail ignores Jacobitism and Byrom: http://www.industrialpowerhouse.co.uk/audioradical.asp.

DISCUSSION DOCUMENT
The Manchester grocer,
(or, where there is a will ...)*

Bob Mather

Most historians of Manchester have, until recently, concentrated on industry-specific issues, such as the cotton industry and the town's role in a regional context, during the late seventeenth and early eighteenth centuries.[1] This article takes a different focus by discussing Manchester's commercial culture for the same period. In particular it stresses the place of retail activity and how we might better understand, for example, occupational activity and the differentiation between retail and wholesale; these distinctions for the industrialising period are far from clear. As Patten puts it, 'We simply do not know if a "tailor", for example, was a great merchant tailor or just some poor "botcher" making a scarce living repairing and mending'.[2] Historians have already addressed these issues by using probate records and, in particular, inventories, since they provide probably the most reliable source of information about what individuals held in their shops, homes or workshops, and the scale of those holdings. They can be used to assess, say, occupational activity, personal wealth and civic status, often in the absence of any other reliable source of such information, and thus provide us with an immense source of historical data.[3] For the Manchester experience, the probate documents for 408 individuals for the period 1681–1700 described as 'of Manchester' or 'of Salford', and 573 for the period 1741–1760,[4] have been examined, with case studies used here in illustration.

Four types of probate document exist: wills, inventories post-mortem, administration bonds (admons)[5] and more rarely, probate accounts. Probate records are further divided into two groups, 'infra' being those estates valued at under £40 and 'supra' for those over. Probate inventories, which, in the main ceased to be deposited after 1750, are lists of personal goods, credits and debts, compiled under oath by the friends and neighbours of the deceased as a central part of the process of proving a will. The inventory would also list debts owed to the deceased as a part of the estate, and often indicate whether a debt was considered 'good', in that it was likely to be paid, or 'desperate', that is, unlikely to be paid. Debts owed by the testator only appear in probate accounts, as discussed later.[6]

In the case of an individual dying intestate, three stages of legal requirements were necessary before the estate could be split up. Firstly letters of administration were sought by either a close member of the family, or by a principal creditor. The ecclesiastical consistory court for the archdeaconry of Chester dealt with all probate issues regarding personal estates in the Chester diocese. In the case of Manchester and Salford, the process was not always carried out by personal attendance at the court in Chester, but through a 'surrogate' appointed by the court to represent its interests. The second stage was the 'exhibition' of the inventory before the court or surrogate. Letters of administration would then be issued as a form of probate. The third stage required the administrator, or in the case of an existing will, the executor, to present a set of accounts showing how the estate had been divided, what debts had been collected and paid, and what expenses had been incurred in the process.

Figure 1: Infra inventory of Robert Burnell, tailor, 1686

Robert Burnell was a Manchester tailor who died intestate in July 1686. In his case, letters of administration were sought by his son Philip. The bond sworn by Philip Burnell is in the sum of £80, and signed by Richard Wroe, warden of the Collegiate Church. The inventory of Burnell's personal estate, his goods and chattels, was made on 17 February 1686/7 by John Newton and Richard Mordon, and showed goods to the value of £8 19s 0d as described in Figure 1. The inventory implies a self-employed individual making garments to order rather than ready-to-wear. As can be seen, no complete garments are listed other than the clothing of the deceased.

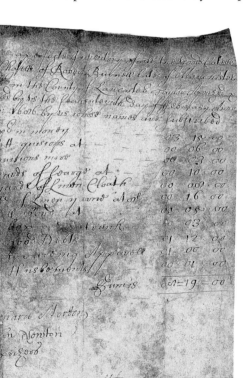

Where a trade such as 'tailor' is given, there is little ambiguity, other than scale, of what an individual saw as his prime occupation. Others can be less clear. What, for example, did a grocer sell? Were their sales limited to 'groceries' as we know them, or were they what Shammas describes as mercers who, along with grocers, sold more cloth and haberdashery (by percentage of inventory value) than groceries or provisions?[7] The 1683 supra will and inventory of Jeremiah Harrison, grocer, of Manchester, can help answer this. In his will he leaves all his personal estate 'of Goods Chattells wares household stuff and Credits whatsoever' to his wife Mary and their children, all of whom were under 21 years of age, to be divided one-third to Mary, two-thirds to the children.[8] There is no mention of the estate, real or personal, being sold off, so it may be assumed that Mary was likely to carry on the business.[9] Mary is made executrix along with Jeremiah's 'dearly beloved' uncle William Bowker, 'grosser'.[10] Harrison also remits to Mary and Bowker along with his 'trusty kinsman' Jonathan Hall 'the Tuition and government of my children and all their portions and rights untill their severall and respective ages of One and Twenty years'. It should be noted, however, that Mary would only remain a trustee 'so long time as my said Wife shall live a Widdow, and after her death or remarriage again then to the said William Bowker and Jonathan Hall only'. The removal of Mary's trusteeship after remarriage may be interpreted as Harrison seeking to ensure that the financial interests of his children did not fall into the hands of a future husband who might choose to exploit them for his own ends.

Figures 2a and b: Inventory of Jeremiah Harrison, grosser, 1683

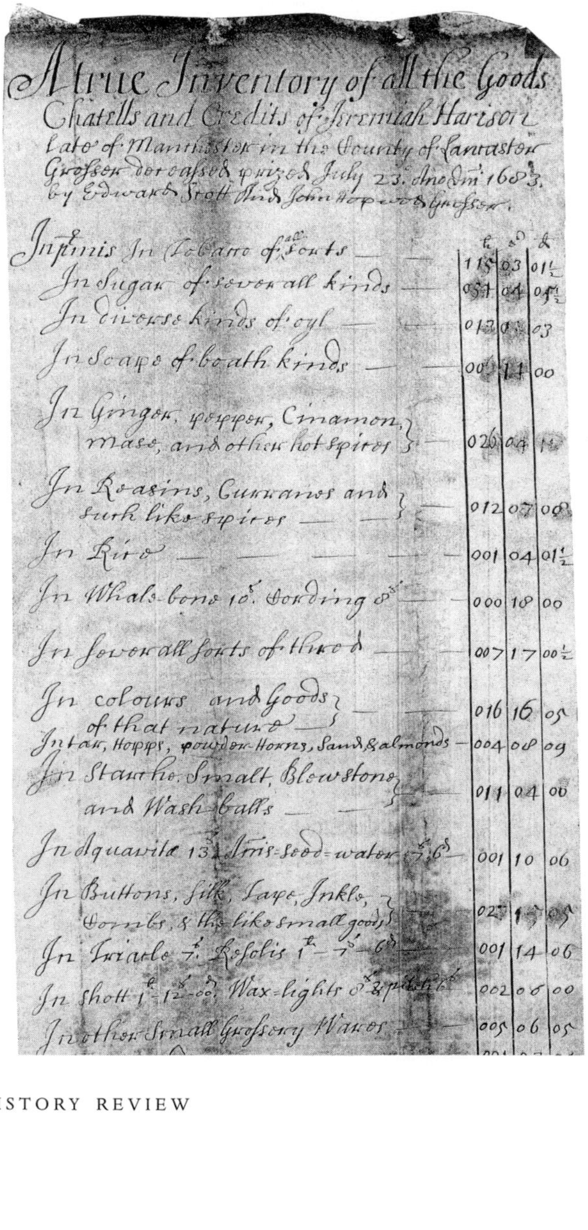

A true Inventory of all the Goods Chatells and Credits of Jeremiah Harison late of Manchester in the County of Lancaster Grosser deceased prized July 23. Ano Dni 1683. by Edward Scott and John Hopwood Grosser.

	£	s	d
Inprimis In Tobacco of all sorts	115	03	01½
In Sugar of severall kinds	051	04	05½
In diverse kinds of oyl	012	[illegible]	03
In Soape of boath kinds	00[illegible]	11	00
In Ginger, pepper, Cinamon, mase, and other hot spices	026	04	[illegible]
In Reasins, Currants and such like spices	012	07	08
In Rice	001	04	01½
In Whale-bone 10s. Cording 8s.	000	18	00
In severall sorts of thred	007	17	00½
In colours and Goods of that nature	016	16	05
In tar, Hopps, powder-Horns, Sand & almonds	004	08	09
In Starch, Small, Blewstone and Wash-balls	011	04	00
In Aquavite 13s. Anis-seed-water 17s. 6d.	001	10	06
In Buttons, silk, Lace, Inkle, Combs, & the like small goods	02[illegible]	[illegible]	05
In Triacle 7s. Rosolis 1£ 7s. 6d.	001	14	06
In Shott 1£ 12s. 00 Wax-lights 8s. [illegible]	002	08	00
In other Small Grosery Wares	005	06	05

Was he a retailer or wholesaler? Throughout the probate documents his occupation is written as 'Grosser'. *The Oxford English Dictionary* gives us two meanings. Firstly, 'Grosser: One who buys and sells in the gross, i.e. large quantities, a wholesale dealer or merchant … in spices and foreign produce' with usage from the fourteenth to the seventeenth century. The second is 'A trader who deals in spices, dried fruits, sugar and … all items of domestic consumption,' with usage from the fifteenth to nineteenth century. In considering Harrison's case, it is his inventory (see Figures 2a and b), taken on 23 July 1683 by John Hopwood, 'grosser', and Edward Scott which attracts our attention, giving a glimpse into the stock-in-trade of a Manchester 'grosser', and also by giving us a base-line comparator with other traders. The total value of the inventory is £489 4s 1½d, a considerable amount; and one must also consider that the value of any real estate that Harrison may have owned is not included.

But what does his tell us? Certainly, as discussed above, that we cannot take for granted the occupation of any individual. With the inclusion of, for example, whalebone, cording, thread, buttons and dyestuffs, Harrison was catering to the needs of either households' making and mending, or to the needs of small textile manufacturers and finishers. Gunpowder, shot and powder horns indicate that firearms were commonplace. Oils, sugar, spices, rice, raisins, currants and the like are items that one would expect to find in grocers' shops. The noticeable absence of any other foodstuffs such as cheese or bread further points to wholesale rather than retail, as these latter items would no doubt be found in specialist shops such as cheese-mongers and bakers. The fact that there was relatively little cash in evidence – £12, with debts owed to Harrison standing at almost ten times that level (£115 15s 2½d) – is a demonstration of the intricate network of credit that existed at the time, which Muldrew describes as 'so extensive and intertwined that it introduced moral factors which provided strong reasons for stressing co-operation within the marketing structures of the period.'[11]

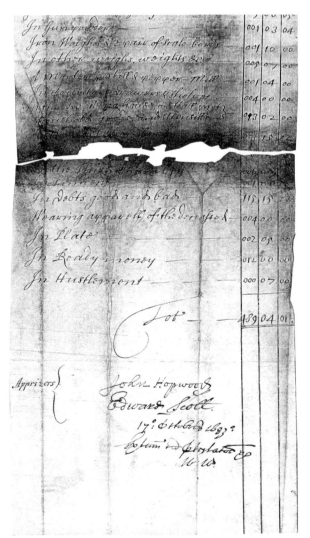

For the purposes of contemporary comparison, during this period (1681–1700) we find probate records for six grocers, only two of whom have inventories included. One is Harrison's, the other that of George Routleech of St. Mary Gate.

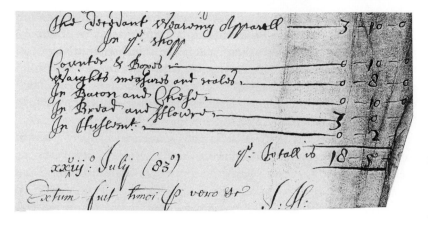

Figure 3: Detail of inventory of George Routleech, grosser, 1683

Routleech's wife Jane swore the infra admon on 28 July 1683 in the sum of £80, before the surrogate John Hulton. An inventory had been taken before she sought letters of administration, as the document shows that it was exhibited before the surrogate (initialled 'J:H:') on the same date. The inventory is quite badly damaged but identifies a personal estate of £18 5s 3d; the extract shown in Figure 3 shows the contents of his shop. Clearly Routleech was not in the same league as Harrison as far as stock values are concerned, and it would not be remiss therefore to describe him as a small retail grocer. The proximity of St. Mary Gate to the Market Place might also suggest that Routleech was little more than a market trader selling from his home.

No other specialist commodity dealers have appeared in the records sampled, other than two tobacconists. For 1681–1700 we find Thomas Harrald[12] whose supra inventory (Figure 4) demonstrates a considerable personal estate of £371 19s 11d. Debts owed to Harrald, and cash in hand, exceed those relating to Harrison, and although not all the contents of the rooms listed would be tobacco, that commodity would certainly have been the most valuable amongst the contents. We are left again with the question of wholesale or retail. Was Harrald a large-scale dealer in tobacco, importing and supplying smaller traders; was tobacco his sole sale-goods; or was he the owner of a retail outlet as we identify with today? To address this we might usefully look to the period 1741–60 and consider the 1744 will and inventory of John Caldwell, a Manchester tobacconist and snuff-maker. His inventory gives quantities and prices of the various grades held as well as the value of the stock held, to the total value of £88 5s 4¼d, as in Figure 5. Comparison with Harrison's stock of tobacco indicates that, with a value of £115 3s 1½d, he was carrying over a ton of tobacco, assuming 9d per pound, and therefore that he was in the wholesale rather than the retail trade.

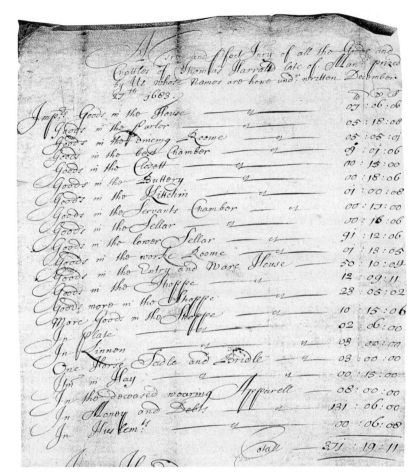

Figure 4: Inventory of Thomas Harrald, tobacconist, 1683

Foster allows us a further commodity comparison by quoting the prices of sugar purchased by the Warburton family at Arley Hall in Cheshire from Robert Patten of Warrington in 1757, with lump sugar at a fraction over 8d per pound, and double-refined sugar at 11¾d per pound.[13] Harrison's stock of sugar 'of severall kinds', valued at £54 4s 5½d, indicates well over half a ton at 8d per pound, and again points to wholesale rather than retail. Foster further relates that 8d was the same as a labourer's daily wage, and 11d that of a craftsman, which suggests that sugar was a luxury item and unlikely to appear in the diet of the majority of the population of Manchester.

According to Spufford, 53,000 sets of probate accounts are known to exist nationally, of which only 26 apply to estates in Manchester and Salford for the period 1589–1799.[14] However, this author has discovered a single set of probate accounts amongst the records at the Lancashire Record Office, of which there is no mention in Spufford's index. The document details the winding up, by his wife, of the estate of John

Figure 5:
Supra inventory of John Caldwell, tobacconist and snuff-maker, 1744

Jackson, ironmonger and grocer of Manchester, dated 22 September 1744, and includes Jackson's supra will, dated 16 September, in which he leaves 'all my Estate and Effects whatsoever of whatever nature kind or Denomination soever unto Catherine my wife', whom he nominates as sole executrix. An endorsement reads 'Above forty Pounds'. Then follows an inventory, firstly of household goods, totalling £18 15s 6d, followed by details of 'Shop goods sold at a publick day of sale to the several persons of Manchester as follows', with a list of purchasers, the quantities of goods and their values. The wide variety of goods sold indicates clearly that 'groceries' were not Jackson's sole stock-in-trade, and that 'grocer' did not fully describe his business interests. This sale realised £152 10s 7d. This is followed by a list of 'Book Debts recd' (see Figure 6) listing sums owed to Jackson, totalling £184 10s 9¼d, and the debtors. This in turn is followed by a list of 'Books Debts not yet recd', and by whom they are owed, amounting to £3 5s 5¼d, the largest amount being 11s 5d from James Harrop[15] of Manchester, who is listed as having already paid the same sum.

The record then continues with a two-page account of the costs incurred by the widow. It is notable that here are listed details of what may be termed the 'private' debts of Jackson. Two such items appear, giving an indication of the practice of borrowing and lending money, common in such 'pre-bank' times:

> Pd. Jeremy Bowers of Manchester Hatter a Debt due to him by Bond from ye sd. Testor principal £12 (no Interest due) ... £12:0:0
> Pd. To Alice Grantham of Manchester, principal £30. Interest of 16s.9d in all ... £30:16:9

From this it can be assumed that private debts and 'book' debts were perceived differently, the one being personal and therefore requiring settlement before the book debts pertaining to the business.

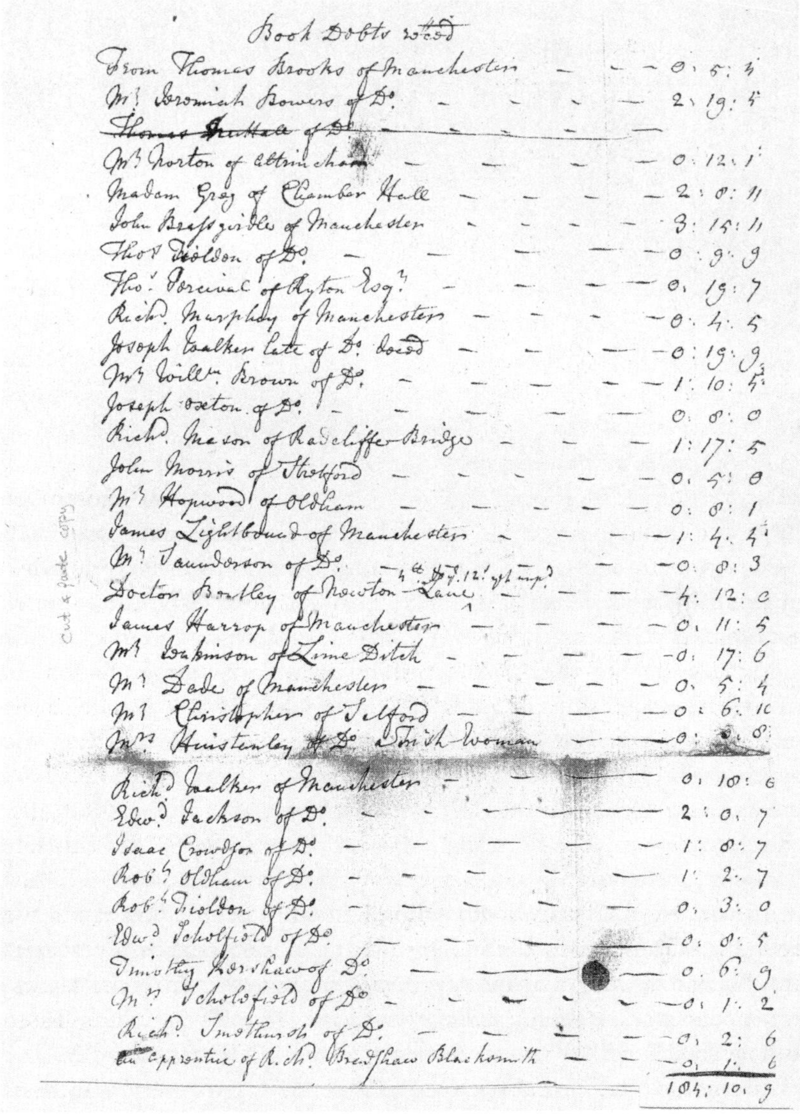

Figure 6: 'Book Debts recd': sums owed to John Jackson, ironmonger and grocer, 1744

Catherine Jackson acknowledges that there is £184 10s 9¼d available, and makes herself chargeable for the payment of debts. The cost of the funeral and the organisation of the sale of goods amounted to £88 5s 9d, whilst the book debts owed by Jackson amounted to £254 10s 11d (see Figure 7). The list of Jackson's creditors gives an excellent illustration of the widespread credit-based trading activity taking place at the time, including distillers, iron mongers and tobacconists in the city of London; sugar bakers, grocers and tobacconists in Warrington and Liverpool; and notably, 'Abraham Derby of Coal Brook in the County of Salop & Company' in the sum of £26 6s 9d, as well as a number of Manchester-based individuals.

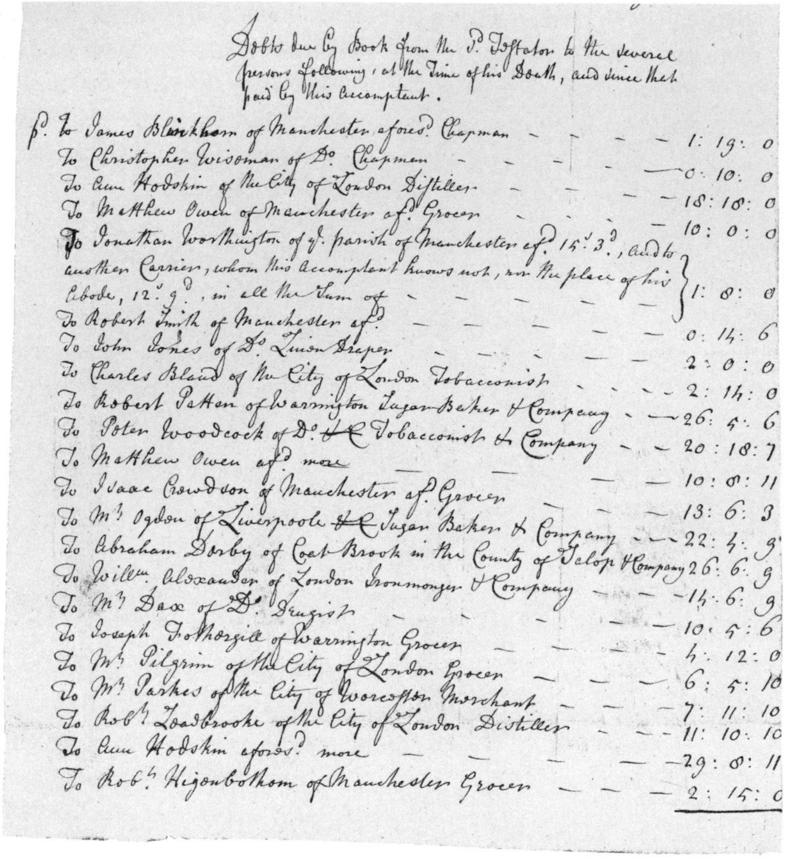
Debts due by Book from the sd. Testator to the several persons following, at the Time of his Death, and since that paid by this Accomptant.

To James Blinkhorn of Manchester aforesd. Chapman — 1: 19: 0
To Christopher Wiseman of Do. Chapman — 0: 10: 0
To Ann Hodgkin of the City of London Distiller — 18: 10: 0
To Matthew Owen of Manchester afd. Grocer — 10: 0: 0
To Jonathan Worthington of ye parish of Manchester afd. 15s. 3d., and to another Carrier, whom this Accomptant knows not, nor the place of his Abode, 12s. 9d., in all the Sum of — 1: 8: 0
To Robert Smith of Manchester afd. — 0: 14: 6
To John Jones of Do. Linen Draper — 2: 0: 0
To Charles Bland of the City of London Tobacconist — 2: 14: 0
To Robert Patten of Warrington Sugar Baker & Company — 26: 5: 6
To Peter Woodcock of Do. Tobacconist & Company — 20: 18: 7
To Matthew Owen afd. more — 10: 0: 11
To Isaac Crowdson of Manchester afd. Grocer — 13: 6: 3
To Mr. Ogden of Liverpoole Sugar Baker & Company — 22: 4: 9
To Abraham Darby of Coat Brook in the County of Salop & Company 26: 6: 9
To Willm. Alexander of London Ironmonger & Company — 14: 6: 9
To Mr. Dax of Do. Drugist — 10: 5: 6
To Joseph Fothergill of Warrington Grocer — 4: 12: 0
To Mr. Pilgrim of the City of London Grocer — 6: 5: 10
To Mr. Parkes of the City of Worcester Merchant — 7: 11: 10
To Robt. Leadbrooke of the City of London Distiller — 11: 10: 10
To Ann Hodgkin aforesd. more — 29: 0: 11
To Robt. Higenbotham of Manchester Grocer — 2: 15: 0

Figure 7: Creditors of John Jackson, ironmonger and grocer, 1744

In total we find that credits amounted to £359 2s 3½d, with costs and debts amounting to £342 16s 8d. That Jackson did not possess any real estate in the form of property is suggested by three entries in the expenses section: £6 16s, being half a year's rent of a house and a shop paid to 'Danl. Fenshaw, Baker',[16] followed by £1 10s to 'Benj. Bowker' for three quarters' rent of two cellars. Richard Middleton was paid 6s for three quarters' 'Water money'. It should not be assumed from this that Jackson had not owned any real estate; property interests were often disposed of through, for example, marriage settlements.

We are still left with a puzzle arising from Jackson's probate accounts. As seen above, the value of household goods is given as £18 15s 6d, the sale of stock realised £152 10s 7d, and book debts received amounted to £184 10s 9¼d. In the preamble to the description of accounts paid by the executrix, it is stated:

> The Charge
> This accomptant chargeth herself with all and singular the Goods

Chattels and Credits of the said Deceased mentioned and as recorded by her comprised in the inventory of the said Deceased by her exhibited, amounting in the Whole to the sum of £184.10.9¼; and she is ready and willing to make herself chargeable, and doth hereby charge herself with the Book Debts unreceived and yet standing out, when she shall receive the same

Since she paid a total of £88 5s 9d as expenses, the question still outstanding is how she was able to discharge book debts of £254 10s 11d from the remainder when she apparently had only £184 10s 9¼d available.

On a more general point, since probate accounts are the main source of information regarding any debts owed by a testator, then it is unfortunate that there are so few to consult. As a consequence, the debts owed to an individual as found detailed in inventories as good or desperate debts can give us a distorted picture of the actual wealth of individuals, such as Harrison and Jackson, although the role of inventories in highlighting the place of credit in trading practices of the time cannot be overstated. Probate accounts can also provide us with further valuable insight into everyday life in Manchester and Salford, for example, the cost and organisation involved with the death of an individual – here we see the prices of individual items such as the £2 2s paid to Edward Jackson[17] for a coffin, and other amounts for mourning wear and catering. The total cost of Jackson's funeral amounted to £13 2s 11d; quite a lavish affair compared to that of, say, the Manchester tapeweaver William Colisson. The infra inventory of Colisson's personal estate gives us details of his funeral expenses, to a total of £1 16s 9½d, of which 5s 3d was paid for his coffin.[18]

It has been shown how probate records can help to illuminate the commercial activities of early modern trades. However, the usefulness of probate records as a source of information must be qualified for a number of reasons. A major factor to be considered is that a large proportion of the population left no testamentary evidence, having little or no personal wealth or property to bequeath. These individuals would probably have been wage earners with few, if any, fixed assets and no stock-in-trade; Stobart records how 'only around 40 per cent of the adult population of southern Lancashire and Cheshire appear to have left any sort of probate record.'[19] Many documents have also failed to survive the depredations of time. The value of surviving probate records to the historian, then, must be reiterated. They contain so much to aid our understanding of other people's lives and circumstances, as shown by the information about traders illustrated above. We find information about the contents of their homes and shops, of their personal possessions such as clothing – often the subject of bequests to family and friends, as well as their real estate, investment interests and occupations.

Acknowledgements

The probate records used for this paper are to be found in the Lancashire Record Office (LRO) at Preston. The search-room staff must be thanked for their help and patience. Images are reproduced by kind permission of the County Archivist, reference WCW. Thanks also to Viscount Ashbrook and Charles Foster of Arley Hall for an introduction to the Warburton family archives; Michael Powell and Jane Muskett at Chetham's Library for assistance with the Chetham's Hospital archives; Craig Horner for comments on earlier drafts; and the anonymous reviewer.

Notes

* This article is a fuller version of a paper presented at the University of York to the annual conference of the Centre for Eighteenth-Century Studies, June 2006. The spellings used throughout in examples are those in the documents. Square brackets indicate assumptions or illegible text or damage.

1. A. P. Wadsworth and J. de L. Mann, *The cotton trade and industrial Lancashire, 1600–1780* (Manchester, 1931); J. K. Walton, *Lancashire: a social history, 1558–1939* (Manchester, 1987); J. Stobart, *The first industrial region: north-west England c. 1700–60* (Manchester, 2004).

2. J. Patten, 'Urban occupations in pre-industrial England', *Transactions of the Institute of British Geographers*, new ser., 2 (1977), p. 306.

3. T. Arkell, 'Interpreting probate inventories', in T. Arkell, N. Evans and N. Goose (eds.), *When death do us part* (Oxford, 2000), p. 72; A. M. Erickson, *Women and property in early modern England* (London, 1993), p. 204; P. Riden (ed.), *Probate records and the local community* (Gloucester, 1984), p. 5; Stobart, *First industrial region*, p. 229; J. S. Moore, (ed.), *The goods and chattels of our forefathers* (Chichester, 1976), pp. 1–2.

4. J. P. Earwaker (ed.), *An index to the wills and inventories now preserved in the Court of Probate at Chester* (Record Society of Lancashire and Cheshire, 18 [1681–1700]; 25 [1741–1760]; [Manchester, 1888, 1892]). The actual documents are held at the LRO, Preston.

5. Arkell suggests that the administrator entered into a bond 'with perhaps two other sureties for about double the estimated value of the personal estate': T. Arkell, 'The probate process', in Arkell, Evans and Goose, *When death*, p. 9.

6. J. D. Marshall, 'Agrarian wealth and social structure in pre-industrial Cumbria', *Economic History Review*, 33:4 (1980), p. 506. J. S. Moore,

'Probate inventories – problems and prospects', in P. Riden (ed.), *Probate records and the local community* (Cambridge, 1984), p. 13.

7. C. Shammas, *The pre-industrial consumer in England and America* (Oxford, 1990), pp. 232–3.

8. There existed a formulaic distribution of an estate until 1692, which involved one third going to the widow, one third to the children, and one third at the decedent's choice: A. Laurence, *Women in England, 1500–1760: a social history* (London, 1995), pp. 228–9.

9. We have no firm record of where Harrison had his premises, but the 1690 Poll Tax record for Manchester does show a Mrs Harrison and a maid living in Market Street Lane, and levied 2s. There is evidence from Court Leet records, probate records and Raffald's *Directory* that many widows did carry on a family business, having gained knowledge and experience whilst jointly operating that business with their husbands. See also Hannah Barker, *The business of women: female enterprise and urban development in northern England, 1760–1830* (Oxford, 2006).

10. Throughout the probate records the word 'Grosser' is spelt with the now obsolete 'long S' In the interests of clarity this has been omitted.

11. C. Muldrew, 'The ethics of credit and community relations', *Social History*, 18:2 (1993), p. 169.

12. Harrald's occupation as tobacconist is derived from other sources, for example, Craig Horner, *The diary of Edmund Harrold, a Manchester wigmaker, fl. 1712–5* (Aldershot, 2008, forthcoming).

13. C. F. Foster, *Capital and innovation* (Northwich, 2004), p. 300-1.

14. P. Spufford (ed.), *The probate accounts of England and Wales*, Vols. 1 and 2 (London, 1999), *passim*.

15. Probably James Harrop (c.1700–1754), joiner, father of the Manchester printer Joseph Harrop: J. Ramwell, 'Joseph and James Harrop of Manchester', *Transactions of the Lancashire and Cheshire Antiquarian Society*, 97, 2001, p. 76.

16. 'Danl. Fanshaw' also appears as a witness to Jackson's will.

17. Edward Jackson, possibly John's brother, makes another appearance in the probate record. As well as being paid for the coffin, he is shown being paid 2s 6d for *'prising the said testators Household Goods'*. The Court Leet record for 1744 identifies him as one of the appointed Appraisers.

18. In the churchwardens' accounts for the seven-week period ending 30 Dec. 1715 we find that a total of £2 17s was paid for 'Coffins and Church Dues' for twelve paupers (eight adults and four children). Adult coffins and dues were 4s and 1s 10d respectively, whilst the total cost for a child was between 2s and 3s 10d: *Church Wardens' and Overseers' Accounts, 1715, 1716*, Manchester Central Library M3/3/2a.

19. J. Stobart, 'Geography and industrialisation: the space economy of north-west England, 1701-1760', *Transactions of the Institute of British Geographers*, new ser., 21 (1996), p. 683.

LIBRARIES
The acquisition of books by Chetham's Library, 1655- 1700: a progress report

Matthew Yeo

Cataloguing Chetham's Library

In a recent article in *The Local Historian*, Fergus Wilde discussed the work undertaken at Chetham's Library towards a detailed catalogue of the Library's holdings and in making this catalogue available on the internet through the Library OPAC.[1] This work is now largely complete, thanks to the generous support of the Heritage Lottery Fund. Such a catalogue is a valuable addition to the resources available to scholars working in Manchester, and also provides a unique opportunity for research into the early history of the Library and of intellectual culture in Manchester in the latter half of the seventeenth century. Working in conjunction with a manuscript copy of the Library's accessions register, this new OPAC has been employed to generate a detailed descriptive bibliographical catalogue of the Library's acquisitions from its foundation after Humphrey Chetham's death in 1655 to the end of the century.[2] This enormous catalogue (c. 230,000 words), a sample of which is provided in Figure 1, has divided the acquisitions into groups according to the date of delivery, and gives each of the Library's acquisitions in this period a numeric identifier. In the OPAC, the dates of acquisition, from August 1655 to December 1700, along with a unique keyword search (*chetacq*, standing for **Chet**ham's **acq**uisition), are visible at the bottom of the relevant pages of the OPAC; *chetacq* 16550802 means that it was acquired in the first delivery by the London bookseller Robert Littlebury on 2 August 1655. This catalogue is the backbone of my forthcoming PhD thesis, the product of a new collaboration between the Library and the School of Languages, Linguistics and Cultures at the University of Manchester, funded by Chetham's Library and the Arts and Humanities Research Council.[3]

Using the catalogue for research purposes

The catalogue of acquisitions by Chetham's Library has generated a wealth of information both about what the Library bought and when it bought it. This information can be employed to identify and explore a number of different but complementary aspects of intellectual life in the period. Created *ab initio* with £1,000 in cash from Chetham's will to spend and, from 1661, the income from land purchased with Chetham's estate, what the Library received in the first six years of its history offers a conspectus of what the trustees regarded as the 'foundational texts' of any good scholarly library. Modelled on Oxford and Cambridge college libraries where most of the Library's readers would have been educated, we can compare its earliest acquisitions very favourably against the cash-strapped Oxford colleges which had to rely on alumni donations for their books.[4] The books the Library purchased were for the most part second-hand titles in Latin imported from the continent, covering theology, law, history and medicine. This was a scholarly library for the use of Manchester's professional classes, and not one of the five Calvinist parish libraries full of 'good English workes' also provided for in Chetham's will.[5] And in terms of its theological acquisitions, Chetham's Library was characterised by an ecumenism not matched at some university college libraries, taking deliveries early on of both the collected works of the Jesuit Francisco Suárez and the intemperate Lutheran *Magdeburg Centuries*.[6] Not that this open-mindedness was entirely favoured by all of Chetham's three trustees. John Tilsley, the most extreme Puritan of the three, had avowed in 1655 that the Library would buy 'no erroneous ... histories etc'.[7] The Library's acquisitions thus articulated confessional conflict between the three men who administered the Library as well as reflecting intellectual trends in English theology and intellectual life after the Restoration, notably under the leadership of Nicholas Stratford, warden of the Collegiate Church and Library trustee from 1667 to 1684.[8] Under him, Chetham's bought a large quantity of material relating to Christian Hebraism, and was instrumental in bringing the findings of the new 'experimental science' to Manchester, including complete sets of the house journal of the Royal Society, the *Philosophical Transactions*.[9] As a catalogue, Chetham's acquisitions are also fascinating in telling us what the Library did not buy. The absence of Arminian scholarship in the early purchases in the 1650s suggests a desire to ignore a volatile field of doctrinal error and to gloss over some of Manchester's recent factional past, although this was rectified later on in the 1680s.[10] More surprising still is the absence of sermons and tracts printed in the 1680s on popery and other topics, including works by Nicholas Stratford himself, published by the Library's main book supplier Robert Littlebury, and which can be ascribed to the Library's desire to get the best editions and scholarship available for their money rather than the temporarily popular or ephemeral.[11]

No.	Entry in accession register and volume title	£	s	d
1	**Augustini Opera vol. 8. Basileae**	07	00	00

(Basileae: Froben, 1541) (fol.) Re-spined contemporary German? dark brown calf binding with wooden bevel-edged boards and remnants of clasps. 10 vols bound in 8. Adams, A2162 *642*.

| 2 | **Aquinatis Summa – Cum Comment.: Cajetani vol: 2.** | 01 | 14 | 00 |

a) (Lugduni: apud Stephanum Michaelem., 1588) (fol.) 3 tom. in 2. Inscription on t.ps. of v. 1 & 2: "Ex dono Gulielmi Pickeringe xiij October A? don 1635". Adams, A1442 *1119*.

b) (Lugduni Lyon: Apud Stephanum Michaelem, 1588) Adams, C127 *1119*.

| 3 | **Aristotelis Opera. Vol.2 gr. lat. Paris. 1619.** | 01 | 18 | 00 |

(Lutetiae Parisiorum: Typis Regiis, 1619) (fol.) MS. note at top of t.p. (T. 1): Both volumes cost 2l–0–0. BM STC French, 1601–1700 A664. *5917*.

| 4 | **Aquinatis Catena in Evangelia.** | 00 | 09 | 00 |

(Parisiis: In aedibus Ioannis Petit sub signo floris lilij aurei, 1540) (fol.) Contemporary full-calf roll binding with wooden boards and metal furniture and clasps (lacking the leather ties). Adams A1476 – 1537 Petit imprint. *419*.

| 5 | **– Comment in Evangelia: et Epistolas. Vol. 2.** | 00 | 17 | 00 |

a) (Parisiis: Apud Dionysium Moreau viâ Iacobaeâ sub Salamandra, 1640) (fol.) *418*.

b) (Parisiis: Apud Dionysium Moreau viâ Iacobaeâ sub Salamandra, 1636) (fol.) MS. note on half-title-page: ':o: s. c'. BM STC French, 1601–1700 B1057. *420*.

| 6 | **– Opuscula Omnia** | 00 | 11 | 00 |

(Parisiis: Apud Guillelmum Pelé viâ Iacobaeâ sub signo Crucis Aureae, 1634) (fol.) *1104*.

| 7 | **– Quaest: disputate de deo, Anima, Angelis &c.** | 00 | 10 | 00 |

(Lugduni: apud Gulielmum Rouillium sub scuto Veneto, 1569) (fol.) Inscription on free endpaper: P. Hooker. col: CC socius. Presumably P. Hooker, BA, 1590–1, MA, 1594, BD. 1604. Late sixteenth-century early seventeenth-century English centrepiece calf binding ... Ker, Pastedowns, centrepiece xiv, with ornament 51. Pearson CC2(b). Armorial bookplate with motto Post Mortem Vita on free endpaper. Printed pastedown on inside of both covers from C15th theology book. Adams, A1409 *1103*.

The best editions available

It is in this sense of the 'best editions available' that the other scholarly aspect of the catalogue comes into its own. Supplied as it was with nearly all of its 3,000 titles by Robert Littlebury (1622–1695), a haberdasher and second-hand bookseller who worked outside the traditional cartel of the Stationers' Company, the Library's acquisitions challenge some of the traditional orthodoxies about the book trade in this period and contribute to previously unexplored areas of study in this field. Firstly, Littlebury was charged by the trustees to supply the Library with the best editions available. Although he was able to dispatch a number of works from the Plantin printing house and those of Estienne in Geneva, many of the titles he sent were incomplete or misbound, such as the Plantin *Biblia Polyglotta*, limiting our understanding of 'availability' to what Littlebury obtained at the time.[12] Of course, availability meant sometimes that Littlebury would send titles to Manchester to rid himself of stock, including works he had a share in publishing; the trustees were not receptive to his offers, and the titles never reached the Library shelves.[13] The problems of this relationship do question our notions of intentional acquisition by the Library, and needs to be addressed in our consideration of the reception of texts in this and any other period.[14] Secondly, Littlebury's work as a publisher, importer and seller in Britain and on the Continent highlights the dangers of the book-historical monopoly accorded to the Stationers' Company in this period, and indicates that such work should move beyond the distorting 'national' boundaries imposed by some recent studies.[15] Finally, Littlebury's work for the Library can be used to explore the previously unconsidered realm of the profit margin for the second-hand book trade. By comparing the prices Littlebury charged for new and second-hand stock against the prices paid by other institutions, we see that far from being a fixed mark-up like that of one-third on new stock, Littlebury used profit margins flexibly as a tool to build up relationships of trust with customers.[16] While claiming in a letter to the Library in 1684 that he charged them the same price as he paid, we can assume that he covered this loss by charging much more than cost price elsewhere to.[17] Profit margins are an area of book trade studies that need much more study; Robert Littlebury's interaction with Chetham's Library can make a small contribution to this field.

Figure 1: Chetham's Library accessions register transcription, f. 02r 2 Aug. 1655, *chetacq 16550802 Robert Littlebury*. Total cost of delivery £238 2s 3d

Conclusion

The work that this research has generated will be submitted as a doctoral thesis in the latter half of 2009. Much more on the character of the Library's acquisitions needs to be done, and there is still a great deal of material on the holdings' provenance and readership history on offer, including the marginalia by the eminent Cambridge Hebraist Thomas Wakefield in the Library's copy of the Bomberg Hebrew Bible.[18] As a first step, the study of the Library's accessions register, in conjunction with the Library's new and detailed on-line catalogue, provides a new and unique insight into the history of the Library at its foundation, the intellectual history of seventeenth-century Manchester, and offers some new perspectives on the book trade and on thinking about the history of the book.

Notes

1. The Library's on-line catalogue is available at www.chethams.org.uk. Cf. Fergus Wilde, 'Chetham's Library, Manchester 1653–2003', *The Local Historian*, 33:4 (2003), pp. 221–5.
2. Chetham's Library accessions register 1655–1720, C/LIB/ACCN/1.
3. Arts and Humanities Project 06/128292, University of Manchester Collaborative Doctoral Award.
4. Michael Powell, 'Endowed libraries for towns', in Giles Mandelbrote and Keith Manley (eds.), *The Cambridge history of libraries in Britain and Ireland: Vol. 2: 1640–1850* (Cambridge, 2006), p. 85.
5. For the terms of Chetham's will, cf. Francis Raines and Charles Sutton, *Life of Humphrey Chetham, founder of the Chetham Hospital and Library, Manchester* (2 vols.), Chetham Society, new ser., 50 (1903), ii, pp. 228–77.
6. Francisco Suárez, *Doctoris Francisci Suarez Granatensis, De Societate Iesu … Varia Opuscula Theologica* (Mainz, 1618), and Matthias Flacius Illyricus, *Ecclesiastica Historia, Integram Ecclesiae Christi Ideam* (Basel, 1559).
7. Chetham's Library papers, Mun A.5.
8. Henry D. Rack, 'Stratford, Nicholas (*bap.* 1633, *d.* 1707)', *Oxford Dictionary of National Biography* (Oxford, 2004) [http://www.oxforddnb.com/view/article/26646, accessed 22 Oct. 2007].
9. *Philosophical Transactions: Giving Some Accompt of the Present Undertakings, Studies and Labours of the Ingenious in Many Considerable Parts of the World* (London, 1665).
10. The collected works of Arminius were not delivered until July 1674. Cf. Jacobus Arminius, *Iacobi Arminii Veteraquinatis Batavi, Ss. Theologiae Doctoris Eximii Opera Theologica* (Frankfurt am Main, 1631).
11. Cf. Nicholas Stratford, *A Sermon Preached at the Assizes Held at Chester, September Xx. 1681* (London, 1681).
12. Benito Arias Montano, *Biblia Sacra, Hebraice, Chaldaice, Graece, & Latine: Philippi Ii. Reg. Cathol. Pietate, Et Studio Ad Sacrosanctae Ecclesiae Vsum* (Antwerp, 1569). Bound in seven volumes, and is incomplete. Vol. 7 replaces Vols. 7–8 (cf. L. Voet, *The Plantin press (1555–84)* [6

vols., Amsterdam, 1980–3]), and begins with 'Communes et familiares Hebraicae linguae idiotismi omnibus Bibliorum interpretationibus' (version B). All 18 of the works belonging to Vol. 8 are bound in after this, but in the wrong order.

13. Chetham's Library Invoices Book, Robert Littlebury to the Library, 9 Aug. 1683, f.43r.

14. David D. Hall, 'What was the history of the book? A response', *Modern Intellectual History*, 4 (2007), pp. 537–44.

15. Michael F. Suarez, 'Historiographical problems and possibilities in book history and national histories of the book', *Studies in Bibliography*, 55 (2003–2004), p. 147.

16. Cf. Appendix to David Stoker, 'Doctor Collinges and the revival of Norwich City Library, 1657–1664', *Library History*, 5:3 (1980); and Chetham's Library Invoices Book, Robert Littlebury to the Library, 30 Aug. 1684, f. 47r.

17. Chetham's Library Invoices Book, Robert Littlebury to the Library, 30 Aug. 1684, f. 47r.

18. James Carley, 'Thomas Wakefield, Robert Wakefield and the Cotton Genesis', *Transactions of the Cambridge Bibliographical Society*, 12:3 (2002), pp. 246–65.

MUSEUMS

Ordsall Hall: One of the oldest and best loved buildings in Greater Manchester

John Sculley

Ordsall Hall is the North West's 'Small Visitor Attraction of the Year' for 2007. Recognised as Salford's 'Historic Gem', its heritage significance is reinforced by its contemporary location: sandwiched between one of the most deprived communities in Greater Manchester (Ordsall and Riverside) and the Salford Quays visitor and tourist attractions; the Lowry, Imperial War Museum North, Manchester United Football Club and Lancashire Cricket Club. The Hall and its grounds are unique assets in a unique location.

Ordsall Hall's value lies not only in its half-timbered façade, but also in the way its history reflects social, political and economic change from the fourteenth century to Salford's spectacular regeneration initiatives of the twenty-first. The first known reference to Ordsall Hall and estate is in the twelfth century, with the earliest part of the house dating from 1346. Ordsall Hall is Grade I-listed and defined as a building of exceptional interest; only 2 per cent of all listed buildings enjoy this status. As well as being one of the oldest timber-framed buildings in the North, its historic value and importance is emphasised by its surviving fourteenth-century domestic apartments, offering significant evidence of medieval family life. In fact, throughout its entire existence, the Hall has grown and developed, illustrating well the human responses to changing domestic expectations of high status households.

Architecturally, the Hall is a gem. Much of its building fabric and decorative features are regarded as nationally significant. The Hall's accurate dating provides a benchmark for the study of similar properties throughout England. As the east-wing bed chambers improve our understanding of medieval construction, so the sixteenth-century Great Hall (one of the largest timber-framed open halls in the region) offers similar exemplary learning opportunities for later building techniques. The Great Hall's architectural importance is seen by its elaborate spere posts, with their moulded stone bases – reminiscent of those at Manchester Cathedral – and the ornamental quatrefoil, which provide the building's architectural tracery both inside and

Ordsall Hall   out and became, together with Tudor self-confidence, an icon of the age. Although later seventeenth-century additions and the complete Victorian remodelling of the South Front are of lesser significance, they help complete the building's first 600-year journey through a range of period styles. As well as its pillars, trusses and quatrefoils, the Hall has some other important – in some cases nationally significant – decorative features. These include two medieval fireplaces; evidence of medieval paintwork; a seventeenth-century plaster ceiling; stained glass; and original oak panelling. In addition, the Hall's archaeological finds are exhibited permanently in a dedicated gallery. Evidence of a moat and outbuilding are recorded here, alongside an eleventh-century log boat (the hall is situated near the banks of the River Irwell), Cistercian ware pottery and, of course, a mountain of animal bones.

No less important than the Hall itself are its connections with many of the country's great moments, such as the Hundred Years War; the Wars of the Roses; the Battle of Crecy; the religious disputes of the Tudor period; the Gunpowder Plot; the English Civil War; and the Victorians. They have all had an impact on Ordsall Hall and its heritage. In its lifetime, the Hall's incarnations have included a self-sufficient estate; a family home; a clergy training school; a working men's club; a wartime radar station; and latterly, an historic house museum.

For its first 300 years the Hall was the family home of the Radclyffes, whose dynasty was confirmed following a murderous episode with the Trafford family on Valentine's Day, 1345. The Radclyffes subsequently secured their importance to the monarchy by distinguishing themselves in battle, usually against the French, and were granted the right to use one of the oldest battlefield mottoes for service to the Crown – 'Caen, Crecy, Calais'. Radclyffe's links with kings and queens of England litter Ordsall's story; Sir John Radclyffe (d.1362) stood proxy at the marriage of the future Edward III, Margaret Radclyffe (d.1599) was a maid of honour to Elizabeth I, and Sir Alexander Radclyffe (d.1654) carried the purple robes at the coronation of Charles I. Creative links with Ordsall Hall are similarly easy to find. The Elizabethan poet Ben Jonson, playwright William Shakespeare and artist friend to the pre-Raphaelites, Frederick J. Shields, all have important links with the Hall.

All of this features in our development proposals. Ordsall Hall has now embarked upon its second-stage Heritage Lottery Fund application. This intends to protect, conserve, enhance and secure the Hall, as well as build on its proven success as a local learning resource and award-winning visitor attraction. The Heritage Lottery Fund and Salford City Council offer Ordsall Hall a fabulous opportunity to stake its claim for the future. Public fundraising for this £6-million project remains crucial. We are fortunate to have considerable local support, especially from the Friends of Salford Museums who are driving the fundraising campaign. Our proposed developments position the Hall at the centre of the area's regeneration. The Hall's potential

An educational visit

contribution to local social cohesion and community pride are equally important to the project's aims, with intelligent access through the careful programming of public visits, private functions and training opportunities. But we still need loads of money. If you would like to help, visit www.salford.gov.uk/ordsallhall and follow the links to the 'Extrardinary Ordsall' campaign.

Today, Ordsall Hall's popularity is seen by its outstanding visitor figures, its over-subscribed schools and community service and, of course, its ghosts. As with all self-respecting historic houses, Ordsall Hall has its 'White Lady'. In fact, the Hall's 'ghost-cam' is the sixth most popular webcam in the world, with over 30,000 hits every month.

Ordsall Hall Museum
Ordsall Lane
Salford M5 3AN
0161-872 0251

Opening Times:
Mon – Fri: 10am – 4.00pm
Sat: Closed
Sun: 1.00 – 4.00pm

ARCHIVES
The Archive of the Booth Charities of Salford

Michael Powell

The charitable foundation known as the Booth Charities is one of the oldest and most effective charities operating in the north-west of England. It was established in 1630/1 when Humphrey Booth the Elder (1580–1635), a rich fustian merchant of Manchester and Salford, granted lands to trustees by a deed of feoffment. The lands comprised five fields and a barn in Manchester with a yearly value of £20, and Booth's intention was that income from these lands should be 'ymployed towards or for the succour aid or relief of such poore aged needie or impotent people as for the tyme being shall inhabit or dwell within the said Borough or Towne of Salford'.[1]

The Charities originally fulfilled these requirements by distributing small money grants and clothing or blankets to the poor. Today the Charities have annual net assets of just under £25 million and give grants of almost £1.3 million a year to a wide range of organi-sations.[2] The charities which make up Booth are without doubt some of the most important charities active in the North West and have a remarkable record of over three centuries of poor relief.

Through the centuries the Charities' trustees have preserved a large and detailed archive of their land holding and activities, an archive which is deposited at Chetham's Library, Manchester. The collection is catalogued and copies are available in local libraries and record offices. More importantly, the catalogue is available on the Access to Archives (A2A) website (http://www.a2a.org.uk), where it can be both browsed and searched.

The Booth Charities Archive provides an essential primary resource for scholarly research on a wide range of studies of the history of Manchester and Salford. In the first place, the collection has much to say about how the trustees acquired their income. The lands which the Charities originally owned are now some of the most important parts of Manchester and Salford, and study of the archive enables us to reconstruct the economic and architectural history of these areas. Lands left by Humphrey Booth the Elder are now covered by buildings around Piccadilly and Oxford Street. In 1776 an Act of Parliament enabled the Booth trustees to let their estates on building leases for terms up to 99 years long. Houses were being built on the land around Piccadilly by 1790, and thus through the centuries the value of the lands increased steadily, enabling the trustees of the charity to adapt their income to changing needs.

Lands left by the founder's grandson, Humphrey Booth the Younger, were situated in Salford at Broken Bank and Gravel Lane. Towards the end of the eighteenth century the trustees developed this area into the Crescent, an elegant line of Georgian houses in an area free from the air pollution and industrial noise of central Manchester. As late as 1841, *Bradshaw's Manchester Journal* could describe the Crescent and its environs as 'one of the most picturesque landscapes in the suburbs of Manchester'.[3] But the area was changing as the suburb became part of Salford's inner city and the green oasis was soon ruined by industrial buildings and cheap housing. Looking at the leases of property we can see the change from the 1790s when the tenants included lawyers, medics and mill-owners, to the 1890s when the now-subdivided properties were home to artisans and labourers. A number of large houses were demolished to make way for public buildings and by 1914 the Crescent's days as residential accommodation were effectively over. Even so the properties still continued to provide the Booth Charities with important income; indeed the fact that a handful of the Crescent's Georgian houses have survived at all is largely due to the fact that the Booth trustees continued to derive benefit from them.

As well as aiding the poor and elderly of Salford financially, Humphrey Booth the Elder was also concerned with their spiritual welfare and he founded the first church in Salford, Trinity Chapel, shortly before his death. He laid the foundation stone in 1634 and the Chapel was completed on 16 May 1635. The chapel, built on the western outskirts of what was then a small town, was created a parish church in 1650 due to the huge population increase in Salford.

Although a sum of 20 pounds had been set aside as the annual stipend for the minister, Humphrey Booth the Elder died before he could plan for the maintenance and repairs which Trinity Chapel would inevitably require. Four decades after Humphrey Booth the Elder's death in 1635, his grandson, Humphrey Booth the Younger, followed his philanthropic example. In his will of 1672 Humphrey the Younger left lands in Salford to provide for the future of the Chapel. His will stated that 'in case there be any overplus then my Will and Mind is that it shall be distributed amongst the Poore of Salford, Att a Christmas as the Money's left by my Grandfather is'. The maintenance of Salford's parish church has been one of the core purposes of the Booth distributors and documents relating to Trinity Chapel, its rebuilding in the 1750s and partial rebuilding in 1874, form a considerable part of the archive.

Trinity Church, Salford, detail from the margin of Casson and Berry's Map of Manchester, c. 1746

The Booth Archive shows both how the trustees derived their income, and how that money was spent. Using the Archive, we are able to explore in detail the central issue of poverty relief in early modern and in industrial society and to chart how a charity founded in the 1630s with lands of five fields and a barn has contributed to the alleviation of poverty in the era of the welfare state. The Archive shows how the relief of the poor can change through the centuries, from handing out blankets to the elderly to funding research in neurological illness within a clinical research centre in gerontology in a university teaching hospital. Moreover, the collection allows us to investigate the relationship between philanthropy and power, to consider how those responsible for administering Booth's bequest attempted to shape policy and to influence the behaviour of the needy. This is not simply a charity which has survived against the odds, but one that has moulded opinions and shaped lives for over 300 years.

Notes

1. Chetham's Library, Booth Charities Archive, 2/1/1/1.
2. Humphrey Booth the Elder's and Grandson's Charities annual reports and consolidated financial statements, year ended 31 Mar. 2005.
3. *Bradshaw's Manchester Journal*, 14 Aug. 1841.

LONG REVIEWS

Hannah Barker
The business of women: female enterprise and urban development in northern England, 1760–1830 Oxford: Oxford University Press, 2006. xi+189pp. ISBN 0190299714.

It is clear from the outset that Hannah Barker intends the conjunction of 'business' and 'women' in her title to be unsettling. On the one hand, by exploring the work of middling women, she diverts us from the well explored channel of historical enquiry that limits the study of women and work during the industrial revolution to the labouring classes. On the other hand, by exploring women's participation in trade and commerce, she diverts us from an equally well explored channel that associates 'business' with men and assumes that middling women were restricted to private, domestic space. The result is a book that should, for starters, make the conjunction of women and business a commonplace, and should, more fundamentally, make us revise our picture of urban society and business during the industrial revolution. Barker sets her enquiry into *The business of women* in three rapidly developing cities of northern England –Manchester, Leeds and Sheffield – during the period from the 1760s to the 1820s. Deeply involved in the industrial development of their regional hinterlands, these cities nonetheless retained significant economic and social diversity, opening up opportunities for women in business.

The conceptual and methodological heart of the book is found in the two chapters that explore women's involvement in business using trade directories and newspaper advertisements. Published periodically in all three of these cities from the 1770s, directories allow Barker to measure the scale of women's involvement in business since they list, in a comprehensive fashion, all of the commercial establishments in town. Taken as a whole, just over 6 per cent of all enterprises in the sample of directories identify a woman as an owner. Moreover, as Barker demonstrates with a host of examples, women's involvement was almost certainly more significant given that directories under-reported women's role in managing businesses listed under the name of a husband, brother, or sons. While the number is not large, Barker's point is that a female business owner would have been unremarkable. (Admittedly more so in some trades than others, for women were concentrated in businesses categorized as clothing, shop keeping, and food.) Barker's systematic survey of advertisements in regional newspapers in this same period cannot say as much about the numbers of women's businesses, but an analysis of their content does reveal something of how women presented themselves to their customers and trading partners. Significantly, Barker finds that these ads make little reference to gender. When women advertised, they identified themselves by an occupational label rather than as a woman, and they claimed the same kinds of attributes for their businesses – quality, value, honesty – as their male competitors.

In the final two chapters, Barker explores evidence from family records and court cases to further develop her thesis that women were an acknowledged element of, and fully integrated into, the economy of these northern industrial cities. The chapter on family explores the role women played in family firms by analyzing evidence about their participation in partnerships and the family business ownership during probate. Convention dictated that women would not normally be identified as a partner to a male relative nor continue the family business after their sons came of age, but the numerous counter-examples clearly indicate that there was a space which women could occupy if circumstances and inclination allowed. The final chapter, 'Family, property, and power', shows that women were quite willing to take economic grievances to court, and, perhaps more significantly, that they could expect the courts to uphold their claims despite the common law doctrine of coverture.

Although there are occasional instances when she overstates the conclusions that the assembled instances will bear, the validity and historiographical value of Barker's work is clear. Most obviously, the book makes an important contribution to the body of work challenging the separate spheres model. Far from being marginalized as mere consumers restricted to the private sphere, Barker's research shows us women who were active as producers and traders; women who were equal, if minority, players in the commercial networks in three of England's most economically vibrant cities. The book is also important simply for its exploration of these three cities, particularly because of its focus on the lower middling, a social group whose role and importance in the history of industrialization has been overlooked.

Finally, *The business of women* is valuable because of the many questions it raises. One relates directly to her central thesis, for having debunked the separate spheres as a model of women's realities, Barker does not attempt to discuss its ideological significance for the lives of the businesswomen we meet in this book. Second, her tendency to stress the inferiority against which women business owners must have been struggling makes it hard for Barker to ask about the realities of women's experiences in commerce. For example, given that trade credit was an essential prop to virtually all business concerns during this period, one wonders whether and to what extent the willingness of male wholesalers to extend credit for raw materials or shop goods might have been a factor constraining women into the relatively narrow range of trades in which we find them. Third, Barker's focus on a group that she herself identifies as the 'lower middling' (a group analogous to the families studied in Margaret Hunt's *The middling sort*) raises a number of questions about boundaries. To what extent did the experience of childbearing – hardly mentioned in the book – serve to distinguish this social group from either labouring women or their wealthier counterparts in the upper middling? How did education (basic numeracy and literacy) define the difference between the woman who could raise a small stock from relations to commence trading on her own, and the woman whose options were confined to labour alone? How did these businesswomen (or their daughters) react to success? Was domesticity something to which they aspired if they could afford it? The answers to all of these questions lie outside the scope of Barker's research, but they indicate the importance of the new channels of historical enquiry opened up by this book.

John Smail
University of North Carolina, Charlotte

Michael L. Bush

The casualties of Peterloo Lancaster: Carnegie Publishing Ltd, 2005. x+166pp. £15.00 hb. ISBN 1859361250.

There have been many books on the events in Manchester on 16 August 1819, the occasion of the 'Peterloo Massacre', but this is different. It provides not a narrative of events but an analysis of those who were killed and injured during – or as a result of – the happenings of that day. Of the 160 pages of text, 62 are devoted to discussion and notes and the remainder to a list of 634 casualties and fatalities of whom at least 167 were women. For each of these, details are provided, where available, of addresses, occupations, injuries, compensation received (if any) and other details, given according to the various and often slightly differing sources. In all, seven different contemporary or near-contemporary sources have been utilised to produce this impressive database, the publication of which in as a definitive a form as seems likely to be achieved will be of great interest not only to general historians of radicalism and working-class movements but also to family and local historians in search of further details of their ancestors or their own locality. The book is extremely well produced, with clear tables and many illustrations and diagrams to illuminate the text. It challenges and reinterprets previous standard accounts and should become essential reading for any future student of the subject.

The introductory analysis of this information is exhaustive to the point of being almost self-defeating or contradictory, as Professor Bush does not shy away from the ambiguities inherent in the evidence and the conflicting interpretations it is possible to place upon it. For example, in arguing that the number of casualties may well have been more than reported, he reasons that since relatively few casualties were sustained by contingents from some of the outlying communities, such as the four casualties among the people from Rochdale, many more casualties must have been treated later at home or escaped the records. Yet, when discussing the disposition of the various contingents at the meeting, he reasons equally validly that the Rochdale contingent were in a thinner part of the crowd where they could have escaped more easily. Both statements are probably true but they illustrate how in the end evidence can be interpreted to make the case of one's choice. That said, this is a highly commendable effort to take up the challenge laid down by G. M. Trevelyan in an article in *History* in 1922 to publish a detailed casualty list, and to subject it to the most detailed scrutiny yet attempted, going beyond the pioneering work of Malcolm and Walter Bee in this journal back in 1989. The latter suggested that the proportion of injuries might be used to form a profile of the total crowd at Peterloo, especially over the matter of how many women were present. Professor Bush is more cautious as he argues that the injuries reflected the fact that many women were concentrated in what turned out to be the most dangerous positions around the hustings and so are likely to have been over-represented in the casualty lists – one quarter of the casualties but possibly only one eighth of the crowd as a whole. The casualty lists also suggest that the crowd contained a large proportion of people from Manchester itself, despite the traditional emphasis on contingents coming from outside the town. Of 596 names with addresses, 364 came from Manchester and immediately surrounding area, 282 of them from the manor of Manchester itself. Again this can partly be explained by where they were standing in the crowd, but the size of the numbers from Manchester does suggest an important new conclusion. A map of where these casualties lived and an analysis of names also supports the view that the Irish were an important group, with at least 97 of the casualties, 63 of them from Manchester. Information on occupation is less readily obtained from the data: no specific occupation is given for 52 per cent of men and all but 7 per cent of women. Among those whose occupation is known, handloom weavers predominated.

The injury lists enable Professor Bush to offer some suggestions not only as to the possible composition of the crowd but also as to the nature of the injuries and by whom they were delivered. For lack of anything better, Henry Hunt's view is accepted that one eighth of the crowd were women; however, with women representing one quarter of the total casualties it is clear that they came in for more than their fair share of punishment. Moreover, while women represented a quarter of those trampled by horses and one fifth of those wounded by weapons, they made up one third of those crushed in the crowd. While women were less likely than men to have been wounded by a weapon, they were slightly more likely to have been injured by a horse and much more likely to have been injured in the crush of the crowd. This reflects where many women were stood, and the difficulty they had in getting away when attacked. The high injury rate also shows that the troops made no attempt to spare the women out of deference to their sex. Professor Bush argues that the fact that the women had turned up to play an active part in a public political meeting had turned them into a double threat to the established order, adding the democratic insolence of gender to that of class. There was also little discrimination with regard to age, though younger people were better at getting away from the crush. The statistics produced to back up each of these findings helps create a vivid picture of what the experience of the crowd was as the troops charged among them, sabres drawn and bayonets at the ready.

But did this amount to a massacre? The conclusion is yes, because the action appears to have been deliberate and sustained, conducted by the regular troops, both cavalry and infantry, as well as the volunteers, with the aim not merely of dispersing the crowd but of punishing it. Almost half the injuries were caused by a weapon, despite later claims that most were inflicted by the crowd itself in its panic to escape. In all eighteen deaths resulted from Peterloo and its aftermath. Discounting two men shot later that day away from the site, and a special constable killed by the mob as a reprisal two days later, two further specials were killed on the day (one sabred and one trampled under a horse), one woman was suffocated in the crowd some distance from St Peter's Fields, and a small baby was accidentally knocked from his mother's arms and killed by a cavalryman. That leaves the eleven casualties usually listed as arising directly out of the events of Peterloo. And as for the number of injuries, Professor Bush's best guess is in excess of 700. That was quite a day!

Edward Royle
University of York

Jon Stobart
The first industrial region: north-west England, c.1700–60 Manchester: Manchester University Press, 2004. 259pp. ISBN 0719064627.

Focusing on the north-west industrial region, taken here to comprise Cheshire and Lancashire south of the Ribble but including Preston, this book is essentially concerned with the role of towns in facilitating early industrialisation. Whilst recognising the importance of the regional dimension in investigating the development of industrial and commercial activity, and of the economic and cultural differentiation that occurred between and within industrial regions, the author contends that insufficient attention has been given to the inter- and intra-regional linkages that helped to promote such differentiation and to generate economic growth, a matter he seeks to rectify by means of theoretically-informed analysis.

The region is conceptualised as comprising urban nodes that integrated with one another and with the surrounding areas over which they had influence. The marked extent to which specialisation of economic activity was evident within north-west localities in the 60 years prior to the classic Industrial Revolution is examined, along with the crucial role played by towns in providing service sector activities and opportunities for information exchange. Chapters dealing with the textile industries and the coal-using industries are used to develop these ideas, the former highlighting the regional role of Manchester in co-ordinating rural textile production throughout Lancashire and north-east Cheshire, as well as linking with external markets, and the latter the emergence of Liverpool as the major industrial centre in south-west Lancashire, not only forming 'a focus and stimulus of growth' in the area, but also strengthening its connections with an emerging industrial hinterland. A further chapter argues for the importance of the growing service sector in understanding the development of the region's economy, noting its urban emphasis and examining its composition in relation to urban hierarchies. The final chapter offers detailed insights into the nature and strength of rural and urban linkages, centring on the opportunities provided by local markets, by transport systems and the services they offered and by personal networks, including those arising through trading and professional contacts.

The evidential basis of the analysis relies strongly on probate records, which confine the periodisation of the study and, because of their well known limitations, bring concerns about the firmness with which some of the conclusions can be drawn and about the depth to which analysis can be undertaken. Thus, whilst the probate evidence on occupations reveals that about three in every ten males in the region selected were employed in manufacturing activity between 1701 and 1760, parish register entries indicate much stronger concentrations in such parishes as Blackburn and Bolton, at least by the mid 1720s. Both probate and parish register evidence is consistent in suggesting that manufacturing activity had reached substantial levels in the region well before the classic Industrial Revolution period, but the generalised form in which the probate evidence is presented may well help to mask appreciable differences at sub-regional level.

Your reviewer also has concerns with regard to the way in which his own observations are represented in the book, especially concerning his comments on the importance that the literature on proto-industry attaches to the role of towns in co-ordinating manufacturing activity in surrounding rural areas, as well as in carrying out the finishing stages of production. My comment that 'rural industry was largely organised from urban centres' does not fit well with the charge that I see 'little to distinguish town and country' even when applied to this matter alone. I remain mindful of the evidence cited by Wadsworth and Mann, especially about the occurrence of rurally-based manufactures and merchant's agents, of which we know all too little in the eighteenth century. On finishing activity, the probate data are helpful in allaying my concern about the lack of an evidential base on which a conclusion can be reached, but the probate evidence does not provide the basis for a final word on the matter. And it also confirms the importance of finishing in rural areas, especially around Manchester, adding to the observation made by Diana Winterbotham about an early concentration of bleaching at Blackley, Moston and Newton to the north-east of Manchester. Indeed, a key point to arise from the probate data is that there may well have been a strong tendency to bleach both yarn and cloth in rural rather than urban locations where suitable land and water provision was available. Nor do I characterise Manchester in the mid seventeenth century simply as a manufacturing town; I merely comment on the relatively high proportion of young males – about 60 per cent – that parish register evidence indicates were employed in manufacturing activity, quoting, too, the proportions engaged in other sectors.

Putting these concerns aside, the book adds considerably to our understanding of the role of urban centres in promoting north-west industrialisation and of the ways they linked with their immediate localities, with each other and with urban centres outside the region. The theoretical perspectives offered provide fresh insights, introducing such useful concepts as 'gateway' towns, and are well tested against the evidential base. The book will certainly appeal to urban and regional historians and should provoke a good deal of thought as to the further lines of investigation that can be usefully pursued.

Geoff Timmins
University of Central Lancashire

Charles F. Foster

Capital and innovation: how Britain became the first industrial modern nation. A study of the Warrington, Knutsford, Northwich and Frodsham area, 1500–1780, with a foreword by Prof Francois Crouzet Northwich, Ches: Arley Hall Press, 2004. xviii+373pp. ISBN 0951838245.

The traditional interpretation of the Industrial Revolution sites it within Lancashire and dates it from the decades of the 1760s. In a pioneering new study, Charles Foster sets this tradition in a much longer time perspective by tracing the rise of a business society back to the 1540s and by reasoning that such a phenomenon was an essential prelude to the Industrial Revolution proper. He also shifts the focus of study away from Lancashire to the pastoral plain of north-west Cheshire. There he has made a notable excursion into the realm of micro-history, using estate archives never before exploited. The massive citation of primary sources provides a striking contrast with all previous studies of the subject. Mr Foster shows how the rural society of the region responded to the opportunities opened up from the era of the Reformation, when new forms of tenure were developed, conferring property rights upon working families. Small landholders became small capitalists and benefited from the equal division of estates amongst heirs and from the lag of rents behind rising prices, as wealth was extensively redistributed in their favour. Such working families in the middling ranks of society developed new staples of trade wherein they enjoyed a comparative advantage. Thus they undertook the large-scale manufacture and export of Cheshire cheese and the salt of Northwich from the 1650s and the sail-cloth of Warrington from the 1740s. Those products were shipped from two of the three legal quays of the port of Liverpool at Frodsham and Sankey Bridge and served to spread the influence of commerce throughout the ranks of local society.

As a subsistence economy was transformed into a market economy, an independent and self-reliant commercial society arose, differing sharply from the gentry culture of southern England, and from the aristocratic culture of Europe. By 1770, Charles Foster estimates that a business society of some 5,000 families, each with assets of £1,000 or more, had been created by the growth of maritime trade in the four counties of Cheshire, Lancashire, Staffordshire and the West Riding. Those families formed 'an industrial-commercial complex in the north-west of England that was larger than anything of the kind that had appeared in the world before' (p. 173). In north-west Cheshire itself,

especially in such trading towns as Warrington and Knutsford, the middling ranks of society had become large, rich and sophisticated. They benefited from the withdrawal of the local gentry from business enterprise from the seventeenth century onwards. They responded eagerly to measures of state policy encouraging particular activities, and they displayed a marked propensity to make and to accept innovation, especially in the sphere of inland navigation.

Charles Foster concludes that the era of the Civil Wars and Commonwealth forms a watershed in the history of the north-west region and that the great divergence of England from the rest of Europe dates at least from the 1650s. Thus he lends powerful support to the argument set forth in the 1960s by D. C. Coleman, E. A. Wrigley and J. R. Harris for a backwards revision in the chronology of the Industrial Revolution. As a socio-cultural explanation of the origins of that revolution his work does seem more convincing than that of any other scholar, including H. J. Perkin. His work is unusual insofar as it is the product of a retired businessman and may be compared in that respect only with the work of W. R. Scott (1868–1940). It forms the fourth and final volume in the Arley Archives series, following upon the publication of *Four Cheshire townships in the eighteenth century* (1992, 88pp.), *Cheshire cheese and farming* (1998, 128pp.), and *Seven households* (2002, 264pp.). Together the four volumes represent an important contribution to the history of the region. This particular volume will be widely welcomed because of its breadth of perspective, its meticulous scholarship and its cogent analysis. It will be assured of an extensive readership.

D. A. Farnie
Manchester Metropolitan University

Jonathan D. Oates

The Jacobite invasion of 1745 in north-west England Lancaster: Centre for North-West Regional Studies, University of Lancaster, 2006. 143pp. ISBN 186220179X.

This book of Dr Oates's is not another account of the inauspicious campaign of Charles Edward Stuart in 1745 nor yet another nostalgic tale of the lost cause in north-west England. It focuses on the 'activity of the men and women' of the four counties of Cumberland, Westmorland, Lancashire and Cheshire during the autumn and winter of 1745 (and after). The author tries to be as fact-abiding and unbiased as possible when he deals with the actions and inactions of the people. He uses the word 'invasion' from the viewpoint of the north west and not 'rebellion' or 'rising' when describing the event in the region. Except for citations he avoids using the words 'Pretender', 'rebel' and 'Hanoverian'. The Jacobite army marched into the region in early November and out in late December, and there was no spontaneous uprising of the residents, in spite of a number of sympathisers and recruits in the region. The author is more interested in describing and analysing the complex reaction of the local people and their response to the changing situation.

The Jacobite invasion is lucidly structured with the author's purpose clearly presented in the 21-page introduction, and his argument concluded briefly at the end of each chapter. He is careful about the varying attitudes of the men and women of the north west and cautious not to draw simplistic conclusions, but instead offers a balanced assessment of opposing evidence 'not subject to sweeping generalisations'. The author delves into the papers at the National Archives, the British Library and the Royal Archives, as well as county and municipal archives, as shown

by his rich quotations. But perhaps the most outstanding document he employs is the memoir of Walter Shairp (1724–87), a merchant and lieutenant of the 'Liverpool Blues', a volunteer force raised among the townsmen of Liverpool to counter the Jacobite threat. The memoir is valuable, first because it is a rare piece of evidence about those engaged in the loyal volunteers in 1745, and second because the Liverpool Blues was the only volunteer force to cross the county border to march to Carlisle in December. Oates himself has edited 'A history of the raising & adventures of the Liverpool regiment of blues', the manuscript memoir by Shairp, now in the custody of Liverpool Central Library. With an extensive introduction and notes, it has been published by the Record Society of Lancashire and Cheshire as *Jacobites and Jacobins: two eighteenth-century perspectives* (vol. 142, 2006).

In the first chapter of *The Jacobite invasion* the author discusses the predominantly loyal north west before autumn 1745, and then he follows chronological and geographical order in the two chapters dealing with the actual invasion; 'November 1745' on the reactions to the invasion in Cumberland, Westmorland, Lancashire and Cheshire in order; and 'December 1745' about those counties with the Jacobite army in retreat. However, these chapters do not deal with the day-to-day progression of the Jacobite army in the region, with the author's primary interest lying with the inactive support and largely ineffective resistance of the residents of the north west including the assumed 'Jacobites' like James Barry and John Byrom. Why was local resistance nominal and why didn't the Jacobites take up arms in November? Were they either cowards or opportunists?

Whig Carlisle and tory Manchester are the two special towns which Oates considers most important and about which he gives detailed evidence. According to Oates, the judgments of the situation by local magistrates showed discretion, since the French collaboration was unforeseen and the British regular forces remote. In addition, more sensible high-churchmen and tories would realize that the complacent Prince Charlie would make an unacceptable head of the enlightened state. After the Fifteen the English had become a more 'polite and commercial people'. Jocular conviviality at various Jacobite clubs and feasts with the toasts of 'Down with the Rump' and 'King' over a bowl of water is a sign of their complacency as well as their disaffection. Jacobite language certainly died hard and continued to bother the government, but it may have been more important as a sentimental bridge to radicalism and Freemasonry (p. 106; P. K. Monod, *Jacobitism and the English people* [1989], pp. 300–5).

There are only a few flaws I could point to. First, Oates relies too much on *Selections from the journals and papers of John Byrom*, edited by Henri Talon (1950), when he discusses John Byrom and his daughter Beppy. Of course Byrom was a key figure not only in Manchester but also in national literary life. For example, Byrom's literary friendship with Sir Oswald Mosley, whig heir-apparent to the lordship of the manor of Manchester, was decisive when Mosley quitted his whig-presbyterian project of the public workhouse and Byrom implemented the miscarriage of the Manchester Workhouse Bill at Westminster in 1730–1 (see this writer's 2007 article in *Historical Research*). Talon groundlessly assumes

Mosley to be a 'strong Jacobite' and edits his *Selections* without knowing the political import of his excerpts. Oates should have used *The private journal and literary remains of John Byrom*, edited by R. Parkinson (Chetham Society, 1854–7), and *The poems of John Byrom*, edited by A. W. Ward (Chetham Society, 1894–1912); Beppy Byrom's journal is included in the *Literary remains*. Those Victorian publications themselves are not immune from some editorial problems, as Timothy Underhill has pointed out, but still they are far better than Talon's misleading *Selections*.

Second, Oates uses the term 'status quo' so often without specifying it. Is it the 'happy revolutionary settlement and the due Hanoverian succession', the 'Erastian Church' or something else? Related to this, he uses the term 'high church' only once (p. 103). Some of the very frequent use of the term 'Jacobite' may well be reasonably changed for 'high church(man)'. Certainly he focuses on the regional situation in the four north-western counties, but some discussion of the national politics, religion, economy and society is indispensable when dealing with the complex response of the men and women. The economic growth and Jacobite emigration overseas in the mid century are beyond the scope of the book.

The volume comprises 143 pages in all. The main text is followed by endnotes and bibliography. It is humbly published as an Occasional Paper of the CNWRS, but it is more than occasional. The book is articulate and inspiring despite its minor flaws. The advantages are its readability and its lavish use of photographs, engravings, documents and diagrams. This is a welcome addition to the regional history of Jacobitism as a complex phenomenon in 1745.

Kazuhiko Kondo
University of Tokyo

Robert Poole (ed.)
The Lancashire Witches: histories and stories Manchester: Manchester University Press, 2002. xiv+226pp. ISBN 9780719062032 (paper), 9780719062049.

Today anyone paying a visit to the Pendle area of north-east Lancashire cannot fail to learn of the trial of seventeen witches from that area at Lancaster in 1612. The local economy now appears to depend upon tourism generated by the events of almost 400 years ago. Indeed the trial of 1612 was and remains one of the best known of all witch-trials held in seventeenth-century England. This is partly because it had a number of unusual features, in particular a large number of defendants for an English trial and, supposedly, accounts of a demonic pact and a witches' meeting, similar to those found in continental and Scottish witch trials but rarely in those held in England. The principal reason for the fame of this particular trial, however, is the way that it and the events leading up to it were described and narrated by Thomas Potts in his *The Wonderfull Discoverie of Witches in the Countie of Lancaster*. Later in the nineteenth century the publication of a modern edition by the Manchester antiquarian James Crossley was used as the basis for a best-selling novel by the popular Victorian writer William Harrison Ainsworth, and later still in 1951 was also used by Robert Neill in his *Mist Over Pendle*. The events of 1612 thus came to enter popular culture in a way that was not true of other witch trials.

Despite this, the trial of the Lancashire witches, and the linked trial of Jennet Preston in York, has not before been the object of a major work or collection of essays. However in 1999 a conference was organised jointly by the Centre for North-West Regional Studies, Lancaster College, and St Martin's College, and this book is the result, collecting the various papers delivered there. Collections of this kind can sometimes lack coherence or be of uneven quality but neither is true in this case. The papers – and hence the book – fall naturally into three sections, reflecting the three principal themes of the conference. The most interesting aspect of the book is the way it deals not only with the actual events of 1612, their context and the contemporary records such as Potts's pamphlet, but also looks at their later representation and the way in which they have continued to be remembered ever since.

Following a very helpful and well organised introduction by James Sharpe, which places the events of 1612 and the papers into a wider historical and historiographical context, the various papers are collected in three sections, each reflecting one of the major themes. The first three, by Stephen Pumphrey, Marion Gibson and Jonathan Lumby, all focus on the local records and in particular the famous work of Potts. The examination of his publication and role in the preparation and conduct of the trial by Pumphrey and Gibson make it clear that we should be very careful in the use we make of this fascinating source. Pumphrey points out the connection between such elements as a demonic pact and something resembling a witches' sabbat, drawn from his account, and the impact of James VI and I, whose strong interest in and support for continental demonology in his own writings in the 1590s was appealed to and used in the work. Gibson shows clearly how we need to see the *Discoverie* as being as much a work of literature as a simple descriptive account. Essentially Potts used the events of the trial as the material for a work in the genre of accounts of witch cases, in a way that also presented the judicial system in a benevolent light. The outstanding paper for this reader, however, is the third by Lumby which, through forensic examination of the local records, shows clearly why there was a connection between the case at Lancaster and the trial of Jennet Preston at York and how the latter derived from a mess of parochial rivalry and bad feeling.

The second section, with papers by John Swain, Michael Mullett and Kirsteen Bardell, explores the local context of the trial. Mullett looks at the way this part of Lancashire was on the front line between the persistence of the old religion and the emergence of an aggressive Protestantism among sections of the elite, which saw itself as surrounded by a mass of unbelief, superstition, popery and worse. The key factor here was the institutional vacuum left by the dissolution of Whalley Abbey and the subsequent holding of the living of the enormous parish of Whalley by a strong conservative. The other two papers both bring out the way in which folk magic and the range of beliefs associated with it were an integral part of the rural folkways and economy of this part of England. When this is combined with the insights provided by the papers in the first section, it becomes clear how the kind of continental-style demonology borrowed by Potts from the king was an alien template forced by members of the local elite onto a mass of local practices and conflicts, deriving in large part from the efforts of some to reform the society they governed. Interestingly, as Sharpe points out, the tide of opinion was already starting to turn and less than a generation later, another scare in the 1630s following a trial would lead not to a mass

execution but the examination and ultimate rejection of the kind of accusations that had earlier led to local panics.

In many ways the most interesting section is the third, which looks at the representation of witchcraft in literature and the way the events of the early seventeenth century persisted in popular memory and, thanks to Thomas Potts and James Crossley, were then made part of a wider popular culture through the medium of a popular novel by William Harrison Ainsworth. The first, by Richard Wilson, looks at the representation of the witches in Macbeth and shows how Shakespeare's play also articulates the kinds of ideas about witches found in Potts and, more arguably, may reflect a possible connection between Shakespeare and Lancashire. (One point to note is that James I was not happy with the play, being upset with both its subject matter, the part played by witchcraft and its representation of his native land.) Alison Findlay looks at the trial of 1634 and its representation in a play to explore the persistence of witchcraft beliefs and the fascination they had for so many people, as indeed they still do. One interesting aspect of the later case is the way the invented accusation it derived from drew upon memories of the earlier trial and its representation, which clearly persisted in the popular mind. It also shows the power and hold of the idea, so that even when a particular accusation was shown to be false (as happened in this case) this did not lead people to doubt the validity of the set of beliefs itself. The two final papers examine the use made of this belief and the events of the seventeenth century in the modern period. Jeffrey Richards shows how Ainsworth interprets the episode through the medium of the Gothic, to produce a work, which like most in that genre, can be understood as, in part, a critique of the rationalist and commercial world of modernity. An excellent paper by Joanne Pearson rounds off the book by examining the use made of the historical events of the early modern witch-hunts, including those in Lancashire, by the modern religion of Wicca. Wiccans claim to be the lineal descendants of those accused of witchcraft in the earlier period and so posit a continuity of conscious belief and practice that historical investigation does not support, while also making use of a modern mythology of the scale and nature of the hunts. As she points out, Wiccans benefit in some ways by identifying themselves with the accused at the trails but also have to cope with the negative baggage that it brings. This is in fact a fascinating example of the use of historical events to create a narrative and myth that is then used to justify and provide content for something that is a novel phenomenon.

Altogether this is an extremely useful and enjoyable collection for anyone interested in either the historical phenomenon of witch-hunts in general or the form these took in one specific case and location in particular. What does come out is the particularity of the circumstances and events in seventeenth-century Pendle, reflecting distinctive local factors, tensions and concerns, as well as the way that these were interpreted and understood by employing ideas and concepts that had a more general origin and relevance. Perhaps most striking is the way it demonstrates the persistence and power of a set of ideas and images, both generic and specific. The one lack is perhaps an account of the way these events have been used by modern commercialism and what this says about images and beliefs about witchcraft and their place in the popular culture of today. This however is a minor quibble about what is otherwise an excellent collection.

Stephen Davies
Manchester Metropolitan University

Dorothy Bentley Smith

A Georgian Gent & Co.: the life and times of Charles Roe Ashbourne: Landmark Publishing, 2005. 656pp. ISBN 1843061759.

Following her two previous books on the history of Macclesfield and its environs, Dorothy Bentley Smith has turned her attention to the life and work of local industrialist Charles Roe (1715–81). Bentley's study is not simply a narrow personal biography of Roe however, but a voluminous antiquarian work offering several centuries' worth of complex local genealogy, minutely detailed commercial and public records, and a thoroughgoing account of the largely neglected industrial fields of copper mining and brass fabrication. In addition, Bentley Smith focuses significantly upon Charles's son and commercial successor William (1747–1827), whose own influence saw him occupy respected positions as a bailiff in Liverpool and as the commissioner of customs for that city.

Charles Roe's successes as silk mill owner, merchant, and latterly, brass manufacturer, along with his active public life as a prominent citizen (and one-time mayor) of Macclesfield locate him within that breed of individuals who made their fortunes and names against the increasingly commercial background of Hanoverian England. In this sense Roe's story fits comfortably into the recent historiography of eighteenth-century commercial culture, and he himself does into the entrepreneurial mould of more well known figures such as Watt, Boulton and Wedgwood. In one particular passage the author yokes these figures together by observing that, 'without the use of brass, Watt would never have been able to build up sufficient pressure in his engines to create far more powerful machines than those built earlier by Newcome' (p. 571). Indeed, it is partly a popularisation of Roe, and perhaps of other marginalised regional figures like him, which informs some of the implicit objectives of the book.

A Georgian Gent & Co. is split into three main sections, but relies most heavily on the longest second section to fill the bulk of its 600 or so pages. The first section discusses the genealogies of several generations of Roes beginning with the Revd William Roe (born in Wem, Shropshire in 1618), and detailing the continued affiliation of the family with the counties of Cheshire and Derbyshire through the troubled English seventeenth century. Section two, the most weighty, focuses on the life of the central figure, Thomas Roe's son, Charles. It covers the period 1700–81 and details the movements of the Roes throughout the Midlands and North West, charting also the shift from their involvement in the silk trade in the first half of the century to the later incursions into brass and copper manufacture. The final section deals with the state of Roe & Co. in the years following Charles's death in 1781, and the activities of his son William who resided primarily in Liverpool.

Somewhat paradoxically both the greatest strengths and the most glaring weaknesses of the text appear to come from the same source, that is, the author's attempts to deal with questions of status; and to establish the possible positions of both Charles and William Roe within the firmament of eighteenth-century entrepreneurs. On the positive side, the lack of a conventional historiographical framework in the book allows the author to avoid some of the occasionally ponderous and controversial typologies of the 'middling orders' during this period, and, by omitting these more qualitative distinctions Bentley Smith presents a series of incredibly detailed sets of information, primarily those concerning the business relationships of the various subjects, and in a relatively neutral format. Rather than becoming overly entangled and perhaps outweighed by a set of questions concerning socio-cultural mobility, the book's inability (or perhaps its refusal – only the author could tell us) to engage with this set of standard academic questions means that for others who do wish to engage in such debates, they have a potentially valuable reference tool.

However, while such a structure might *potentially* provide direction for future research, *A Georgian Gent & Co.* is also problematic for this, among other, reasons. The lack of said framework means that during the points at which Bentley Smith's narrative actually does touch upon the concerns of other historians, including the enduring significance of religion during this supposedly secular age, the book struggles to situate itself more broadly. Equally, because the narrative operates largely at a microcosmic level, it rarely makes any successful connections between the commercial life of the subjects and their personal beliefs or cultural *mentalités*.

Furthermore, the text offers a rather impressionistic account of the links between the individuals it presents and the wider socio-economic and political changes which took place over the course of the long eighteenth century. The author guesses, for instance, that 'Thomas Roe [Charles Roe's father] must have sensed a restlessness emerging in the small town of Macclesfield. A good strong personality was needed, someone of sufficient stature to command respect from all sections of the community, and until that person presented himself, a struggle for power would develop over the next few years' (p. 42). Yet the reader is told nothing about why Thomas Roe must have 'sensed' this, and from what kind of evidence this assumption is derived. This is perhaps not the fault of the author (that her subjects recorded virtually nothing of their interior states), but in order to enhance our ability to 'read' these people, the book may have benefited from comparisons with other diarists of the period, or with a greater familiarity with similar material.

What is perhaps most baffling about the book is the question of its intended audience. The lack of scholarly apparatus means that it is unlikely to be studied by academic historians, and yet the length and absolute density of information would presumably also make it inaccessible to the casual reader. Additionally, despite offering a wealth of information and being written by someone with an obvious passion for the topic, the book's accessibility is confounded in both markets because of the lack of a strong editorial hand. Much of the material is given too much room within the text and this results in sections which omit no detail, no matter how small, thus demanding continual perseverance where perhaps a more streamlined version could have been simultaneously entertaining and educative. On balance, although there are a number of issues which mar the delivery of information in this book, it is still a piece of work which demands respect for both its scale and its engagement with previously neglected material.

Stephen Connolly
University of Manchester

SHORT REVIEWS

G. K. Fox *The line – part one: Stockport, Davenport, and Hazel Grove to Disley, New Mills (Newtown) and Whaley Bridge* Foxline, 2006. Illus. Maps. 144pp. £16.95. ISBN 1870119851.

This new Foxline examines the railway between Stockport and Whaley Bridge during the 1950s and 1960s through the records of one enthusiast. It provides a fascinating insight into both passenger and freight services that used the line. After a short introduction tracing its history, the many well reproduced photographs are accompanied by informative captions and plans of sidings and junctions, almost all of which have since been removed. This is a book that should appeal to those who are interested in the history of the line and its contribution to the transport of the area.

I. R. Smith and G. K. Fox *Manchester London Road to Hayfield via Reddish, Bredbury, Romiley, Marple and New Mills* Foxline, 2005. Illus. Maps. 136pp. £15.95. ISBN 1870119738.

For many people in the days before almost everyone had their own car, the easiest way to reach Hayfield to walk in the Peak District, especially in the area around Kinder Scout, was by train. Today, the line from New Mills to Hayfield has disappeared, although part of it is a pleasant walk. This book traces the journey from Manchester to Hayfield with many well reproduced photographs and informative captions of the stations, engines and rolling stock used on the route. As with other books in the series, there is a useful and informative historical introduction.

E. M. Johnson *Manchester's Central Station and the Great Northern goods warehouse* Foxline[, 2005]. Illus. Maps. 78pp. £12.95. ISBN 1870119797.

Two of the most prominent buildings in central Manchester are the former Central Station and the adjacent Great Northern warehouse. Both have survived into the twenty-first century with new uses having been found for them. This book traces the history of both buildings from their origins to their modern day use. Unlike most of the books in this series, it is not a collection of photographs, but one where the text is of greater importance as it covers many aspects, not only of the building of the two structures but also their operation. The photographs are not solely of engines and trains and are again well reproduced and accompanied by informative captions. This book is one of which all those interested in the transport history of Manchester should take note as it is the only substantial publication on these two former railway buildings.

Ruth Z. Roskell *Glimpses of Glasson Dock and vicinity* Blackpool: Landy Publishing, 2005. 72pp. Illus. £8. ISBN 1872895344.

This is the first pictorial book about Glasson Dock, an important transport centre at the mouth of the Lune. It is an area that is often overlooked, yet it is one which has a rich and varied history. The book has a wide range of photographs, from views of the docks and shipping to school photographs and ones of individual local characters. Each is accompanied by informative and well written captions which add to the interest of the book itself. Many of the illustrations have come from local people and are therefore part of their personal archive, but they should be praised for allowing them to be used as they also form part of the history of Glasson Dock and its vicinity.

Betty Gilkes and Stan Pickles *Traipsing from a Lancashire toll bar: Bretherton, Croston, Hesketh Bank, Hoole, Tarleton and Walmer Bridge in focus* Blackpool: Landy Publishing, 2005. 72pp. Illus. £8. ISBN 1872895654.

This book starts at the now-demolished toll house at Bretherton on the Liverpool to Preston road and visits several nearby villages which were in the parish of Croston, but now in different boroughs. There are many fascinating photographs in this book that show life in these Lancashire villages. As well as photographs, the author has made use of items for variety such as programmes for events and advertisements for local firms. The many photographs are accompanied by well written and informative captions which help to bring the book alive.

Sylvia McHale *Time to stand and stare: Tottington memories, 1939–1943* Stonecloough: Richardson, 2005. 43pp. Illus. £5.25. ISBN 1852161639.

The beginning of September 1939 was a traumatic time for many children as, with the outbreak of war, they were evacuated from their homes to safer places. The experiences of each evacuee were different: some enjoyed their time whilst others hated it. This publication recounts the experiences of the author during the four years she was an evacuee at Tottington. It provides an insight into what life was like for those who were accepted by the host family, and who stayed on after many had returned home. It is well illustrated and an important addition to the material available on the experience of Manchester's evacuees.

Nigel Drum and Roger Dowson *Hell let loose: the 1/7th (Salford) Territorial Battalion Lancashire Fusiliers, 1914–1915* Stonecloough: Richardson, 2005. 91pp. Illus. £6.25. ISBN 1852161620.

This is the story of one of the English battalions involved in the Gallipoli campaign that resulted in many casualties from the Salford area. The book outlines the movements of the battalion, as well as giving details of the casualties. It offers a list of the men who were members of the battalion with details of their war service, and where possible, what they did when they returned to civilian life. It is another very useful addition to the material on local involvement in the First World War.

D. Rendell (comp.) *Photographers in the Altrincham area* Altrincham: privately published, 2006. 132pp. Illus. £15. ISBN 0951256025.

Most towns have their photographers, but very often little is known about them and their work. This book examines the work of those photographers, some well known and others not so well known, who lived and worked in the Altrincham area from the middle of the nineteenth century to the present day. It not only includes photographs of the area much beloved by local historians, but also the commercial and professional photographers whose work might appear in exhibitions, newspapers, magazines and family photograph albums.

The book provides a brief history of the development of photography before outlining the work of the local photographers with examples of their work. As well as the photographers, there are sections on postcards, Thornton-Pickard and those who specialized in industrial photographs. This book is a valuable addition to the material available not only on the Altrincham area, but also on the history and development of photography. Available from Northern Writers' Advisory Services, 77 Marford Crescent, Sale, Cheshire M33 4DN.

D. Bayliss *A town in crisis: Altrincham in the mid nineteenth century* Hale: privately published, 2006. 82pp. Maps. Illus Bibliog. £9.

This book is based on fifteen maps produced in 1852 to help with the improvement of Altrincham, then suffering from a lack of housing for the poor, a high death rate and a lack of efficient local government. In order to improve conditions, a local board of health was set up in 1851 which ordered a set of large-scale maps of the area to help with the improvement work. After an introduction – setting the scene of what Altrincham was like in the mid nineteenth century – the author takes each of the fifteen sheets in turn, outlining the features of the area and then taking a small section of the sheet and examining this in more detail, making use of census detail and information from the *Book of reference*. This book is a fascinating insight into conditions in Altrincham as it provides a snap-shot of the town in 1852 and shows how the basis for improvements and future development was laid down.

Available from the author at 51 Chiltern Drive, Hale, Cheshire WA15 9PN; or Northern Writers' Advisory Services, 77 Marford Crescent, Sale, Cheshire M33 4DN.

T. Wray *Manchester Victoria station* Hereford: Peter Taylor Publications and the Lancashire and Yorkshire Railway Society, 2004. 132pp. Illus. Diags. Maps. £16.95. ISN 0954945107.

Today, Victoria station is a shadow of its former self, the number of trains using it much reduced, but many of the buildings – especially the entrance to the station – remain as a reminder of the importance of railway travel in a by-gone era. This well illustrated and well written book might be said to be an account of the rise and fall of this once important station. The author traces the history of the site and station from the 1840s to the 1990s with the arrival of the Metrolink in 1992 and beyond. The book also examines the operation of the station and deals with aspects such as signalling, electrification, carriage storage and relations between the L&Y and LNWR as they affected Victoria station. This book is a worthy addition to the literature on Manchester's buildings and railway history.

H. L. Holliday *Moston colliery, Manchester: a Victorian super-pit* Ashbourne: Landmark Publishing, 2005. 123pp. Illus. Maps. £14.95. ISBN 1843061848.

Although many people know there was a colliery in the Bradford area of Manchester, few realise that there was once a colliery in Moston that survived until 1950. This book on the Moston colliery traces the history of mining in the area from the early nineteenth century to the closure of this mine. In addition to the history of the colliery, the author has included information about the geology of the area and its influence on the way the pit developed and was worked after it was re-opened following a serious flood in 1884. This book is a useful addition to the literature available on the coal mines of Manchester and their importance to Manchester and the south-east Lancashire coal field as a whole.

R. Freethy *Lancashire, 1939–1945: the secret war* Newbury: Countryside Books, 2005. 176pp. Illus. £9.99. ISBN 1853069337.

During the Second World War the civilian population at home did much to assist those who were serving in the armed services, producing a wide range of products that eventually went on to help win the war. Much of the work done was undertaken with a varying amount of secrecy, such as the production of PLUTO and the Mulberry Harbour. In addition, there were plans for what should happen if the country were invaded. This book looks at some of the developments that took place in Lancashire in the war effort and the plans made to counter an invasion. The book provides a different approach to the Second World War from that taken in the past where the emphasis has been on major events such as evacuation and the blitz. This is a useful addition to the literature available on the Second World War and makes use of personal recollections of those involved.

P. Holme *Play up, Higher Walton: football in a Lancashire village from 1882 to 2005* Blackpool: Landy Publishing, 2006. 80pp. Illus. Bibliog. £6. ISBN 1872895670.

During the late nineteenth century, a large number of football teams were formed by factories, Sunday schools and other organisations. Some went on to become professional teams with household names, but others stayed close to their roots. One such team was Higher Walton FC which started playing in 1882 and was eventually disbanded in 2005. This book traces the history of the club, and its successes and failures over its 123 years. As well as the history of the club, the author has included chapters on the setting of Higher Walton and the growth of football in Lancashire during the late nineteenth century, providing an interesting and useful background to the story of Higher Walton FC.

D. Eastwood *The Booths of Dunham Massey* Leek: Churnet Valley Books, 2004. 192pp. Illus. Bibliog. £9.95. ISBN 1904546161.

The original Dunham Hall was built by the Booth family in the seventeenth century and rebuilt in the early eighteenth century by the same family. This book traces the history of the Booths over a period of about 100 years from the time the first Sir George Booth built the original house to its rebuilding by George Booth, second earl of Warrington. It is not only the story of an important Cheshire landed family, but also of the politics of a turbulent period in English history with the Civil War, the Interregnum, the Restoration and the overthrow of James II in 1688. The Booth family was involved in some way or another in all these national events, which Eastwood traces both at the local and national level. It is a book that will interest not only those who want to know about Dunham and the Booth family, but also those who are interested in the Civil War and local involvement in the events of the period.

M. Baggoley *Strangeways: a century of hangings in Manchester* Barnsley: Wharncliffe Books, 2006. 176pp. Illus. Bibliog. £10.99. ISBN 1903425972.

Strangeways Prison was opened in 1868 and the first execution took place the following year. From then until 1964, 100 people were executed there. This book re-tells the stories behind fourteen of the executions that took place within the walls of the prison. In each case the author outlines the crime that led to the execution and a summary of the police investigation and trial, using contemporary sources. It is a book that recalls some famous cases in Lancashire as well as others which were not so well known.

S. Richardson (ed.) *The recollections of three Manchesters in the Great War* Stoneclough: Richardson, 2006. 79pp. Illus. Maps. £5.75. ISBN 1852161655.

The original edition of this book was published in 1985 and has now been revised with material added. It is based on recordings made by Frank Heaton with the three men involved, each being members of different regiments during the war, including one of whom was a member of the original force to be sent to Belgium in 1914 and who died in 1999. This is a fascinating set of accounts by men who had served at the fronts in France, Italy and Gallipoli and who recalled their experiences of the 'war to end all wars'. These personal accounts are important as they add to the bare bones of official accounts and bring home to the reader the difficulties and hardships which soldiers faced during this war. A useful feature is the addition of brief pen portraits on some of the local men killed whilst serving with the 2nd Manchesters,

1/7th Manchesters and 20th Manchesters, including details of where they were born, their pre-war occupations and when they were killed or died. This latest book from Richardson is a worthy addition to his other publications, especially those on war-time recollections.

The Tameside Local History Forum *History alive: Tameside* Issue 1, 2006. 64pp. Illus. Maps. Free.

This is a new annual publication about the many aspects of Tameside's history. It consists of a series of short articles on a wide range of subjects such as mining in Mottram, William Kenyon's of Dukinfield, the stained glass at Dukinfield old Chapel (Unitarian), Cotton Street in the nineteenth century, Gee Cross and World War One, and many others. The articles are well written and a source of valuable information which might not be found elsewhere. It is an encouragement to what others groups can do in publishing research that has been carried on in a particular area and for which publication can be difficult.

J. Edgar (ed.) *From smoke to grass: Gamesley, the birth of a new community* Derbyshire County Council, 2004. 85pp. Illus. Map. £3.50. ISBN 0903463776.

During the 1960s, as slum clearance made progress in Manchester, it was necessary to move the residents from the clearance areas to new homes on what became known as 'overspill estates'. One of these was Gamesley near Glossop. This publication 'takes the reader on a journey with the people of Gamesley; their lives in Manchester, the first view of their new homes, living on the estate and the changes it brought for them, and their hopes for the future' as seen through the eyes of those involved. It makes interesting reading and records for posterity the views of those involved as opposed to that given in official reports and press reports.

R. Bullock *Salford in the nineteen-twenties* Stoneclough: Richardson, 2005. 95pp. Illus. Map. £5.95. ISBN 1852161647.

This is another one in the excellent series that Bullock has compiled of events in Salford during the twentieth century based on local newspaper reports. This volume covers the 1920s and includes a wide range of events from the opening of new buildings to visits by distinguished visitors to Salford, from the commemoration of events of the First World War to sporting events and the activities of the city council. Like others in the series, this book contains a wealth of material and will provide an endless source of information for local historians and others.

G. Cooper *The Wharncliffe companion to Manchester: an A to Z of local history* Barnsley: Wharncliffe Books, 2005. 173pp. Illus. Map. £10.99. ISBN 1903425743.

This book consists of a collection of alphabetically-arranged items relating to Manchester. Some of the entries refer to historic events, persons and buildings whilst others cover more recent events, buildings or people. However, there are many potential entries that ought to have been included and are not, such as Edward Walters, Lydia Becker, the Gentlemen's Concert Hall and the Boer War Memorial, a fact that restricts the usefulness of the book. It should also be noted that the information in some of the entries is suspect, being legend or otherwise inaccurate. For instance, the author refers to Manchester's 'Lord Mayor' when talking about the Cromwell Statue; Manchester did not get a lord mayor until 1893. It would also have been nice to have included a little more detail on some of the entries such as the date the Free Trade Hall opened. Although the book is meant to deal with Manchester, there are a number of entries that are not Manchester and should have been excluded. This is a book that requires great care when being used and there is a need to cross-check information.